Relational
Database Design
Clearly
Explained

Second Edition

Relational Database Design Clearly Explained
Second Edition

Jan L. Harrington

Morgan Kaufmann Publishers
An Imprint of Elsevier Science

Amsterdam   London   New York   Oxford   Paris   Tokyo
Boston   San Diego   San Francisco   Singapore   Sydney

Academic Press
An Imprint of Elsevier Science
525 B Street, Suite 1900, San Diego, California 92101-4495, USA
http://www.academicpress.com

Academic Press
32 Jamestown Road, London NW1 7BY, UK
http://www.academicpress.com

Morgan Kaufmann
An Imprint of Elsevier Science
340 Pine Street, Sixth Floor, San Francisco, California 94104-3205, USA
http://www.mkp.com

Library of Congress Catalog Card Number: 2002101250

International Standard Book Number: 0-1-55860-820-6

Printed in the United States of America

02   03   04   05   06   07   MV   9   8   7   6   5   4   3   2   1

Contents

Chapter 4: The Relational Data Model   73

Chapter 5: Normalization   93

Part Two: Practice

Chapter 9: Using SQL to Implement a Relational Design   177

Preface to the Second Edition

My favorite opening line for the database courses I teach is: "Probably the most misunderstood term in all of business computing is *database*, followed closely by the word *relational*." At that point, the students often snicker, because they are absolutely, positively sure that they know what a database is and that they also know what it means for a database to be relational. Unfortunately, the popular press, with the help of some software developers, long ago distorted the meaning of both those terms, which led many businesses to think that designing a database is a task that could be left to a clerical worker who had taken a few days training in using database software. As you will see throughout this book, nothing could be further from the truth.

> *Note: By the same token, I have received applications for adjunct faculty positions from people who say they know how to use a specific piece of database software and therefore believe*

*they are qualified to teach a database theory course. From where
I sit, that is pretty scary.*

Before preparing the first edition of this book, I had wanted to write
a book like this for a long time. We teach relational database design
theory to college students, but it is a rare pleasure to get the chance
to share that theory—and the practice of that theory—with the
business community, with people who are actually doing such designs in their jobs. It's just as great a pleasure to be able to prepare
a second edition, giving me a chance to correct some nasty typos
and add material that reviewers have indicated was lacking.

This book is intended for anyone who has been given the responsibility of designing or maintaining a relational database. The first
part will teach you how to look at the environment your database
serves and to tailor the design of that database to the environment.
It will also teach you ways of designing the database so that it provides accurate and consistent data, avoiding the problems that are
common to poorly designed databases. In addition, you will read
about design compromises that you might choose to make in the interest of database application performance and the consequences of
making such choices.

The second edition introduces a chapter on the history of data management. This chapter will show you just how far the IT industry
has come in the past 40 years or so in terms of handling business data. It may also help you appreciate why so many people prefer relational databases to any other alternative. The placement of this new
chapter is somewhat problematic. Ideally, it should be Chapter 0,
but it requires concepts that are taught in Chapter 2. Therefore, although it is slightly out of place, it appears as Chapter 3.

Part II looks at the more practical aspects of performing database
design, covering the implementation of a design using SQL and using a CASE tool to help document and support the design process.
In addition, Part II contains three large database design case studies, each of which presents one or more design challenges that you
may encounter when designing relational databases.

Probably the biggest trend in relational database design since the first edition of this book appeared is the integration of objects into relational databases. The major relational DBMSs on the market have embraced this hybrid object-relational approach. You will therefore find an entire chapter on the object-oriented paradigm and how it has been merged with a relational database. Each of the case studies in Part II also concludes with an example of an object-relational solution.

What You Need to Know

Because this book deals primarily with database design, you do not need any special computing background to read it. You should, however, have some basic computer literacy. If you know how to get around your computer's operating system and how to run programs someone has written for you, then you know enough to understand the material in Part I and most of Part II of this book. To get the most out of Chapter 9 (using SQL to implement a relational design), you should be familiar with some type of database environment that provides an interface for sending SQL commands to a database.

Acknowledgments

Writing a book for the folks at Morgan Kaufman is always a joy. I would therefore like to thank the following individuals who helped make this one possible:

- Diane Cerra, editor at Morgan Kaufman
- Mona Buelher, editorial assistant at Morgan Kaufman
- Debbie Liehs, project manager
- Edward Wade, assistant publishing services manager
- Mei Levenson, production coordinator
- Adrienne Rubello, copy editor
- Tara Masih, proofreader

- ♦ The three reviewers:
  - Sheldon Barry, Memorial University of Newfound-land
  - Karen Watterson, industry consultant
  - Russell Belfer, independent software developer/consultant

And above all, to my very active two-year-old son, Sean, who slept long enough for me to finish this book.

JLH

Relational Database Design Clearly Explained

Second Edition

Part One

Theory

The first part of this book considers the theoretical aspects of relational database design. You will read about identifying data relationships in your database environment, the details of the relational data model, and how to translate data relationships into a well-designed relational database that avoids most of the problems associated with bad designs.

1

Introduction

Many of today's businesses rely on their database systems for accurate, up-to-date information. Without those repositories of mission-critical data, most businesses are unable to perform their normal daily transactions, much less create summary reports that help management make strategic corporate decisions. To be useful, the data in a database must be accurate, complete, and organized in such a way that data can be retrieved when needed and in the format required.

Well-written database application programs—whether they execute locally, run over a local area network, or feed information to a Web site—are fundamental to timely and accurate data retrieval. However, without a good underlying database design, even the best program cannot avoid problems with inaccurate and inconsistent data. That is what this book is all about: to help you learn to design good relational databases that avoid many of the problems inherent in poor database design.

Good database design means that you take time to plan your database before you put it into use. It means that you focus on the way your business works and tailor that database to your own organization's specifications. What do you get for all this work? You get a database that accurately supports the needs of your company, that provides everyone who uses it with accurate, complete information.

Effects of Poor Database Design

To make it a bit clearer why the design of a database matters so much, let us take a look at a business that has a very bad design, and the problems that the poor design brings. The business is named Lasers Only.

> *Note: We will leave the precise definition of a database for later. As you will see, the data storage used by Lasers Only is not precisely a database.*

Back in the early 1980s, when most people were just discovering video tapes, Mark Watkins and Emily Stone stumbled across a fledgling technology known as the laser disc. There were several competing formats, but by 1986 the industry had standardized on a 12-inch silver platter on which either 30 or 60 minutes of video and audio could be recorded. Although the market was still small, it was at that time that Watkins and Stone opened Lasers Only, a business that sold and rented laser discs.

Today, Lasers Only carries laser discs, audio CDs, and DVDs. (There is still great disagreement between videophiles as to whether the DVDs are better than the 12-inch laser discs.) The company rents titles from its single retail store. However, the largest part of its business comes from sales, both in the store and through mail order.

In 1990, when the store began its mail order business, Watkins created a "database" to handle the orders and sales. Customers were (and still are) enticed to order titles before the official release date by offering a 15 to 20 percent discount on preorders. (All titles are always discounted 10 percent from the suggested retail price.) The mail order database therefore needed to include a way to handle backorders so that preordered items could be shipped as soon as they came into the store.

At the time we visit Lasers Only, they are still using the software Watkins created. The primary data entry interface is a form like that in Figure 1-1. Each time a customer orders a single title, an employee of the store fills out the entire form.

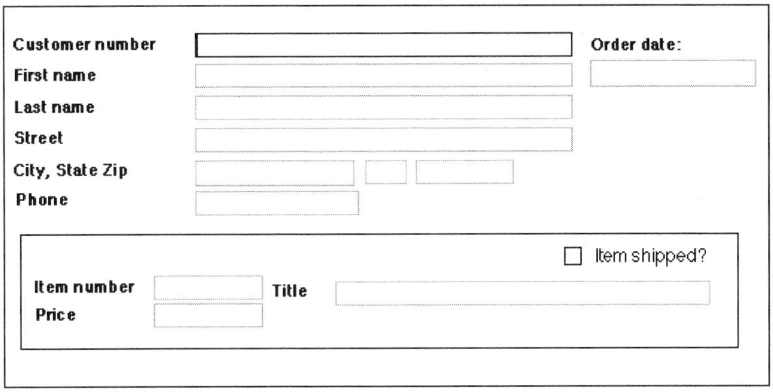

Figure 1-1: The data entry form used by Lasers Only for their mail order business

Customer numbers are created by combining the customer's zip code, the first three letters of his or her last name, and a three-digit sequence number. For example, if Stone lives in zip code 12345 and she is the second customer in that zip code with a last name beginning with STO, then her customer number is 12345STO002. The sequence number ensures that no two customer numbers will be alike.

When a new title comes into the store, an employee searches the database to find all people who have preordered that title. The employee prints a packing slip from the stored data and then places an X in the "Item shipped?" check box.

At first glance, the Lasers Only software seems pretty simple and straightforward. Should work just fine, right? Well, it worked for a while, but after a year or two, serious problems began to arise.

Unnecessary Duplicated Data and Data Consistency

The Lasers Only database has a considerable amount of unnecessary duplicated data:

- ◆ A customer's name, address, and phone number are duplicated for every item the customer orders.
- ◆ A merchandise item's title is duplicated every time the item is ordered.

What is the problem with this duplication? When you have duplicated data in this way, the data should be the same throughout the database. In other words, every order for a given customer should have the same name, address, and phone number, typed exactly the same way. Every order for a single title should have the same title, typed exactly the same way. We want the duplicated data to be consistent throughout the database.

As the database grows larger, this type of consistency is very hard to maintain. Most business-oriented database software is *case sensitive*, in that it considers upper- and lowercase letters to be different characters. In addition, no one is a perfect typist. A difference in capitalization or even a single mistyped letter will cause database software to consider two values to be distinct.

When a Lasers Only employee performs a search to find all people who have ordered a specific title, the database software will retrieve only those orders that match the title entered by the employee exactly. For example, assume that a movie named *Summer Days* is scheduled to be released soon. In some orders, the title is stored correctly as "Summer Days." However, in others it is stored as "summer days" or even "Sumer Days." When an employee searches for all the people to whom the movie should be shipped, the orders for "summer days" and "Sumer Days" will not be retrieved. Those customers will not receive their orders, causing disgruntled customers and probably lost business.

The current Lasers Only software has no way to ensure that duplicated data are entered consistently. There are two solutions. The first is to eliminate as much of the duplicated data as possible. (As you will see, it is neither possible nor desirable to eliminate all of it.) The second is to provide some mechanism for verifying that when data must be duplicated, they are entered correctly. A well-designed database will do both.

> *Note: Unnecessary duplicated data also take up extra disk space, but given that disk space is relatively inexpensive today, that is not a major reason for getting rid of the redundant data.*

Data Insertion Problems

Lasers Only prepares its catalog of forthcoming titles by hand. Each month when the announcements of new releases arrive from the distributors, an employee does a manual "cut and paste" operation to assemble a 16-page booklet that can be duplicated and mailed to customers. In 1995, however, Stone realized that this was a very cumbersome process and thought it would be much better if the catalog could be generated from the database.

Why not get a list of forthcoming titles from the database and have a database program generate the entire catalog? As she discovered, it could not be done. There are two major reasons.

First, the current database does not contain all the information needed for the catalog, in particular a synopsis of the content of the disc. This problem could be remedied by adding that information to the current database. However, doing so would only exacerbate the problem with unnecessary duplicated data if the company were to include the summary with every order. If the summary were to be included only once, how would the company know which order contained the summary?

Second, and by far more important, there is no way to enter data about a title unless someone has ordered it. This presents a rather large Catch-22. Lasers Only can't insert data about a title until it has been ordered at least once, but customers won't know that it is available to be ordered without receiving the computer-generated catalog. But the catalog can't contain data about the new title until someone can get the data into the database, and that can't happen until the title has been ordered.

> Note: This problem is more formally known as an "insertion anomaly," and you will learn about it more formally throughout this book.

Data Deletion Problems

Lasers Only also has problems when it comes to deleting data. Assume, for example, that a customer orders only one item. After the order has been processed, the item is discontinued by the manufacturer. Lasers Only therefore wants to delete all references to the item from its database because the item is no longer available.

When the orders containing the item are deleted, information about any customer who has ordered only that item is also deleted. No other orders remain in the database for that customer. Lasers Only will be unable to send that customer any more catalogs and therefore loses the chance of getting any more business from that customer.

> Note: This problem is more formally known as a "deletion anomaly." It, too, will be discussed in greater depth throughout this book.

Meaningful Identifiers

The Lasers Only database has another major problem: those customer numbers. It is very tempting to code meaning into identifiers
and it usually works well — until the values on which the identifiers are based change.

Consider what happens when a Lasers Only customer moves. The
person's customer number must change. At that point, there will be
orders for the same customer with two different customer numbers
in the same database.

If a customer who has moved since first ordering from the store
calls and asks for a list of all items he or she has on order, the first
thing the employee who answers the telephone does is ask the customer for his or her customer number. The customer, of course, provides the current value, which means that anything ordered under
the old customer number will be missed during a search. The customer may assume that titles ordered under the old customer number are not on order. As a result, the customer may place another
order, causing two copies of the same item to be shipped. Lasers
Only is then faced with another disgruntled customer who has to
make the effort to send back the duplicate and get the second
charge removed from his or her credit card.

What You Will Find in This Book

The purpose of this book is to help you avoid the types of problems
about which you have just read. A well-designed database provides
ways to eliminate much data redundancy, enforce data consistency,
allow data entry as needed without requiring you to enter "extra"
data, and allow data deletion without accidentally losing data you
want to keep.

In Chapter 2 we begin by looking at the foundation of database design: identifying logical data relationships in the environment the
database will serve, without reference to the software you will be

using. Chapter 3, which is new to the second edition, covers methods of handling data that preceded the relational data model. You do not need to read Chapter 3 to understand the rest of the book, although it does provide some background for the case studies in Part II.

In Chapter 4, we turn to data models, the formal way in which you express data relationships to database software. There you will meet the relational data model for the first time and begin to understand what it means for a database to be relational. In Chapters 4 through 7, we'll explore the details of the relational data model. Chapter 8, the second new chapter in this book's second edition, concerns the way in which a number of relational products have integrated aspects of the object-oriented data model. You will find an introduction to object-oriented concepts as well. If you choose, you do not need to read this chapter to follow the remainder of this book.

The discussion of relational concepts concludes in Chapter 9, in which you will learn how to use SQL (the standard language for interacting with relational databases) to create the relational database elements about which you have been reading. You also see some extensions to SQL that have been implemented (although not standardized) for integrating objects. Along the way we will redesign and expand the Lasers Only database to give the company a workable design on which to build database applications.

In Chapter 10 you will be introduced to the role of software tools that support database design activities. Chapters 11 through 13 contain database design case studies that present a variety of database design challenges that you may encounter. Each of these chapters has been expanded to include coverage of the integration of objects into the case study databases.

2

Entities and Data Relationships

In this chapter we will explore the fundamental concept behind all databases: There are things in a business environment about which we need to store data, and those things are related to one another in a variety of ways. In fact, to be considered a *database*, the place where data are stored must contain not only the data but also information about the relationships between those data.

The idea behind a database is that the user—either a person working interactively or an application program—has no need to worry about the way in which data are physically stored on disk. The user phrases data manipulation requests in terms of data relationships. A piece of software known as a *database management system* (DBMS) then translates between the user's request for data and the physical data storage.

11

The formal way in which you express data relationships to a DBMS is known as a *data model*. The relational data model, about which you will learn in this book, is just such a formal structure. However, the underlying relationships in a database environment are independent of the data model and therefore also independent of the DBMS you are using. Before you can design a database for any data model, you need to be able to identify data relationships.

> *Note: Most DBMSs support only one data model. Therefore, when you choose a DBMS, you are also choosing your data model.*

In this chapter we will explore data relationships and their characteristics. You will also learn a DBMS-independent technique for documenting those relationships known as the *entity–relationship diagram* (ER diagram).

Entities and Their Attributes

An *entity* is something about which we store data. A customer is an entity, as is a merchandise item stocked by Lasers Only. Entities are not necessarily tangible. For example, an event such as a concert is an entity; an appointment to see the doctor is an entity.

Entities have data that describe them (their *attributes*). For example, a customer entity is usually described by a customer number, first name, last name, street, city, state, zipcode, and phone number. A concert entity might be described by a title, date, location, and name of the performer.

When we represent entities in a database, we actually store only the attributes. Each group of attributes that describes a single real-world occurrence of an entity acts to represent an *instance* of an entity. For example, in Figure 2-1, you can see four instances of a customer entity stored in a database. If we have 1000 customers in our database, then there will be 1000 collections of customer attributes.

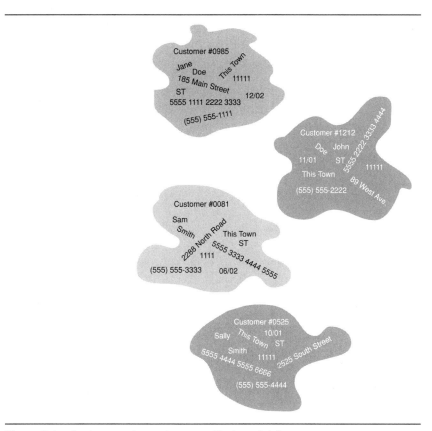

Figure 2-1:   Instances of a customer entity in a database

*Note: Keep in mind that we are not making any state-
ments about how the instances are physically stored.
What you see in Figure 2-1 is purely a conceptual representation.*

Entity Identifiers

The only purpose for putting the data that describe an entity into a
database is to retrieve the data at some later date. This means that
we must have some way of distinguishing one entity from another
so that we can always be certain that we are retrieving the precise
entity we want. We do this by ensuring that each entity has some

attribute values that distinguish it from every other entity in the database (an *entity identifier*).

Assume, for example, that Lasers Only has two customers named John Smith. If an employee searches for the items John Smith has on order, which John Smith will the DBMS retrieve? In this case, both of them. Because there is no way to distinguish between the two customers, the result of the query will be inaccurate.

Lasers Only solved the problem by creating unique customer numbers. That is indeed a common solution to identifying instances of entities where there is no simple unique identifier suggested by the data themselves.

Another solution would be to pair the customer's first and last names with his or her telephone number. This combination of columns (a *concatenated identifier*) would also uniquely identify each customer. There are, however, two drawbacks to doing so. First, the identifier is long and clumsy; it would be easy to make mistakes when entering any of the parts. Second, if the customer's phone number changes, then the identifier must also change. As you read in Chapter 1, changes in an entity identifier can cause serious problems in a database.

Some entities, such as invoices, come with natural identifiers (the invoice number). We assign unique, meaningless numbers to others — especially accounts, people, places, and things. Still others require concatenated identifiers.

> Note: We will examine the issue of what makes a good unique identifier more closely in Chapter 4, when we talk about "primary keys."

When we store an instance of an entity in a database, we want the DBMS to ensure that the new instance has a unique identifier. This is an example of a *constraint* on a database, a rule to which data must adhere. The enforcement of a variety of database constraints helps us to maintain data consistency and accuracy.

Single-Valued versus Multivalued Attributes

Because we are eventually going to create a relational database, the attributes in our data model must be *single-valued*. This means that for a given instance of an entity, each attribute can have only one value. For example, a customer entity allows only one telephone number for each customer. If a customer has more than one phone number and wants them all included in the database, then the customer entity cannot handle them.

> Note: While it is true that the entity–relationship model of a database is independent of the formal data model used to express the structure of the data to a DBMS, we often make decisions on how to model the data based on the requirements of the formal data model we will be using. Removing multivalued attributes is one such case. You will also see an example of this when we deal with many-to-many relationships between entities.

The existence of more than one phone number turns the phone number attribute into a *multivalued attribute*. Because an entity in a relational database cannot have multivalued attributes, you must handle those attributes by creating an entity to hold them.

In the case of the multiple phone numbers, we could create a phone number entity. Each instance of the entity would include the customer number of the person to whom the phone number belonged along with the telephone number. If a customer had three phone numbers, then there would be three instances of the phone number entity for the customer. The entity's identifier would be the concatenation of the customer number and the telephone number.

> Note: There is no way to avoid using the telephone number as part of the entity identifier in the telephone number entity. As you will come to understand as you read this book, in this particular case there is no harm in using it in this way.

What is the problem with a multivalued attribute? Multivalued attributes can cause problems with the meaning of data in the database, significantly slow down searching, and place unnecessary restrictions on the amount of data that can be stored.

Assume, for example, that you have an Employee entity with attributes for the names and birthdates of dependents. Each attribute is allowed to store multiple values. How will you associate the correct birthdate with the name of the dependent to which it applies? Will it be by the position of a value store in the attribute (i.e., the first name is related to the first birthdate, and so on)? If so, how will you ensure that there is a birthdate for each name and a name for each birthdate? How will you ensure that the order of the values is never mixed up?

When searching a multivalued attribute, a DBMS must search each value in the attribute, most likely scanning the contents of the attribute sequentially. A sequential search is the slowest type of search available.

In addition, how many values should a multivalued column be able to store? If you specify a maximum number, what will happen when you need to store more than the maximum number of values? For example, what if you allow room for 10 dependents in the Employee entity just discussed and you encounter an employee with 11 dependents? Do you create another instance of the Employee entity to handle that person? Consider all the problems that doing so would create, particularly in terms of the unnecessary duplicated data.

> Note: Although it is theoretically possible to write a DBMS that will store an unlimited number of values in an attribute, the implementation would be difficult and searching much slower than if the maximum number of values were specified in the database design.

As a general rule, if you run across a multivalued attribute, this is a major hint that you need another attribute. The only way to handle multiple values of the same attribute is to create an entity of which you can store multiple instances, once for each value of the attribute. In the case of the Employee entity, we would need a Dependent entity that could be related to the Employee entity. There would be one occurrence of the Dependent entity related to an occurrence of the Employee entity for each of an employee's dependents. In this way, there is no limit to the number of an employee's dependents. In addition, each occurrence of the Dependent entity would contain the name and birthdate of only one dependent, eliminating any confusion about which name was associated with which birthdate. Searching would also be faster because the DBMS could use fast search techniques on the individual Dependent entity occurrences, without resorting to the slow sequential search.

Avoiding Collections of Entities

When you first begin to work with entities, the nature of an entity can be somewhat confusing. Consider, for example, the merchandise inventory handled by Lasers Only. Is "inventory" an entity? No. Inventory is a collection of the merchandise items handled by the store. The entity is actually the merchandise item. Viewing all of the instances of the merchandise item entity as a whole provides the inventory.

To make this a bit clearer, consider the attributes you would need if you decided to include an inventory entity: merchandise item number, item title, number in stock, retail price, and so on. But because you are trying to describe an entire inventory with a single entity, you need multiple values for each of those attributes. As you read earlier, however, attributes cannot be multivalued. This tells you that inventory cannot stand as an entity. It must be represented as a collection of instances of a merchandise item entity.

As another example, consider a person's medical history maintained by a doctor. Like an inventory, a medical history is a collection of more than one entity. A medical history is made up of appointments and the events that occur during those appointments. Therefore, the history is really a collection of instances of appointment entities and medical treatment entities. The "history" is an output that a database application can obtain by gathering the data stored in the underlying entity instances.

Documenting Logical Data Relationships

Entity-relationship diagrams provide a way to document the entities in a database along with the attributes that describe them. There are actually several styles of ER diagrams. The two most commonly used styles are Chen (named after the originator of ER modeling, Dr. Peter P. S. Chen) and Information Engineering (IE), which grew out of work by James Martin and Clive Finkelstein. It does not matter which you use, as long as everyone who is using the diagram understands its symbols.

Both the Chen and Information Engineering models use rectangles to represent entities. Each entity's name appears in the rectangle and is expressed in the singular, as in

The original Chen model has no provision for showing attributes on the ER diagram itself. However, many people have extended the model to include the attributes in ovals:

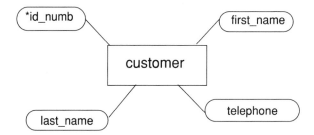

The entity's identifier is the attribute preceded by an asterisk (*id_numb).

The Information Engineering model includes the attributes in the rectangle with the entity:

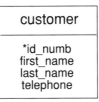

Because the Information Engineering model tends to produce a less cluttered diagram, we will be using it for most of the diagrams in this book, although you will be introduced to elements of both models throughout this chapter.

Entities and Attributes for Lasers Only

The major entities and their attributes for the Lasers Only database can be found in Figure 2-2. As you will see, the design will require additional entities as we work with the relationships between those already identified. In particular, there is no information in Figure 2-2 that indicates which items appear on which orders because that information is a part of the logical relationship between orders and items.

The entities in Figure 2-2 and the remainder of the ER diagrams in this book were created with a special type of software known as a *CASE tool* (computer-aided software engineering). CASE tools provide a wide range of data and systems modeling assistance. You will find more detail on how CASE tools support the database design process in Chapter 9.

Note: The specific product used for these diagrams was MacA&D, which provides capabilities typical of most professional CASE tools.

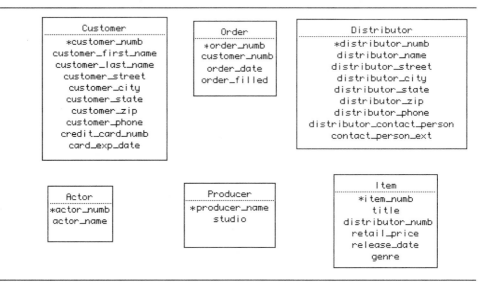

Figure 2-2:   **Major entities and their attributes for the Lasers Only database**

Domains

Each attribute has a *domain,* an expression of the permissible values for that attribute. A domain can be very small. For example, a T-shirt store might have a Size attribute for its merchandise items with the values L, XL, and XXL comprising the entire domain. In contrast, an attribute for a customer's first name is very large and might be specified only as "text" or "human names."

A DBMS enforces a domain through a *domain constraint.* Whenever a value is stored in the database, the DBMS verifies that it comes from its attribute's specified domain. Although in many cases we cannot specify small domains, at the very least the domain assures us that we are getting data of the right type. For example, a DBMS can prevent a user from storing 123x50 in an attribute whose domain is currency values. Most DBMSs also provide fairly tight domain checking on date and time attributes, which can help you avoid illegal dates such as February 30.

Documenting Domains

The common formats used for ER diagrams do not usually include domains on the diagrams themselves, but store the domains in an associated document (usually a *data dictionary*, something about which you will read much more throughout this book). However, the version of the Chen method that includes attributes can also include domains by placing an expression of the domain underneath each attribute. Notice in Figure 2-3 that three of the domains are fairly general (integer and character), while the domain for the telephone number attribute includes a very specific format. Whether a domain can be constrained in this way depends on the DBMS.

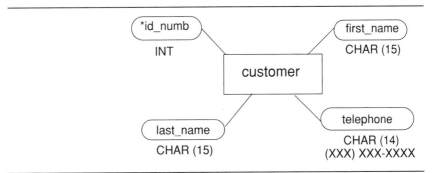

Figure 2-3: Indicating domains on an ER diagram

> *Note: There is no specific syntax for indicating domains. However, if you know which DBMS you will be using, consider using the column data types supported by that product as domains in an ERD to simplify the later conversion to the DBMS's requirements.*

Practical Domain Choices

The domains that Lasers Only chooses for its attributes should theoretically be independent of the DBMS that the company will use. In practical terms, however, it makes little sense to assign domains that you cannot implement. Therefore, the database designer working for Lasers Only takes a look at the DBMS to see what column data types are supported.

Most relational DBMSs that use SQL as their query language provide the following among their column data types, any of which can be assigned as a domain to an attribute:

- ◆ CHAR: A fixed-length string of text, usually up to 256 characters.
- ◆ VARCHAR: A variable-length string of text, usually up to 256 characters.
- ◆ INT: An integer, the size of which varies depending on the operation system.
- ◆ DECIMAL and NUMERIC: Real numbers, with fractional portions to the right of the decimal point. When you assign a real number domain, you must specify how many digits the number can contain (including the decimal point) and how many digits should be to the right of the decimal point (the value's *precision*). For example, currency values usually have precision of two, so a number in the format XXX.XX might have a domain of DECIMAL (6,2).
- ◆ DATE: A date.
- ◆ TIME: A time.
- ◆ DATETIME: The combination of a date and a time.
- ◆ BOOLEAN: A logical value (either true or false).

Many of today's DBMSs also support a data type known as a BLOB (binary large object), which can store anything binary, such as a graphic.

Choosing the right domain can make a big difference in the accuracy of a database. For example, a U.S. zip code is made up of five or nine digits. Should an attribute for a zip code therefore be given a domain of INT? No, for two reasons. First, it would be nice to be able to include the hyphen in nine-digit zip codes. Second, and more important, zip codes in the northeast begin with a zero. If they are stored as a number, the leading zero disappears. Therefore, we always choose a CHAR domain for zip codes. Since we never do arithmetic with zip codes, nothing is lost by using character rather than numeric storage.

By the same token, it is important to choose domains of DATE and TIME for chronological data. As an example, consider what would happen if the dates 01/12/2000 and 08/12/1999 were stored as characters. If you ask the DBMS to choose which date comes first, the DBMS will compare the character strings in alphabetical order, and respond that 01/12/2000 comes first, because 01 alphabetically precedes 08. The only way to get character dates to order correctly is to use the format YYYY/MM/DD, a format that is rarely used anywhere in the world. However, if the dates were given a domain of DATE, then the DBMS would order them properly. The DBMS would also be able to perform date arithmetic, finding the interval between two dates or adding constants (for example, 30 days) to dates.

Basic Data Relationships

Once you have a good idea of the basic entities in your database environment, your next task is to identify the relationships among those entities. There are three basic types of relationships that you may encounter: one-to-one, one-to-many, and many-to-many.

Before turning to the types of relationships themselves, there is one important thing to keep in mind: The relationships that are stored in a database are between instances of entities. For example, a Lasers Only customer is related to the items he or she orders. Each instance of the customer entity is related to instances of the specific items ordered (see Figure 2-4).

> Note: As you look at Figure 2-4, once again remember that this is a purely conceptual representation of what is in the database and is completely unrelated to the physical storage of the data.

When we document data relationships, such as when we draw an ER diagram, we show the types of relationships among entities. We

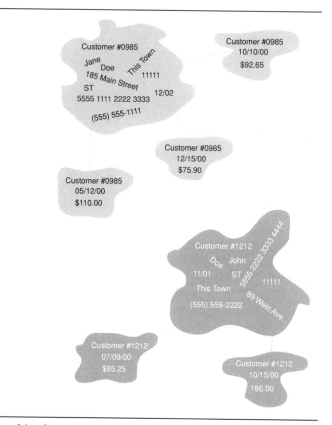

Figure 2-4:   Relationships between instances of entities in a database

are showing the possible relationships that are allowable in the database. Unless we specify that a relationship is mandatory, there is no requirement that every instance of every entity be involved in every documented relationship. For example, Lasers Only could store data about a customer without the customer having any current orders to which it is related.

One-to-One Relationships

Consider, for a moment, an airport in a small town and the town in which the airport is located, both of which are described in a database of small town airports. Each of these might be represented as an instance of a different type of entity. The relationships between the two instances can then be expressed as "The airport is located in one and only one town and the town contains one and only one airport."

This is a true *one-to-one relationship* because at no time can a single airport be related to more than one town and no town can be related to more than one airport. (Although there are municipalities that have more than one airport, the towns in this database are too small for that to ever happen.)

If we have two instances of two entities (A and B) called A_i and B_i, then a one-to-one relationship exists if at all times A_i is related to no instances of entity B or one instance of entity B, and B_i is related to no instances of entity A or one instance of entity A.

True one-to-one relationships are very rare in business. For example, assume that Lasers Only decides to start dealing with a new distributor of laser discs. At first, the company orders only one specialty title from the new distributor. If we peered inside the database, we would see that the instance of the distributor entity was related to just the one merchandise item instance. This would then appear to be a one-to-one relationship. However, over time Lasers Only may choose to order more titles from the new distributor, which would violate the rule that the distributor must be related to no more than one merchandise item. What we have is therefore not a true one-to-one relationship. (This is an example of a one-to-many relationship, which is discussed in the next section of this chapter.)

By the same token, what if Lasers Only created a special credit card entity to hold data about the credit cards that renters used to secure their rentals? Each customer has only one credit card on file with the store. There would therefore seem to be a one-to-one relationship between the instance of a customer entity and the instance of the credit card entity. However, in this case we are really dealing with a single entity. The credit card number, the type of credit card, and the credit card's expiration date can all become attributes of the customer entity. Given that only one credit card is stored for each customer, the attributes are not multivalued; no separate entity is needed.

If you think you are dealing with a one-to-one relationship, look at it very carefully. Be sure that you are not really looking at a one-to-many relationship or that what you think is two entities should really be one.

One-to-Many Relationships

The most common type of relationship is a *one-to-many relationship*. (In fact, most relational databases are constructed from the rare one-to-one relationship and numerous one-to-many relationships.) For example, Lasers Only typically orders many titles from each distributor and a given title comes from only one distributor. By the same token, a customer places many orders but an order comes from only one customer.

If we have instances of two entities (A and B), then a one-to-many relationship exists between two instances (A_i and B_i) if A_i is related to zero, one, or more instances of entity B and B_i is related to zero or one instance of entity A.

Other one-to-many relationships include that between a daughter and her biological mother. A woman may have zero, one, or more biological daughters; a daughter has only one biological mother. As another example, consider a computer and its CPU. A CPU may not be installed in any computer or it may be installed in at most one computer; a computer may have no CPU, one CPU, or more than one CPU.

The example about which you read earlier concerning Lasers Only and the distributor from which the company ordered only one title is actually a one-to-many relationship where the "many" is currently "one." Remember that when we are specifying data relationships, we are indicating possible relationships and not necessarily requiring that all instances of all entities participate in every documented relationship. There is absolutely no requirement that a distributor be related to any merchandise item, much less one or more merchandise items. (It might not make much sense to have a distributor in the database from whom the company did not order, but there is nothing to prevent data about that distributor from being stored.)

Many-to-Many Relationships

Many-to-many relationships are also very common. There is, for example, a many-to-many relationship between an order placed by a Lasers Only customer and the merchandise items carried by the store. An order can contain multiple items; each item can appear on more than one order. The same is true of the orders placed with distributors. An order can contain multiple items and each item can appear on more than one order.

A many-to-many relationship exists between entities A and B if for two instances of those entities (A_i and B_i), A_i can be related to zero, one, or more instances of entity B and B_i can be related to zero, one, or more instances of entity A.

Many-to-many relationships bring two major problems to a database's design. These issues and the way in which we solve them are discussed in the next major section of this chapter ("Dealing with Many-to-Many Relationships").

Weak Entities and Mandatory Relationships

As we have been discussing types of data relationships, we have defined those relationships by starting each with "zero," indicating that the participation by a given instance of an entity in a relationship is optional. For example, Lasers Only can store data about a customer in its database before the customer places an order. Therefore, an instance of the customer entity does not have to be related to any instances of the order entity.

However, the reverse is not true in this database: An order *must* be related to a customer. Without a customer, an order cannot exist. An order is therefore an example of a *weak entity*, one that cannot exist in the database unless a related instance of another entity is present and related to it. An instance of the customer entity can be related to zero, one, or more orders. However, an instance of the order entity must be related to one and only one customer. The "zero" option is not available to a weak entity. The relationship between an instance of the order entity and the customer is therefore a mandatory relationship.

Identifying weak entities and their associated mandatory relationships can be very important for maintaining the consistency and integrity of the database. Consider the effect, for example, of storing an order without knowing the customer to which it belongs. There would be no way to ship the item to the customer, causing a company to lose business.

By the same token, we typically define the relationship between an order and the order lines (the specific items on the order) as one-to-many because we don't want to allow an order line to exist in the database without it being related to an order. (An order line is meaningless without knowing the order to which it belongs.)

In contrast, we can allow a a merchandise item to exist in a database without indicating the supplier from which it comes (assuming that there is only one source per item). This lets us store data about a new item before we have decided on a supplier. In this case, the relationship between a supplier and an item is actually zero-to-many.

Documenting Relationships

The Chen and Information Engineering methods of drawing ER diagrams have very different ways of representing relationships, each of which has its advantages in terms of the amount of information it provides and its complexity.

The Chen Method

The Chen method uses diamonds for relationships and lines with arrows to show the type of relationship between entities. For example, in Figure 2-5 you can see the relationship between a Lasers Only customer and an order. The single arrow pointing toward the customer entity indicates that an order belongs to at most one customer. The double arrow pointing toward the order entity indicates that a customer can place one or more orders. The word within the relationship diamond gives some indication of the meaning of the relationship.

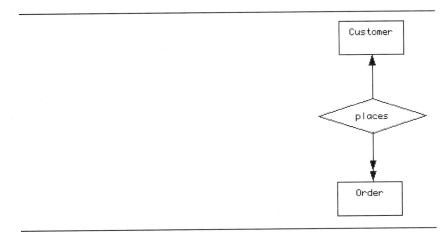

Figure 2-5:   Using the Chen method with relationship diamonds and arrows

There are two alternative styles within the Chen method. The first (for example, Figure 2-6) replaces the arrows with numbers and letters. A "1" indicates that an order comes from one customer. The "M" (or an "N") indicates that a customer can place many orders.

The second alternative addresses the problem of trying to read the relationship in both directions when the name of the relationship is within the diamond. "Customer places order" makes sense, but "order places customer" does not. To solve the problem, this alternative removes the relationship name from the diamond and adds both the relationship and its inverse to the diagram, as in Figure 2-7. This version of the diagram can be read easily in either direction:

"A customer places many orders" and "An order is placed by one customer."

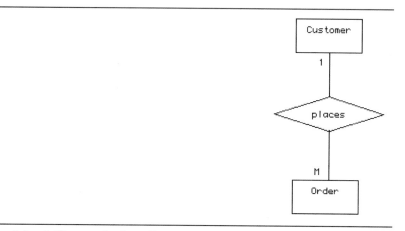

Figure 2-6:   A Chen method ER diagram using letters and numbers rather than arrows to show relationships

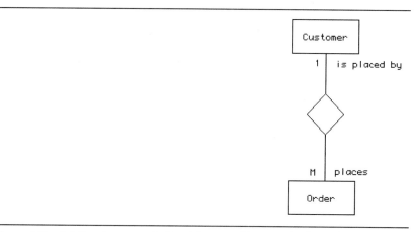

Figure 2-7:   Adding inverse relationships to a Chen method ER diagram

There is one major limitation to the Chen method of drawing ER diagrams: There is no obvious way to indicate weak entities and mandatory relationships. For example, an order should not exist in the database without a customer. Therefore, order is a weak entity and its relationship with a customer is mandatory.

Some database designers have therefore added a new symbol to the Chen method for a weak entity — a double-bordered rectangle:

Whenever a weak entity is introduced into an ER diagram, it indicates that the relationship between that entity and at least one of its parents is mandatory. However, if the entity does happen to have multiple parents, then there is no way to determine simply by looking at the diagram which of the relationships are mandatory.

The Information Engineering Method

The Information Engineering (IE) method exchanges simplicity in line ends for added information. As a first example, consider Figure 2-8. This is the same one-to-many relationship we have been using to demonstrate the Chen method ER diagrams. However, in this case the ends of the lines indicate which relationships are mandatory.

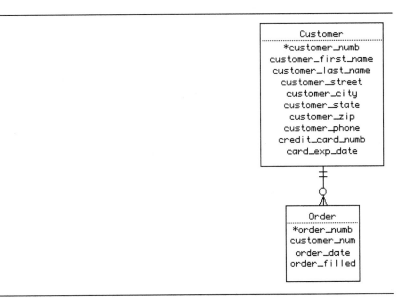

Figure 2-8:   A one-to-many relationship using the IE method

The double line below the customer entity means that each order is related to one and only one customer. Because zero is not an option, the relationship is mandatory. In contrast, the 0 and three-legged teepee connected to the order entity mean that a customer may have zero, one, or more orders.

There are four symbols used at the ends of lines in an IE diagram:

- | |: One and one only (mandatory relationship)
- 0 |: Zero or one
- > |: One or more (mandatory relationship)
- >0: Zero, one, or more

Although we often see the symbols turned 90 degrees, as they are in Figure 2-8, they are actually readable if viewed sideways as in the preceding list.

An IE method ER diagram often includes attributes directly on the diagram. As you can see in Figure 2-8, entity identifiers are marked with an asterisk.

Basic Relationships for Lasers Only

The major entities in the Lasers Only database are diagrammed in Figure 2-9. You read the relationships in the following way:

- One customer can place zero, one, or more orders. An order comes from one and only one customer.
- An order has one or more items on it. An item can appear on zero, one, or more orders.
- An actor appears in zero, one, or more items. An item has zero, one, or more actors in it. (There may occasionally be films that feature animals rather than human actors; therefore it is probably unwise to require that every merchandise item be related to at least one actor.)
- Each item has zero, one, or more producers. Each producer is responsible for zero, one, or more items. (Although in practice you would not store data about a

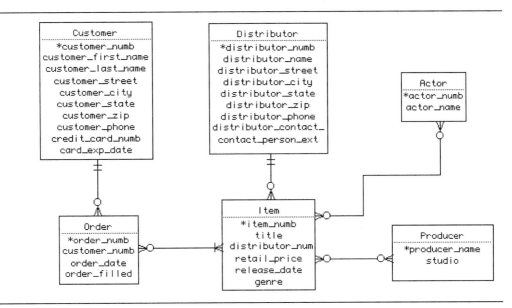

Figure 2-9:   **The major entities and the relationships between them in the Lasers Only database**

producer unless that producer was related to an item, leaving the relationship between a producer and an item as optional means that you can store producers without items if necessary.)

The major thing to notice about this design is that there are three many-to-many relationships: order to item, actor to item, and producer to item. Before you can map this data model to a relational database, they must be handled in some way.

Dealing with Many-to-Many Relationships

As you read earlier, there are problems with many-to-many relationships. The first is fairly straightforward: The relational data model cannot handle many-to-many relationships directly; it is limited to one-to-one and one-to-many relationships. This means that you must replace the many-to-many relationships that you have identified in your database environment with a collection of one-to-many relationships if you want to be able to use a relational DBMS.

The second is a bit more subtle. To understand it, consider the relationship between an order Lasers Only places with a distributor and the merchandise items on the order. There is a many-to-many relationship between the order and the item because each order can be for many items and, over time, each item can appear on many orders. Whenever Lasers Only places an order for an item, the number of copies of the item varies, depending on the perceived demand for the item at the time the order is placed.

Now the question: Where should we store the quantity being ordered? It cannot be part of the order entity because the quantity depends on which item we are talking about. By the same token, the quantity cannot be part of the item entity because the quantity depends on the specific order.

What you have just seen is known as *relationship data*, data that apply to the relationship between two entities rather than to the entities themselves. Relationships, however, cannot have attributes. We therefore must have some entity to represent the relationship between the two, an entity to which the relationship data can belong.

Composite Entities

Entities that exist to represent the relationship between two other entities are known as *composite* entities. As an example of how composite entities work, consider the relationship between an order placed by a Lasers Only customer and the items on the order. There is a many-to-many relationship between an item and an order: An order can contain many items and over time the same item can appear on many orders.

What we then need is an entity that tells us that a specific title appears on a specific order. If you look at Figure 2-10, you will see three order instances and three merchandise item instances. The first order for customer 0985 (Order #1) contains only one item

(item 09244). The second order for customer 0985 (Order #2) contains a second copy of item 02944 as well as item 10101. Order #3, which belongs to customer 1212, also has two items on it (item 10101 and item 00250).

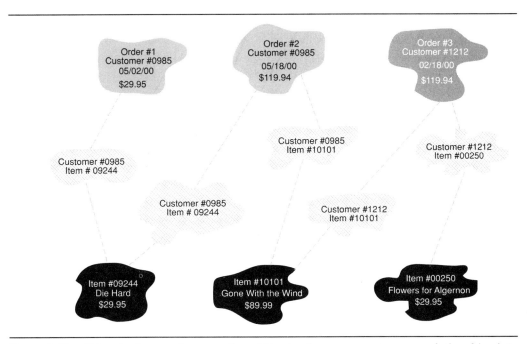

Figure 2-10: **Using instances of composite entities to change many-to-many relationships into one-to-many relationships**

There are five items ordered among the three orders. The middle of the diagram therefore contains five instances of a composite entity we will call a "line item" (thinking of it as a line item on a packing slip). The line item entity has been created solely to represent the relationship between an order and a merchandise item.

Each order is related to one line item instance for each item on the order. In turn, each item is related to one line item instance for each order on which it appears. Each line item instance is related to one and only one order; it is also related to one and only one merchandise item. As a result, the relationship between an order and its line items is one-to-many (one order has many line items) and the relationship between an item and the orders on which it appears is one-to-many (one merchandise item appears in many line items). The presence of the composite entity has removed the original many-to-many relationship and turned it into two one-to-many relationships.

If necessary, the composite entity can be used to store relationship data. In the preceding example, we might include an attribute for the quantity ordered, a flag to indicate whether it has been shipped, and a shipping date.

Documenting Composite Entities

In some extensions of the Chen method for drawing ER diagrams, the symbol for a composite entity is the combination of the rectangle used for an entity and the diamond used for a relationship:

The Information Engineering method, however, has no special symbol for a composite entity.

Resolving Lasers Only's Many-to-Many Relationships

To eliminate Lasers Only's many-to-many relationships, the database designer must replace each many-to-many relationship with a composite entity and two one-to-many relationships. As you can see in Figure 2-11, the three new entities are as follows:

♦ Order lines: The order lines entity represents one item appearing on one order. Each order can have many "order lines," but an order line must appear on one and only one order. By the same token, an order line contains one and only one item but the same item can appear on many order lines, each of which corresponds to a different order.

♦ Performance: The performance entity represents one actor appearing in one film. Each performance is for one and only one film although a film can have many performances (one for each actor in the film). Conversely, an actor is related to one performance for each film in which he or she appears although each performance is in one and only one film.

♦ Production: The production entity represents one producer working on one film. A producer may be involved in many productions, although each production relates to one and only one producer. The relationship with item indicates that each film can be produced by many producers but that each production relates to only one item.

Note: If you find sorting out the relationships in Figure 2-11 a bit difficult, keep in mind that if you rotate the up-and-down symbols 90 degrees, you will actually be able to read the relationships.

Because composite entities exist primarily to indicate a relationship between two other entities, they must be related to both of their parent entities. This is why the relationship between each composite entity in Figure 2-11 and its parents is mandatory.

Relationships and Business Rules

In many ways, database design is as much an art as a science. Exactly what is the "correct" design for a specific business depends on the business rules; what is correct for one organization may not be correct for another.

As an example, assume that you are creating a database for a retail establishment that has more than one store. One of the things you are being asked to model in the database is an employee's schedule. Before you can do that, you need to answer the question of the relationship between an employee and a store: Is it one-to-many or many-to-many? Does an employee always work at only one store—

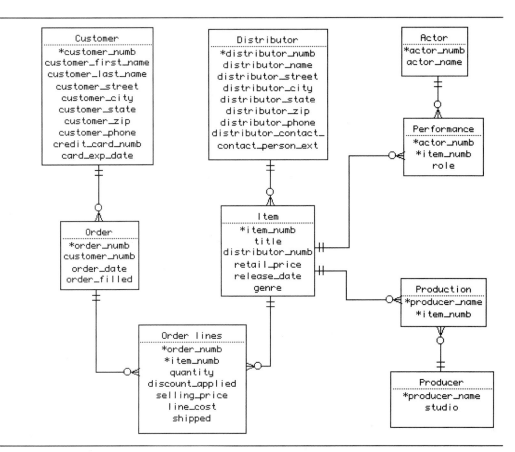

Figure 2-11:   The complete ER diagram for the Lasers Only database

in which case the relationship is one-to-many—or can an employee split his or her time between more than one store, producing a many-to-many relationship? This is not a matter of right or wrong database design, but an issue of how the business operates.

The bottom line is that no matter how much you know about database design, you will not have a good database unless the relationships depicted in that database are an accurate reflection of the relationships in the database environment.

Data Modeling versus Data Flow

One of the most common mistakes people make when they are beginning to do data modeling is to confuse data models with data flows. A *data flow* shows how data are handled within an organization, including who handles the data, where the data are stored, and what is done to the data. In contrast, a *data model* depicts the internal, logical relationships between the data, without regard to who is handling the data or what is being done with them.

Data flows are often documented in data flow diagrams (DFDs). For example, in Figure 2-12 you can see a top-level data flow diagram for Lasers Only. The squares represent the people who are handling the data. Circles represent *processes*, or things that are done with the data. A place where data are stored (a *data store*) appears as two parallel lines, in this example containing the words "Main database." The arrows on the lines show the way in which data pass from one place to another.

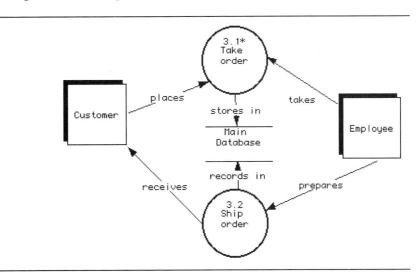

Figure 2-12:   A top-level data flow diagram for Lasers Only

Data flow diagrams are often exploded to show more detail. For example, Figure 2-13 contains an explosion of the "Take Order" process from Figure 2-12. You can now see that the process of taking an order involves two major steps: getting customer information and getting item information.

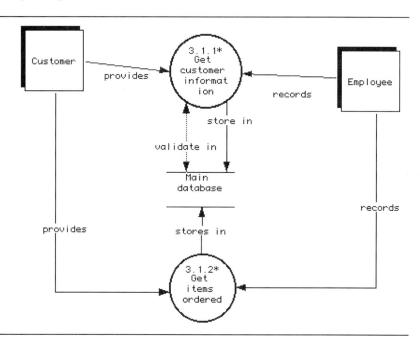

Figure 2-13:   An explosion of the Take order process from Figure 2-12

Each of the processes in Figure 2-13 can be exploded even further to show additional detail (see Figure 2-14 and Figure 2-15). At this point, the diagrams are almost detailed enough so that an application designer can plan an application program.

Where do the database and its ER diagram fit into all of this? The entire ER diagram is buried inside the "Main database." In fact, most CASE tools allow you to link your ER diagram to a database's representation on a data flow diagram. Then, you can simply double-click on the database representation to bring the ER diagram into view.

> *Note: Don't forget that you can read a great deal more about using a CASE tool in Chapter 9.*

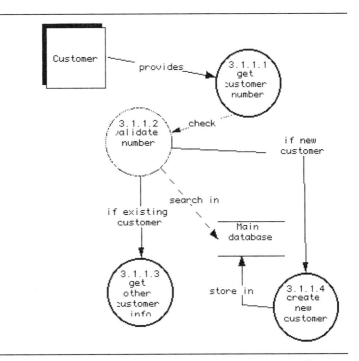

Figure 2-14:   An explosion of the "Get customer information" process from Figure 2-13

There are a few guidelines you can use to keep data flows and data models separate:

♦ A data flow shows who uses or handles data. A data model does not.

♦ A data flow shows how data are gathered (the people or other sources from which they come). A data model does not.

♦ A data flow shows operations on data (the processes through which data are transformed). A data model does not.

♦ A data model shows how data entities are interrelated. A data flow does not.

♦ A data model shows the attributes that describe data entities. A data flow does not.

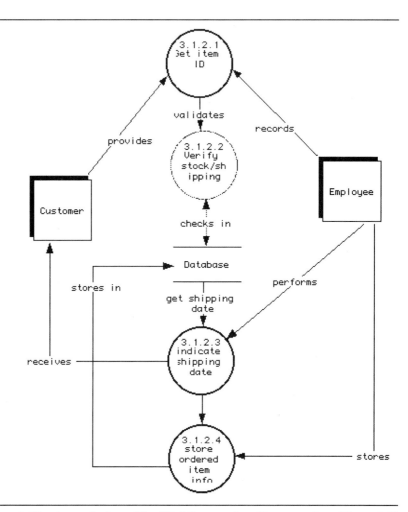

Figure 2-15:   An explosion of the "Get items ordered" process from Figure 2-13

The bottom line is this: A data model contains information about the data being stored in a database (entities, attributes, and entity relationships). If data about an entity are not going to be stored in the database, then that entity should not be part of the database. For example, although the Lasers Only data flow diagram shows the Lasers Only employee who handles most of the data, no data about employees are going to be stored in the database. Therefore, there is no employee entity in the ER diagram.

Schemas

A completed entity-relationship diagram represents the overall, logical plan of a database. In database terms, it is therefore known as a *schema*. This is the way in which the people responsible for maintaining the database will see the design. However, users (both interactive users and application programs) may work with only a portion of the logical schema. And both the logical schema and the users' views of the data are at the same time distinct from the physical storage.

The underlying physical storage, which is managed by the DBMS, is known as the *physical schema*. It is for the most part determined by the DBMS. (Only very large DBMSs give you any control over physical storage.) The beauty of this arrangement is that both database designers and users do not need to be concerned about physical storage, greatly simplifying access to the database and making it much easier to make changes to both the logical and physical schemas.

Because there are three ways to look at a database, some databases today are said to be based on a *three-schema architecture* (see Figure 2-16). Systems programmers and other people involved with managing physical storage deal with the physical schema. Most of today's relational DBMSs provide almost no control over the file structures used to store database data. However, DBMSs designed to run on mainframes to handle extremely large datasets do allow some tailoring of the layout of internal file storage.

> Note: As you will see in Chapter 3, DBMSs based on earlier data models were more closely tied to their physical storage than relational DBMSs. Therefore, systems programmers were able to specify physical file structures to a much greater extent.

Database designers, database administrators, and some application programmers are aware of and use the logical schema. End users working interactively and application programmers who are creating database applications for them work with user views of the database.

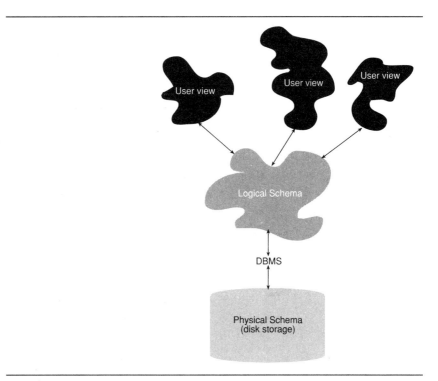

Figure 2-16:   The three-schema architecture

Throughout the rest of this book we will be focusing on the design of the logical schema. You will also learn how to create and use database elements that provide users with limited portions of the database.

For Further Reading

The entity–relationship model was developed by Dr. Peter P. S. Chen. If you want to learn more about its early forms and how the model has changed, see the following:

Chen, P. "The Entity-Relationship Model: Toward a Unified View of Data," *ACM Transactions on Database Systems*. Vol. I, No. 1, March, 1976.

Chen, P. *The Entity-Relationship Approach to Logical Database Design*. QED Information Sciences, Data Base Monograph Series, No. 6, 1977.

Chen, P. *Entity-Relationship Approach to Information Modeling*. E-R Institute, 1981.

The original work that described Information Engineering can be found in the following:

Martin, James. *Information Engineering, Book I: Introduction, Book II: Planning and Analysis, Book III: Design and Construction*. Prentice Hall, 1989.

Finkelstein, Clive. *An Introduction to Information Engineering*. Addison-Wesley, 1989.

For more recent, in-depth coverage of ER diagramming, you can consult either of the following:

Barker, Richard. *Case*Method: Entity Relationship Modelling*. Addison-Welsey, 1990.

Thalheim, Richard. *Entity-Relationship Modeling: Foundations of Database Technology*. Springer Verlag, 2000.

3

Historical Antecedents

In the beginning, there were data files … and from the need to manage the data stored in those files arose a variety of data management methods, most of which preceded the relational data model and, because of their shortcomings, paved the way for the acceptance of relational databases.

This chapter provides an overview of data management organizations used prior to the introduction of the relational data model. Although you do not need to read this chapter to understand the rest of the book, some of the case studies in Part II mention concepts discussed here.

File Processing Systems

The first commercial computer—ENIAC—was designed to help process the 1960 census. Its designers thought that all computers could do was crunch numbers; the idea that computers could handle text data came later. Unfortunately, the tools available to handle data weren't particularly sophisticated. In most cases, all the computing staff had available was some type of storage (at first tapes and later disks) and a high-level language compiler.

Early File Processing

Early file processing systems are made up of a set of data files—most commonly text files—and application programs that manipulate those files directly without the intervention of a DBMS. The files are laid out in a very precise, fixed format. Each individual piece of data (a first name, last name, street address, and so on) is known as a *field*. The data that describe a single entity are collected into a *record*. A data file is therefore made up of a collection of records.

Each field is allocated a specific number of bytes. The fixed field lengths mean that no delimiters are required between fields or at the end of records, although some data files do include them. A portion of such a data file might appear like Figure 3-1.

The programs that store and retrieve data in the data files locate data by their byte positions in the file. Assuming that the first record in a file is numbered 0, a program can locate the start of any field with the computation

```
record_number * record_length + starting_position_of_field
```

This type of file structure therefore is very easy to parse (i.e., separate into individual fields). It is also simplifies the process of writing the application programs that manipulate the files.

```
 1  John        Smith       25 W. Main  Street  ..
 2  Jane        Johnson     120 Elm Lane ...
 3  Edward      Smith       44 Pine Heights ...
 4  Louis       Johnson     250 W. Main Street ...
 5  John        Jones       RR1 Box 250B ...
 6  Theresa     Jones       Anderson Road ...
 7  Thomas      Smith       12589 Highway 25 South ..
 8  Jane        Smith       45 Roxbury Court ...
 9  Edward      Jones       10101 Binary Road ...
10  Emily       Johnson     202 Somerset Blvd. ...
11  Thomas      Johnson     25 N. Main Street ...
12  Louis       Smith       918 Bayleaf Terrace ...
```

Figure 3-1: A portion of a fixed field length data file

If the file is stored on tape, then access to the records is sequential. Such a system is well suited for batch processing *if* the records are in the order in which they need to be accessed. If the records are stored on disk, then the software can perform direct access reads and writes. In either case, however, the program needs to know exactly where each piece of data is stored and is responsible for issuing the appropriate read and/or write commands.

> *Note: Some tape drives are able to read backward to access data preceding the last written or read location. However, those that cannot read backward need to rewind completely and then perform a sequential scan beginning at the start of the tape to find data preceding the previous read/write location. Understandably, random access to data is unacceptably slow for interactive data processing.*

These systems are subject to many problems, including all of those discussed in Chapter 1. In addition, programmers struggle with the following limitations:

♦ Changing the layout of a data file (e.g., changing the size of a field or record) requires changing all of the programs that access that file as well as rewriting the file to accommodate the new layout.

♦ Access is very fast when processing all records sequentially in the physical order of the file. However, searches for specific records, based on some matching criteria, also have to be performed sequentially, a very slow process. This holds true even for files stored on disk.

The major advantage to a file processing system is that it's cheap. An organization that installs a computer typically has everything it needs: external storage and a compiler. In addition, a file processing system is relatively easy to create, in that it requires little advance planning. However, as you have read, the myriad problems resulting from unnecessary duplicated data as well as the close coupling of programs and physical file layouts and the serious performance problems that arise when searching the file, soon drove data management personnel of the 1950s and 1960s to search for alternatives.

ISAM Files

Prior to the introduction of true database management systems, programmers at IBM developed an enhanced file organization known as *Indexed Sequential Access Method* (ISAM), which supported quick sequential access to data for batch processing but also provided indexes to fields in the file for fast access searches.

An ISAM file is stored on a disk. It is written initially to disk with excess space left in each cylinder occupied by the file. This allows records to be added in sequential key order. When a cylinder fills up, records are written to an overflow area and linked back to where they appear in the sequence in the file's primary storage areas (see Figure 3-2).

> *Note: Hard drives write files to a single track on a single surface in a disk drive. When the track is full, then the drive writes to the same track on another surface. The same tracks on all the surfaces in a stack of platters in a disk drive are known as a cylinder. By filling a cylinder before moving to another track on the same surface, the disk drive can avoid moving the access arm to which read/write heads are attached, thus saving time in the read or write process.*

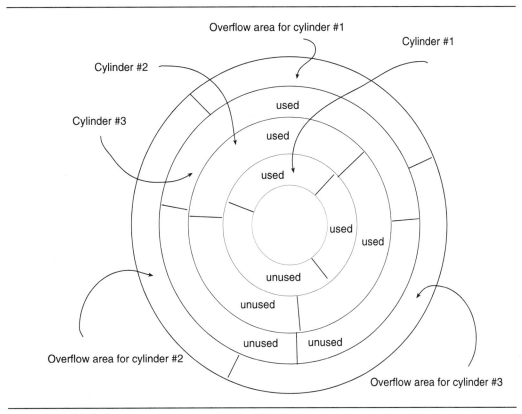

Figure 3-2: ISAM file organization

When the overflow area fills up, the file must be *reblocked*. During the reblocking process, the file size is increased and records are re-written, once again leaving expansion space on each cylinder occupied by the file. No data processing can occur using the file while reblocking is in progress.

Depending on the implementation, indexes to ISAM files may be stored in the same file as the data or in separate files. When the data files are stored separately, the functions that manipulate the files treat the indexes and data as if they were one logical file.

> *Note: Although ISAM files have largely fallen into disuse, the DBMS Informix continues to use its own version of ISAM— c-isam—for data storage.*

Limitations of File Processing

File processing, regardless of whether it uses simple data files or ISAM files, is awkward at best. In addition to the problems mentioned earlier in this section, there are two more major drawbacks to file processing.

First, file processing cannot support *ad hoc* queries (queries that arise at the spur of the moment, cannot be predicted, and may never arise again). Because data files are created by the organization they are serving, there is no common layout to the files from one organization to another. There is therefore no reasonable way for a software developer to write a language that can query any data file; a language that would query file A probably won't work with file B because there is no similarity between the layout of the files. Therefore, access is limited to preplanned queries and reports that are provided by application programs.

So much of today's data access requires ad hoc querying capabilities. Consider, for example, an ATM machine, perhaps the penultimate ad hoc query device. When you walk up to the machine, there is no way for the machine's software to predict which account you will access. Nor is there any way to predict who will use a particular machine nor what that person will request from the machine. Therefore, the software must be able to access data at any time, from any location, from any account holder, and perform any requested action.

Second, when a file processing system is made up of many files, there is no simple way either to validate cross references between the files or to perform queries that require data from multiple files. This cross-referencing issue is a major data integrity concern. If you store customer data in file A and orders in file B, you want the customer data in file B (even if it's only a customer number) to match the customer data in file A. Whenever data are duplicated, they must remain consistent. Unfortunately, when data are stored in multiple files, there is no easy way to perform this type of validation: The only way is to write a program the uses both files and explicitly verifies that the customer data in file B matches data in file

A. Although this can certainly be done, file processing systems rarely perform this type of validation.

By the same token, queries or reports that require data to be extracted from multiple files are difficult to prepare. The application program that generates the output has to be created to read all necessary files, resulting in a program that iss difficult to debug and maintain due to its complexity.

The solution is to look for some way to separate physical storage structures from logical data access. In other words, the program or user manipulating data shouldn't need to be concerned about physical placement of data in files, but should be able to express data manipulation requests in terms of how data logically relate to one another. This separation of logical and physical data organization is the hallmark of a database system.

File Processing on the Desktop

One of the problems with data management software written for PCs has been that both developers and users often didn't understand the exact meaning of the term database. As a result, the word was applied to any piece of software that managed data stored in a disk file, regardless of whether the software could handle logical data relationships.

The trend was started in the early 1980s by a product called *pfs:File*. The program was a simple file manager. You defined your fields and then used a default form for entering data. There was no way to represent multiple entities or data relationships. Nonetheless, the product was marketed as a database management system and the confusion in the marketplace began.

> *Note: Even more egregious was the use of the word database to describe a rectangular area on a spreadsheet. This misuse, too, is still extant.*

A number of products have fallen into this trap. One such product—*FileMaker Pro*—began as a file manager and has been upgraded to database status. Others, such as the data management segments of integrated packages such as *Microsoft Works* and *ClarisWorks* (aka *AppleWorks*) continue to exist as file managers.

You may often hear products such as those in the preceding paragraph described as "flat-file databases," despite the term "database" being a misnomer. Nonetheless, desktop file managers can be useful tools for applications such as maintaining a mailing list, customer contact list, and so on.

> *Note: Access, which is a part of Microsoft Office for Windows, is a true database management system, although it is intended as a desktop product rather than a client-server product.*

The issue here is not to be a database snob, but to ensure that consumers actually understand what they are buying and the limitations that accompany a file manager. The term database is still misused in software marketing and you need to pay special attention to the capabilities of a product when you are considering a purchase.

The Hierarchical Data Model

The first true database data model to be developed was the *hierarchical data model*, which appeared as the basis of a commercial product in 1966. Like the two network data models that followed, it was a *navigational data model*, meaning that access paths were constrained by predeclared pointer structures in the schema.

Characteristics of the Hierarchical Data Model

A database that is designed to use the hierarchical data model is restricted to one-to-many relationships. In addition, no child entity may have more than one parent entity. The implications of this last restriction are significant.

As an example, consider the ER diagram in Figure 3-3, which contains two hierarchies, or *trees*. The first relates departments to their employees and their projects. The second relates employees to projects. There is a one-to-many relationship between an employee and a department, but a many-to-many relationship between projects and employees. The relationship between department and project is one-to-many.

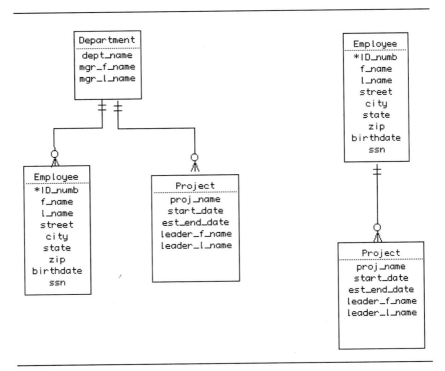

Figure 3-3: Sample hierarchies

Ideally, we would like to be able to use a composite entity to handle the many-to-many relationship. Unfortunately, the hierarchical data model does not permit the inclusion of composite entities. (There is no way to give a single entity two parent entities.) The only solution is to duplicate entity occurrences. This means that a project occurrence must be duplicated for every employee that works on the project. In addition the project and employee entities are duplicated in the department hierarchy as well.

By their very nature, hierarchies include a great deal of duplicated data. This means that hierarchical databases are subject to the data consistency problems that arise from unnecessary data duplication.

There is another major limitation to the hierarchical data model. Access is only through the entity at the top of the hierarchy, the *root*. From each root occurrence, the access path is from top down and left to right. This means that the path through the department hierarchy, for example, is through a department, to all of its employees, and only then to its projects. For example, see Figure 3-4, which contains two occurrences of the department/employee/project hierarchy. The arrows on the dashed lines connecting the entity occurrences represent the traversal order.

The relationships between the entities in an occurrence of a hierarchy are maintained by pointers embedded in the data. As a result, traversing a hierarchy in its default order is very fast. However, if you need random access to data, then access can be extremely slow because you must traverse every entity occurrence in the hierarchy preceding a needed occurrence to reach that needed occurrence. Hierarchies are therefore well suited to batch processing in tree traversal order, but are not suitable for applications that require ad hoc querying.

The hierarchical data model is a giant step forward from file processing systems, including those based on ISAM files. It allows the user to store and retrieve data based on logical data relationships. It therefore provides some independence between the logical and physical data storage, relieving application programmers to a large extent of the need to be aware of the physical file layouts.

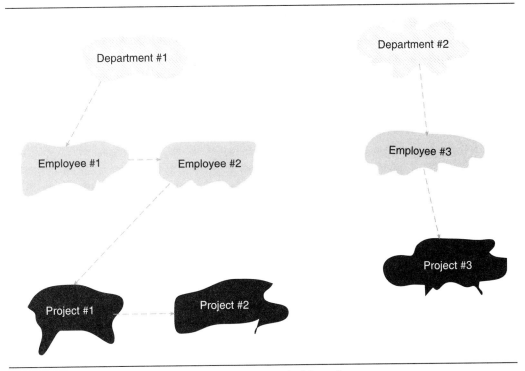

Figure 3-4: Tree traversal order in two occurrences of a hierarchy

IMS

The most successful hierarchical DBMS has been IMS, an IBM product. Designed to run on IBM mainframes, IMS has been handling high-volume transaction-oriented data processing since 1966. Today, IBM supports IMS legacy systems, but actively discourages new installations. In fact, many tools exist to help companies migrate from IMS to new products or to integrate IMS into more up-to-date software.

IMS does not adhere strictly to the theoretical hierarchical data model. In particular, it does allow multiple parentage in some very restrictive situations. As an example, consider Figure 3-5. There are actually two hierarchies in this diagram: the department to project hierarchy and the hierarchy consisting of just the employee.

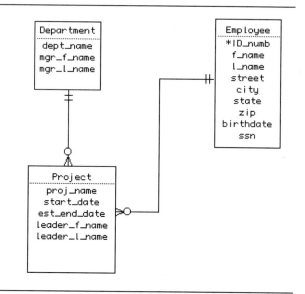

Figure 3-5: Two IMS hierarchies with permitted multiple parentage

> *Note: IMS refers to each hierarchy as a database and each entity*
> *as a segment.*

The multiple parentage of the project entity is permitted because the second parent—the employee entity—is in another hierarchy and is at a higher level in the hierarchy. Despite the restrictions on multiple parentage, this easing of the rules goes a long way to removing unnecessary duplicated data.

IMS does not support a query language. All access is through application programs that are usually written in COBOL. Like a true hierarchical DBMS, it is therefore best suited to batch processing in tree-traversal order. It has been heavily used in large businesses with heavy operational transaction processing loads, such as banks and insurance companies.

The Simple Network Data Model

At the same time IBM was developing IMS, other companies were working on DBMSs that were based on the simple network data model. The first DBMS based on this model appeared in 1967 (IDS from GE) and was welcomed because it directly addressed some of the limitations of the hierarchical data model. In terms of business usage, simple network databases had the widest deployment of any of the pre-relational data models.

> Note: The network data models—both simple and complex—predate computer networks as we know them today. In the context of a data model, the term "network" refers to an interconnected mesh, such as a network of neurons in the brain or a radio or television network.

Characteristics of a Simple Network

A simple network database supports one-to-many relationships between entities. There is no restriction on multiple parentage, however. This means that the employees/departments/projects database we have been using as an example could be designed as in Figure 3-6.

In this example, the project acts as a composite entity between department and employee. In addition, there is a direct relationship between department and employee for faster access.

Given the restrictions of the hierarchical data model, the simple network was a logical evolutionary step. It removed the most aggregious limitation of the hierarchical data model, that of no multiple parentage. It also further divorced the logical and physical storage, although as you will see shortly, simple network schemas still allowed logical database designers to specify some physical storage characteristics.

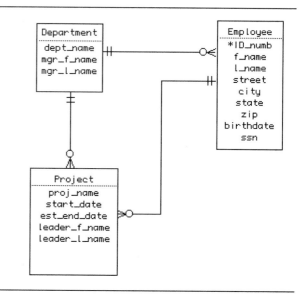

Figure 3-6: A simple network data model

Simple network databases implement data relationships either by embedding pointers directly in the data or through the use of indexes. Regardless of which strategy is used, access to data is restricted to the predefined links created by the pointers unless a fast access path has been designed to a particular type of entity. In this sense, a simple network is navigational, just like a hierarchical database.

There are two types of fast access paths available to the designer of a simple network. The first—*hashing*—involves the strategy used to place entity occurrences in a data file. When an entity occurrence is hashed into a data file, the DBMS uses a key (the value of one or more attributes) to compute a physical file locator (usually known as the *database key*). To retrieve the occurrence, the DBMS recomputes the hash value. Occurrences of related entities are then *clustered* around their parent entity in the data file. The purpose of this is twofold: It provides fast access to parent entities and puts child entities on the same disk page as their parents for faster retrieval. In the example we are using, a database designer might choose to hash department occurrences and cluster projects around their departments.

> *Note: An entity occurrence either can be clustered or hashed; it can't be both because the two alternatives determine physical placement of data in a file.*

The second type of fast access path is an index, which provides fast, direct access to entity occurrences containing secondary keys.

> *Note: For an in-depth explanation of indexing, see "Indexing" on page 122.*

If occurrences are not hashed and have no indexes, then the only way to retrieve them is by traversing down relationships with parent entity occurrences.

To enable traversals of the data relationships, a simple network DBMS must keep track of where it is in the database. For every program running against the database, the DBMS maintains a set of *currency indicators*, each of which is a system variable containing a database key of the last entity occurrence accessed of a specific type. For example, there are currency indicators for each type of entity, for the program as a whole, and so on. Application programs can then use the contents of the currency indicators to perform data accesses relative to the program's previous location in the database.

Originally, simple network DBMSs did not support query languages. However, as the relational data model became more popular, many vendors added relational-style query languages to their products. If a simple network database is designed like a relational database, then it can be queried much like a relational database. However, the simple network is still underneath and the database is therefore still subject to the access limitations placed on a simple network.

Simple network databases are not easy to maintain. In particular, changes to the logical design of the database can be extremely disruptive. First, the database must be brought offline; no processing can proceed against it until the changes are complete. Once the database is down, then the following process occurs:

1. Back up all data or save the data in text files.
2. Delete the current schema and data files.
3. Compile the new database schema, which typically is contained in a text file, written in a *database definition language* (DDL).
4. Reallocate space for the data files.
5. Reload the data files.

In later simple network DBMSs, this process was largely automated by utility software, but considering that most simple network DBMSs were mainframe-based, they involved large amounts of data. Changes to the logical design could take significant amounts of time.

There are many simple network DBMSs in use today as legacy systems. However, it would be highly unusual for an organization to decide to create a new database based on this data model.

CODASYL

In the mid 1960s, government and industry professionals organized into the Committee for Data Systems Languages (CODASYL). Their goal was to develop a business programming language, the eventual result of which was COBOL. As they were working, the committee realized that they had another output besides a programming language: the specifications for a simple network database. CODASYL spun off the Database Task Group (DBTG), which in 1969 released its set of specifications.

The CODASYL specifications were submitted to the American National Standards Institute (ANSI). ANSI made a few modifications to the standard to further separate the logical design of the database from its physical storage layout. The result was two sets of very similar, but not identical, specifications.

Note: It is important to understand that CODASYL is a standard rather than a product. Many products were developed to adhere to the CODASYL standards. In addition, there have been simple network DBMSs that employ the simple network data model but not the CODASYL standards.

A CODASYL DBMS views a simple network as a collection of two-level hierarchies known as *sets*. The database in Figure 3-6 requires two sets: one for department->employee and department->project and the second for employee->project. The entity at the "one" end of the relationships is known as the *owner* of the set; entities at the "many" end of relationships are known as *members* of the set. There can be only one owner entity, but many member entities, of any set. The same entity can be an owner of one set and a member of another, allowing the database designer to build a network of many levels. In fact, there is no limit to the number of sets to which an entity can belong.

As mentioned in the previous section, access is either directly to an entity occurrence using a fast access path (hashing or an index) or in traversal order. In the case of a CODASYL database, the members of each set occurrence have an order that is specified by the database designer.

If an entity is not given a fast access path, then the only way to retrieve occurrences is through the owners of some set. In addition, there is no way to retrieve or search all occurrences of an entity unless all of those occurrences are members of the same set, with the same owner.

Each set provides a conceptual linked list, beginning with the owner occurrence, continuing through all member occurrences, and linking back to the owner. Like the occurrences of a hierarchy in a hierarchical database, the occurrences of a set are distinct and unrelated, as in Figure 3-7. This particular illustration contains two occurrences of the set that department owns—members are employee and project—and three occurrences of the set that employee owns—member is project.

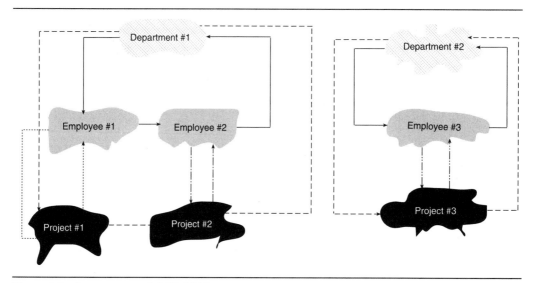

Figure 3-7: Occurrences of CODASYL sets

Note: Early CODASYL DBMSs actually implemented sets as linked lists. The result was complex pointer manipulation in the data files, especially for entities that were members of multiple sets. Later products represented sets using indexes, with database keys acting as pointers to the storage location of owner and member records.

The independence of set occurrences presents a major problem for entities that aren't a member of any set, such as the department occurrences in Figure 3-7. To handle this limitation, CODASYL databases support a special type of set—often called a *system set*—that has only one owner occurrence, the database system itself. All occurrences of an entity that is a member of that set are connected to the single owner occurrence. Employees and projects would probably be included in a system set also to provide the ability to access all employees and all projects. The declaration of system sets is left up to the database designer.

Any DBMS that was written to adhere to either set of CODASYL standards is generally known as a CODASYL DBMS. This represents the largest proportion of simple network products that were marketed.

Arguably, the most successful CODASYL DBMS was IDMS, originally developed by Cullinet. IDMS was a mainframe product that was popular well into the 1980s. As relational DBMSs began to dominate the market, IDMS was given a relational-like query language and marketed as IDMS/R. Ultimately, Cullinet was sold to Computer Associates, which markets and supports the product under the name CA-IDMS.

> *Note: Although virtually every PC DBMS on the market today claims to be relational, many are not. Some, such as FileMaker Pro and Panorama, are actually simple networks. These are client/server products, robust enough for small business use. They allow multiple parentage with one-to-many relationships and represent those relationships with preestablished links between files. These are simple networks. As you become familiar with the relational data model, you will understand why such products aren't relational. It doesn't mean that they aren't good products, but simply that they don't meet the minimum requirements for a relational DBMS.*

The Complex Network Data Model

The complex network data model was developed at the same time as the simple network. It allows direct many-to-many relationships without requiring the introduction of a composite entity. The intent of the data model's developers was to remove the restriction against many-to-many relationships imposed by the simple network data model. However, the removal of this relationship comes with a steep price.

As you will remember from Chapter 2, there are at least two major problems associated with the inclusion of direct many-to-many relationships. Consider first the database segment in Figure 3-8. Notice that there is no place to store data about the quantity of each item being ordered. The need to store relationship data is one reason why we replace many-to-many relationships with a composite entity and two one-to-many relationships.

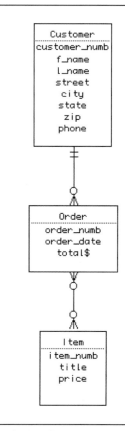

Figure 3-8: A complex network lacking a place to store relationship data

Nonetheless, if we examine an occurrence diagram for Figure 3-8 (see Figure 3-9), you can see that there is no ambiguity in the relationships. However, assume that we now add another entity to the design, as in Figure 3-10. In this case, each item can appear on many shipments and each shipment can contain many items.

The problem with this design becomes clear when you look at the occurrences in Figure 3-11. Notice, for example, that it is impossible to determine the order to which Shipment #1 and Shipment #2 belong. After you follow the relationships from the shipment occurrences to Item #1, there is no way to know which order is correct.

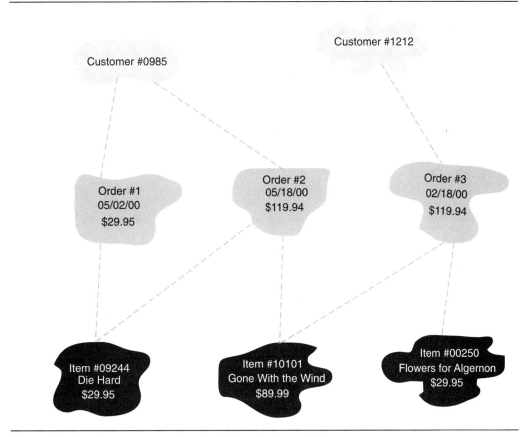

Figure 3-9: Sample occurrences for the design in Figure 3-8

There are two solutions to this problem. The first is to introduce an additional relationship to indicate which shipment comes from which order, as in Figure 3-12. Although this is certainly a viable solution, the result is increased complexity for storing and retrieving data.

The other solution is to abandon the use of the complex network altogether and introduce composite entities to reduce all the many-to-many relationships to one-to-many relationships. The result, of course, is a simple network.

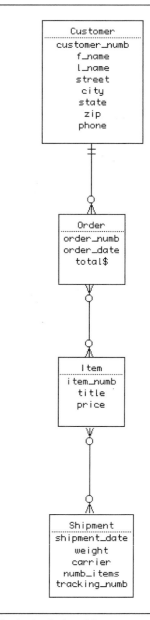

Figure 3-10: A complex network with ambiguous logical relationships

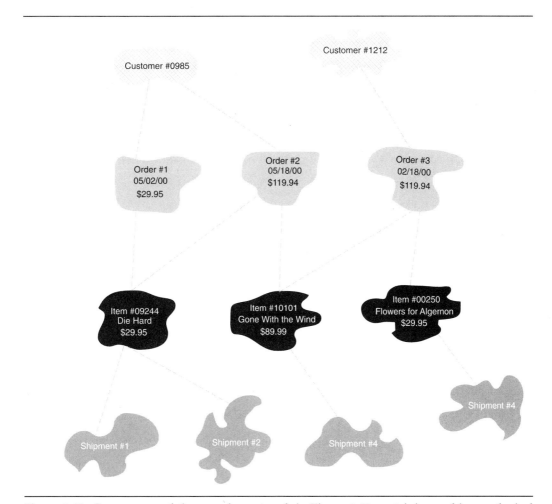

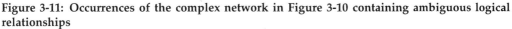

Figure 3-11: Occurrences of the complex network in Figure 3-10 containing ambiguous logical relationships

> *Note: As you will see in Chapter 4, a relational DBMS can represent all the relationships acceptable in a simple network—including composite entities—but does so in a nonnavigational manner. Like a sample network, it can capture all of the meaning of a many-to-many relationship and still avoid data ambiguity.*

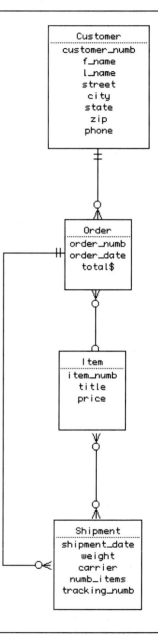

Figure 3-12: Using an additional relationship to remove logical ambiguity in a complex network

Because of the complexity of maintaining many-to-many relationships and the possibility of logical ambiguity, there have been no widely successful commercial products based on the complex network data model. However, the data model remains in the literature and provides some theoretical completeness to traditional data modeling.

> Note: Although it is marketed as a relational DBMS and is typically used as one, Microsoft Access can actually function as a complex network. It does allow direct many-to-many relationships. Fortunately, most database developers who work with the product know better than to try to use this "feature."

> Note: In terms of the sequence of the development of data models, the relational data model followed the network data models. Since the development of the relational data model, two additional data models have appeared: the object-oriented data model (covered in Chapter 8 as it relates to the relational data model) and multidimensional databases (usually known as online analysistical processing [OLAP] or star schema databases). Multidimensional databases are designed primarily for use with data warehouses and are therefore beyond the scope of this book.

4

The Relational Data Model

Once you have a completed ER diagram, you can translate that conceptual logical schema into the formal data model required by your DBMS. Today, most new database installations are based on the relational data model. We call databases that adhere to that model *relational databases*.

> Note: The older data models—in particular the hierarchical data model and the simple network data model—are still in use in many legacy database systems. However, it is rare to find a business creating a new one. On the other hand, the object-oriented data model is still relatively new, and although it has not replaced the relational data model and does not appear to be doing so, some new installations are either object-oriented or a combination of relational and object-oriented. You can find details about how objects have been integrated into relational databases in Chapter 8.

A relational database is a database whose logical structure is made up of nothing but a collection of *relations*. Although you may have read somewhere that a relational database has "relationships between files," nothing could be further from the truth. In this chapter, you will learn exactly what a relation is and how relations provide representations of data relationships.

> *Note: Remember from Chapter 2 that we said that a DBMS isolates database users from physical storage. A logical data model therefore has absolutely nothing to do with how the data are stored in files on disk.*

The relational data model is the result of the work of one man — Edgar (E. F.) Codd. During the 1960s, Dr. Codd, although trained as a mathematician, was working with existing data models. His experience led him to believe that they were clumsy and unnatural ways of representing data relationships. He therefore went back to mathematical set theory and focused on the construct known as a relation. He extended that concept to produce the relational database model, which he introduced in a seminal paper in 1970.

> *Note: You will find the citation for Codd's original paper and his other writings on the relational data model in the For Further Reading section at the end of this chapter.*

Understanding Relations

In mathematical set theory, a *relation* is the definition of a table with columns (*attributes*) and rows (*tuples*). (The word "table" is used synonymously with "relation.") The definition specifies what will be contained in each column of the table, but does not include data. When you include rows of data, you have an *instance* of a relation, such as the small Customers relation in Figure 4-1.

At first glance, a relation looks much like a flat file or a rectangular portion of a spreadsheet. However, because it has its underpinnings in mathematical set theory, a relation has some very specific

Customer number	First name	Last name	Phone
0001	Jane	Doe	(555) 555-1111
0002	John	Doe	(555) 555-2222
0003	Jane	Smith	(555) 555-3333
0004	John	Smith	(555) 555-4444

Figure 4-1: A sample Customers relation

characteristics that distinguish it from other rectangular ways of looking at data. Each of these characteristics forms the basis of a constraint that will be enforced by the DBMS.

Columns and Column Characteristics

A column in a relation has the following properties:

♦ A name that is unique within the table: Two or more tables within the same relational schema may have columns with the same names—in fact, as you will see shortly, in some circumstances this is highly desirable—but a single table must have unique column names. When the same column name appears in more than one table and tables that contain that column are used in the same data manipulation operation, you qualify the name of the column by preceding it with the name of the table and a period, as in:

```
customers.customer_number
```

♦ A domain: The values in a column are drawn from one and only one domain. As a result, relations are said to be *column homogeneous*. In addition, every column in a table is subject to a domain constraint. Depending on your DBMS, the domain constraint may be as simple as a data type, such as integers or dates. Alternatively, your DBMS may allow you to create your own, very specific, domains that can be attached to columns.

Rows and Row Characteristics

A row in a relation has the following properties:

♦ Only one value at the intersection of a column and row: A relation does not allow multivalued attributes.
♦ Uniqueness: There are no duplicate rows in a relation.

Note: For the most part, DBMSs do not enforce the unique row constraint automatically. However, as you will see in the next bullet, there is another way to obtain the same effect.

♦ A primary key: A *primary key* is a column or combination of columns that uniquely identifies each row. As long as you have unique primary keys, you will ensure that you also have unique rows. We will look at the issue of what makes a good primary key in great depth in the next major section of this chapter.

Types of Tables

A relational database works with two types of tables. *Base tables* are relations that are actually stored in the database. These are the tables that make up your schema.

However, relational operations on tables produce additional tables as their result. Such tables, which exist only in main memory, are known as *virtual tables*. Virtual tables may not be legal relations—in particular, they may have no primary key—but because virtual tables are never stored in the database, this presents no problem in terms of the overall design of the database.

The use of virtual tables benefits a DBMS in several ways. First, it allows the DBMS to keep intermediate query tables in main memory rather than storing them on disk, enhancing query performance. Second, it allows tables that violate the rules of the relational data model to exist in main memory without affecting the integrity of stored data. Finally, it helps avoid fragmentation of database files and disk surfaces by avoiding repeated write, read, and delete operations of temporary tables.

> Note: SQL, the language used to manage most relational DBMSs, also supports "temporary base tables." Although called base tables, temporary tables are actually virtual tables in the sense that they exist only in main memory for a short time and are never stored in the physical database.

A Notation for Relations

You will see instances of relations throughout this book used as examples. However, we do not usually include data in a relation when documenting that relation. One common way to express a relation is as follows:

```
relation_name (primary_key, non_primary_key_column, …)
```

For example, the Customers relation that you saw in Figure 4-1 would be written as:

```
customers (customer_numb, first_name, last_name, phone)
```

The preceding expression is a true relation, an expression of the structure of a relation. It correctly does not contain any data. (If data are included, you have an *instance* of a relation.)

Primary Keys

As you just read, a unique primary key makes it possible to uniquely identify every row in a table. Why is this so important? The issue is the same as with entity identifiers: You want to be able to retrieve every single piece of data you put into a database.

As far as a relational database is concerned, you should need only three pieces of information to retrieve any specific bit of data: the name of the table, the name of the column, and the primary key of the row. If primary keys are unique for every row, then we can be sure that we are retrieving exactly the row we want. If they are not unique, then we are retrieving only *some* row with the primary key value, which may not be the row containing the data for which we are searching.

> *Note: Notice how the preceding significantly distinguishes a relational database from one based on a navigational data model. You can retrieve any piece of data directly with only three pieces of information, whereas in a navigational database, a significant traversal of entity occurrences might be required to locate the same piece of data.*

Along with being unique, a primary key must not contain the value *null*. Null is a special database value meaning "unknown." It is not the same as a zero or a blank. If you have one row with a null primary key, then you are actually all right. However, the minute you introduce a second one, you have lost the property of uniqueness. We therefore forbid the presence of nulls in any primary key columns. This constraint, known as *entity integrity*, will be enforced by a DBMS whenever data are entered or modified.

Selecting a good primary key can be a challenge. As you may remember from Chapter 2, some entities have natural primary keys, such as purchase order numbers. These are arbitrary, meaningless, unique identifiers that a company attaches to the orders it sends to vendors and are therefore ideal primary keys.

Primary Keys to Identify People

What about a primary key to identify people? The first thing that pops into your mind might be a social security number. Every person in the United States over the age of 12 months has one, right? And the U.S. government assigns them so they are unique, right? Unfortunately, the answer to both questions is "no."

The Social Security Administration has been known to give everyone in an entire town the same SSN; over time, SSNs are reused.

However, these are minor problems compared to the issue of the social security number being null.

Consider what happens at a college that uses social security numbers as student numbers when international students enroll. Upon entry into the country, the international students do not have social security numbers. Because primary keys cannot be null, the international students cannot sign up for classes, or even be enrolled in the college, until they have some sort of SSN.

The college's solution is to give them "fake" numbers in the format 999-999-XXXX, where XXXX is some number currently not in use. Then, when the student receives a "real" SSN from the government, the college supposedly replaces the fake value with the real one. Sometimes, however, the process does not work. A graduate student ended up with his first semester's grades being stored under the fake SSN but the rest of his grades under his real number. (Rather than changing the original data, someone created an entire new transcript for the student.) When the time came to audit his transcript to see if he had satisfied all his graduation requirements, he was told that he was missing an entire semester's worth of courses.

This example leads us to two important desirable qualities of primary keys:

- ◆ A primary key should be some value that is highly unlikely ever to be null.
- ◆ A primary key should never change.

Although social security numbers initially look like good natural identifiers, you will be much better off in the long run using arbitrary numbers for people—such as student numbers or account numbers—than relying on social security numbers.

Note: There is also a very important privacy issue associated with the use of SSNs in environments where no reporting of income is necessary. This has nothing to do with the design of a database but is often a significant social consideration.

Avoiding Meaningful Primary Keys

It can be very tempting to code meaning into a primary key. For example, assume that Lasers Only wants to assign codes to its distributors rather than giving them arbitrary distributor numbers. Someone might create codes such as TLC for The Laser Club and JS for Jones Services. At first, this may seem like a good idea: The codes are short and by looking at them you can figure out which distributor they reference.

But what happens if one of the companies changes its name? Perhaps Jones Services is renamed to Jones Distribution House. Do you change the primary key of the distributor's table? Do you change the code so that it reads JDH? If the distributor's table were all that we cared about, that would be the easy solution.

However, consider that the table that describes merchandise items contains the code for the distributor so that Lasers Only can know which distributor provides the item. (You'll read a great deal more about this concept in the next major section of this chapter.) If you change the distributor code, you must change the code for every merchandise item that comes from that distributor. Without that change, Lasers Only will not be able to match the code to a distributor and get information about the distributor. It will appear that the item comes from a nonexistent distributor!

> *Note: This is precisely the problem about which you read in Chapter 1 concerning Lasers Only's identifiers for their customers.*

Meaningful primary keys tend to change and therefore introduce the potential for major data inconsistencies between tables. Resist the temptation to use them at all costs. Here, then, is yet another property of a good primary key:

♦ A primary key should avoid using meaningful data. Use arbitrary identifiers or concatenations of arbitrary identifiers wherever possible.

It is not always possible to use completely meaningless primary keys. You may find, for example, that you need to include dates or times in primary keys to distinguish between events. The suggestion that you should not use meaningful primary keys is therefore not a hard-and-fast rule but a guideline to which you should try to adhere whenever it is realistic to do so.

Concatenated Primary Keys

Some tables have no single column in which the values never duplicate. As an example, look at the sample order lines table in Figure 4-2. Because there is more than one item on an order, order numbers are repeated; because the same item can appear on more than one order, order numbers are repeated. Therefore, neither column by itself can serve as the table's primary key.

Order number	Item number	Quantity
10991	0022	1
10991	0209	2
10991	1001	1
10992	0022	1
10992	0486	1
10993	0209	1
10993	1001	2
10994	0621	1

Figure 4-2: A sample order lines table

However, the combination of an order number and an item number *is* unique. We can therefore concatenate the two columns to form the table's primary key.

It is true that you could also concatenate all three columns in the table and still ensure a unique primary key. However, the quantity column is not necessary to ensure uniqueness and therefore should not be used. We now have some additional properties of a good primary key:

♦ A concatenated primary key should be made up of the smallest number of columns necessary to ensure the uniqueness of the primary key.

♦ Wherever possible, the columns used in a concatenated primary key should be meaningless identifiers.

All-Key Relations

It is possible to have a table in which every column is part of the primary key. As an example, consider a library card catalog. Each book title carried by a library has a natural unique primary key—its ISBN (International Standard Book Number). Each ISBN is assigned one or more subject headings in the library's catalog; each subject heading is also assigned to one or more books. We therefore have a many-to-many relationship between books and subject headings.

A relation to depict this relationship might be:

```
subject catalog (isbn, subject heading)
```

All we need to do is pair a subject heading with a book identifier. No additional data are needed. Therefore, all columns in the table become part of the primary key.

There is absolutely no problem with having all-key relations in a database. In fact, they occur whenever a database design contains a composite entity that has no relationship data. They are not necessarily an error and you can use them wherever needed.

Representing Data Relationships

In the preceding section we alluded to the use of identifiers in more than one relation. This is the way in which relational databases represent relationships between entities. To make this concept clearer, take a look at the three tables in Figure 4-3.

Items

Item number	Title	Distributor number	Price
1001	Gone with the Wind	002	69.95
1002	Star Wars: Special Edition	002	39.95
1003	Die Hard	004	29.95
1004	Bambi	006	29.95

Orders

Order number	Customer number	Order date
11100	0012	12/18/00
11101	0186	12/18/00
11102	0056	12/18/00

OrderLines

Order number	Item number	Quantity	Shipped?
11100	1001	1	Y
11100	1002	1	Y
11101	1002	2	Y
11102	1002	1	N
11102	1003	1	N
11102	1001	1	N

Figure 4-3:   Three relations from the Lasers Only database

Each table in the illustration is directly analogous to the entity by the same name in the Lasers Only ER diagram. The orders table (the orders entity) is identified by an order number, an arbitrary unique primary key assigned by Lasers Only. The items table (the items entity) is identified by an item number, another arbitrary unique primary key.

The third table—order lines (the order lines entity)—tells the company which items are part of which order. As you saw earlier in this chapter, this table requires a concatenated primary key because multiple items can appear on multiple orders. The selection of this primary key, however, has more significance than simply uniquely identifying each row: It also represents a relationship between the order lines, the orders on which they appear, and the items being ordered.

The item number column in the order lines relation is the same as the primary key of the item table. This indicates a one-to-many relationship between the two tables. By the same token, there is also a one-to-many relationship between the orders and order lines tables because the order number column in the order lines table is the same as the primary key of the orders table.

When a table contains a column that is the same as the primary key of a table, the column is called a *foreign key*. The matching of foreign keys to primary keys represents data relationships in a relational database. As far as the user of a relational database is concerned, there are no structures that show relationships other than the matching columns.

> Note: This is why the idea that relational databases have "relationships between files" is so absurd. The relationships in a relational database are between logical constructs—tables—and nothing else. Such structures make absolutely no assumptions about physical file storage.

Foreign keys may be a part of a concatenated primary key or they may not be part of their table's primary key at all. Consider, for example, a pair of simple Lasers Only customers and orders relations:

```
customers (customer number, first name, last name, phone)
orders (order number, customer number, order date)
```

The customer number column in the orders table is a foreign key that matches the primary key of the customers table. It represents the one-to-many relationship between customers and the orders they place. However, the customer number is not part of the primary key of its table; it is a nonkey attribute that is nonetheless a foreign key.

Technically, foreign keys need not have values unless they are part of a concatenated primary key; they can be null. However, in this particular database, Lasers Only would be in serious trouble if customer numbers were null: There would be no way to know which customer placed an order!

A relational DBMS uses the relationships indicated by matching data between primary and foreign keys. For example, assume that a Lasers Only employee wanted to see what titles had been ordered on order number 11102. First, the DBMS identifies the rows in the line items table that contain an order number of 11102. Then, it takes the item numbers from those rows and matches them to the item numbers in the items table. In the rows where there are matches, the DBMS finally retrieves the associated title.

Referential Integrity

The procedure described in the preceding paragraph works very well—unless for some reason there is no order number in the orders table to match a row in the order lines table. This is a very undesirable condition, because there would be no way to ship the ordered item because there would be no way to find out which customer placed the order.

The relational data model therefore enforces a constraint called *referential integrity*, which states that *every nonnull foreign key value must match an existing primary key value*. Of all the constraints on a relational database, this is probably the most important because it ensures the consistency of the cross-references among tables.

Referential integrity constraints are stored in the database and enforced automatically by the DBMS. As with all other constraints, each time a user enters or modifies data, the DBMS checks the constraints and verifies that they are met. If the constraints are violated, the data modification will not be allowed.

Foreign Keys and Primary Keys in the Same Table

Foreign keys do not necessarily need to reference a primary key in a different table; they need only reference a primary key. As an example, consider the following employee relation:

```
employee (employee ID, first name, last name, department, manager ID)
```

A manager is also an employee. Therefore, the manager ID, although named differently from the employee ID, is actually a foreign key that references the primary key of its own table. The DBMS will therefore always ensure that whenever a user enters a manager ID, that manager already exists in the table as an employee.

Views

The people responsible for developing a database schema and those who write application programs for use by technologically unsophisticated users typically have knowledge of and access to the entire schema, including direct access to the database's base tables. However, it is usually undesirable to have end users working directly with base tables, primarily for security reasons.

The relational data model therefore includes a way to provide end users with their own window into the database, one that hides the details of the overall database design and prohibits direct access to the base tables.

The View Mechanism

A view is not stored with data. Instead, it is stored under a name in the data dictionary along with a database query that will retrieve its data. A view can therefore contain data from more than one table, selected rows, and selected columns.

Note: Although a view can be constructed in just about any way that you can query a relational database, many views can be used only for data display. As you will learn in Chapter 9, only views that meet a strict set of rules can be used to modify data.

The real beauty of storing views in this way, however, is that whenever the user includes the name of the view in a data manipulation language statement, the DBMS executes the query associated with the view name and recreates the view's table. This means that the data in a view will always be current.

A view table remains in main memory only for the duration of the data manipulation statement in which it was used. As soon as the user issues another query, the view table is removed from main memory to be replaced by the result of the most recent query. A view table is therefore a virtual table.

Note: Some end user DBMSs give the user the ability to save the contents of a view as a base table. This is a particularly undesirable feature, as there are no provisions for automatically updating the data in the saved view table whenever the tables on which it was based change. The view table, therefore, quickly will become out of date and inaccurate.

Why Use Views?

There are three good reasons to include views in the design of a database:

- ◆ As mentioned earlier, views provide a significant security mechanism by restricting users from viewing portions of a schema to which they should not have access.
- ◆ Views can simplify the design of a database for technologically unsophisticated users.
- ◆ Because views are stored as named queries, they can be used to store frequently used, complex queries. The queries can then be executed by using the name of the view in a simple query.

Like other structural elements in a relational database, views can be created and destroyed at any time. However, because views do not contain stored data, but only specification of a query that will generate a virtual table, adding or removing view definitions has no impact on base tables or the data they contain. Removing a view will create problems only when that view is used in an application program and the program is not modified to work with a different view or base table.

The Data Dictionary

The structure of a relational database is stored in the database's *data dictionary*, or *catalog*. The data dictionary is made up of a set of relations, identical in properties to the relations used to hold data. They can be queried using the same tools used to query data-handling relations. No user can modify the data dictionary tables directly. However, data manipulation language commands that create and destroy database structural elements work by modifying rows in data dictionary tables.

You will typically find the following types of information in a data dictionary:

- Definitions of the columns that make up each table
- Integrity constraints placed on relations
- Security information (which user has the right to perform which operation of which table)
- Definitions of other database structural elements, such as views (discussed further in Chapter 7) and user-defined domains

When a user attempts to access data in any way, a relational DBMS first goes to the data dictionary to determine whether the database elements the user has requested are actually part of the schema. In addition, the DBMS verifies that the user has the access rights to whatever he or she is requesting.

When a user attempts to modify data, the DBMS also goes to the data dictionary to look for integrity constraints that may have been placed on the relation. If the data meet the constraints, the modification is permitted. Otherwise, the DBMS returns an error message and does not make the change.

Because all access to a relational database is through the data dictionary, relational DBMSs are said to be *data dictionary driven*.

Sample Data Dictionary Tables

The precise tables that make up a data dictionary depend somewhat on the DBMS. In this section you will see one example of a typical way in which one specific DBMS (Sybase SQL Anywhere) organizes its data dictionary.

The linchpin of the data dictionary is actually a table that documents all the data dictionary tables (syscatalog, the first few rows of which can be found in Figure 4-4). From the names of the data dictionary tables, you can probably guess that there are tables to store data about base tables, their columns, their indexes, and their foreign keys.

creator	tname	dbspace	tabletype	ncols	primary_key
SYS	SYSTABLE	SYSTEM	TABLE	12	Y
SYS	SYSCOLUMN	SYSTEM	TABLE	14	Y
SYS	SYSINDEX	SYSTEM	TABLE	8	Y
SYS	SYSIXCOL	SYSTEM	TABLE	5	Y
SYS	SYSFOREIGNKEY	SYSTEM	TABLE	8	Y
SYS	SYSFKCOL	SYSTEM	TABLE	4	Y
SYS	SYSFILE	SYSTEM	TABLE	3	Y
SYS	SYSDOMAIN	SYSTEM	TABLE	4	Y
SYS	SYSUSERPERM	SYSTEM	TABLE	10	Y
SYS	SYSTABLEPERM	SYSTEM	TABLE	11	Y
SYS	SYSCOLPERM	SYSTEM	TABLE	6	Y

Figure 4-4:   A portion of a syscatalog table

The syscatalog table describes the columns in each table (including the database dictionary tables). In Figure 4-5, for example, you can see a portion of a syscolumns table that describes the Lasers Only merchandise items table.

creator	Cname	Tname	Coltype	Nulls	Lenth	InPrimaryKey	Colno
DBA	item_numb	items	integer	N	4	Y	1
DBA	title	items	varchar	Y	60	N	2
DBA	distributor_numb	items	integer	Y	4	N	3
DBA	release_date	items	date	Y	6	N	4
DBA	retail_price	items	numeric	Y	6	N	5

Figure 4-5:   Selected rows from a syscolumns table

Keep in mind that these data dictionary tables have the same structure and must adhere to the same rules as base tables. They must have nonnull unique primary keys; they must also enforce referential integrity among themselves.

A Bit of History

When Codd published his paper describing the relational data model in 1970, software developers were bringing hierarchical and simple network DBMSs to market. The software was becoming relatively mature and was being widely installed. Although many theorists recognized the benefits of the relational data model, it took some time before relational systems actually appeared.

IBM had a working prototype of its System R by 1976. This product, however, was never released. Instead, the first relational DBMS to feature SQL—an IBM development—was Oracle, released by the company of the same name in 1977. IBM didn't actually market a relational DBMS until 1981, when it released SQL/DS.

Oracle debuted on minicomputers running UNIX. SQL/DS ran under VM (often specifically using CMS on top of VM) on IBM mainframes. There was also a crop of early products that were designed specifically for PCs, the first of which was dBase II, from a company named Ashton-Tate. Released in 1981, the product ran on IBM PCs and Apple II+s.

Note: It is seriously questionnable whether dBase was ever truly a relational DBMS. However, most consumers do consider it to be the first relational product for PCs.

In 1982, IBM released DB/2 for MVS. This product, still mainframe-only at that time, brought significant legitimacy to the relational data model and, despite all the faults in initial releases, firmly entrenched relational databases in large corporate environments. Today, DB/2 runs on a variety of platforms, from desktop servers to mainframes.

Oracle was joined by a large number of competing products in the UNIX market, including Informix and Ingres. Oracle has been the biggest winner in this group because it now runs on virtually every OS/hardware platform combination imagineable. It is probably safe to say that there are more copies of Oracle running on computers in the world than any other DBMS.

The PC market for relational DBMSs has been flooded with products. As always with software, the best has not necessarily become the most successful. In 1983, Microrim release its R:BASE product, the first truly relational product for a PC. With its support for standard SQL, a powerful integrity rules facility, and a capable programming language, R:BASE was a robust product. It succumbed, however, to the market penetration of dBase. The same can be said for Paradox (a Borland product, now owned by Corel) and FoxPro (a Fox Software product, originally named FoxBase).

dBase faded from prominece after being purchased by Borland in 1991. FoxPro, dBase's major competitor, was purchased by Microsoft in 1992. It, too, is no longer a major player on the desktop. Instead, the primary end user desktop DBMS for Windows today is Access, first released by Microsoft in 1993.

For Further Reading

If you want to follow the history of Codd's specifications for relational database, consult the following:

Codd, E. F. "A Relational Model of Data for Large Shared Databanks," *Communications of the ACM*. Vol. 13, No. 6, June 1970.

Codd, E. F. "Extending the Relational Model to Capture More Meaning," *Transactions on Database Systems*. Vol. 4, No. 4, December 1979.

Codd, E. F. "Relational Database: A Practical Foundation for Productivity," *Communications of the ACM*. Vol. 25, No. 2, February 1982.

Codd, E. F. "Is Your DBMS Really Relational?" *Computerworld*. October 14, 1985: ID/1–ID/9.

Codd, E. F. *The Relational Data Model, Version 2*. Addison-Wesley, 1989.

There are also many books that discuss the details of specific relational DBMSs. After you finish reading this book, you may want to consult a book that deals with your specific product to help you learn to develop applications using that product's tools.

5

Normalization

Given any pool of entities and attributes, there is a large number of ways you can group them into relations. In this chapter, you will be introduced to the process of *normalization*, through which you create relations that avoid most of the problems that arise from bad relational design.

There are at least two ways to approach normalization. The first is to work from an ER diagram. If the diagram is drawn correctly, then there are some simple rules you can use to translate it into relations that will avoid most relational design problems. The drawback to this approach is that it can be difficult to determine whether your design is correct. The second approach is to use the theoretical concepts behind good design to create your relations. This is a bit more difficult than working from an ER diagram, but often results in a better design.

In practice, you may find it useful to use a combination of both approaches. First, create an ER diagram and use it to design your relations. Then, check those relations against the theoretical rules for good design.

Translating an ER Diagram into Relations

An ER diagram in which all many-to-many relationships have been transformed into one-to-many relationships through the introduction of composite entities can be translated directly into a set of relations. To do so:

- ◆ Create one table for each entity.
- ◆ For each entity that is only at the "one" end of one or more relationships, and not at the "many" end of any relationship, create a single-column primary key, using an arbitrary unique number if no natural primary key is available.
- ◆ For each entity that is at the "many" end of one or more relationships, include the primary key of each parent entity (those at the "one" end of the relationships) in the table as foreign keys.
- ◆ If an entity at the "many" end of one or more relationships has a natural primary key (for example, an order or invoice number), use that single column as the primary key. Otherwise, concatenate the primary key of its parent or parents with any other column or columns needed for uniqueness to form the table's primary key.

Following these guidelines, we end up with the following tables for the Lasers Only database:

```
customer (customer_numb, customer_first_name, customer_last_name,
    customer_street, customer_city, customer_state, customer_zip,
    customer_phone, credit_card_numb, card_exp_date)
item (item_numb, title, distributor_numb, retail_price,
    release_date, genre)
order (order_numb, customer_numb, order_date, order_filled)
```

```
order_lines (order_numb, item_numb, quantity, discount_applied,
    selling_price, line_cost, shipped)
distributor (distributor_numb, distributor_name,
    distributor_street, distributor_city, distributor_city,
    distributor_state, distributor_zip, distributor_phone,
    distributor_contact_person, contact_person_ext)
actor (actor_numb, actor_name)
performance (actor_numb, item_numb, role)
producer (producer_name, studio)
production (producer_name, item_numb)
```

Note: You will see these relations reworked a bit throughout the remainder of the first part of this book to help illustrate various aspects of database design. However, the preceding is the design that results from a direct translation of the ER diagram.

Normal Forms

The theoretical rules that the design of a relation meet are known as *normal forms*. Each normal form represents an increasingly stringent set of rules. Theoretically, the higher the normal form, the better the design of the relation.

As you can see in Figure 5-1, there are six nested normal forms, indicating that if a relation is in one of the higher, inner normal forms, it is also in all of the normal forms below it.

In most cases, if you can place your relations in third normal form (3NF), then you will have avoided most of the problems common to bad relational designs. Boyce-Codd (BCNF) and fourth normal form (4NF) handle special situations that arise only occasionally. However, they are conceptually easy to understand and can be used in practice if the need arises.

Fifth normal form (5NF), however, is a complex set of criteria that is extremely difficult to work with. It is, for example, very difficult to verify that a relation is in 5NF. Most practitioners do not bother with 5NF, knowing that if their relations are in 3NF (or 4NF if the situation warrants), then their designs are generally problem free.

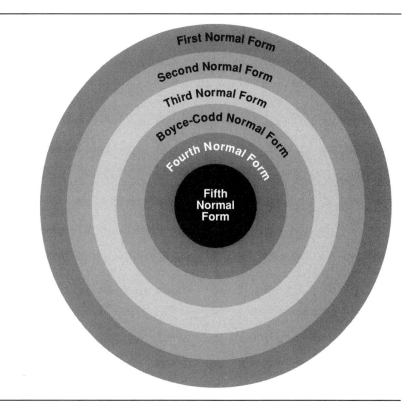

Figure 5-1: Nested normal forms

> *Note: In addition to the six normal forms in Figure 5-1, there is another normal form — domain/key normal form — that is of purely theoretical importance and, to this date, has not been used as a practical design objective.*

First Normal Form

A table is in first normal form (1NF) if it meets the following criteria:

The data are stored in a two-dimensional table with no repeating groups.

The key to understanding 1NF is therefore understanding the nature of a repeating group of data.

Understanding Repeating Groups

A *repeating group* is an attribute that has more than one value in each row. For example, assume that you were working with an employees relation and needed to store the names and birthdates of the employees' children. Because each employee can have more than one child, the names of children and the children's birthdates each form a repeating group.

> Note: A repeating group is directly analogous to a multivalued attribute in an ER diagram.

There is actually a very good reason why repeating groups are disallowed. To see what might happen if they were present, take a look at Figure 5-2, an instance of the employees relation we were just discussing.

Emp. ID	First	Last	Children's Names	Children's Birthdates
1001	Jane	Doe	Mary, Sam	1/1/92, 5/15/94
1002	John	Doe	Mary, Sam	1/1/92, 5/15/94
1003	Jane	Smith	John, Pat, Lee, Mary	10/5/94, 10/12/90, 6/6/96, 8/21/94
1004	John	Smith	Michael	7/4/96
1005	Jane	Jones	Edward, Martha	10/21/95, 10/15/89

Figure 5-2: A relation with repeating groups

Notice that there are multiple values in a single row in both the children's names and children's birthdates columns. This presents two major problems:

♦ There is no way to know exactly which birthdate belongs to which child. It is tempting to say that we can associate the birthdates with the children by their positions in the list, but there is nothing to ensure that the relative positions will always be maintained.

♦ Searching the table is very difficult. If, for example, we want to know which employees have children born before 1995, the DBMS will need to perform data manipulations to extract the individual dates from the birthdates column before it can evaluate the dates themselves. Given that there is no way to know how many birthdates there are in the column for any specific row, the processing overload for searching becomes even greater.

The solution to these problems is, of course, to get rid of the repeating groups altogether.

Handling Repeating Groups

There are two ways to get rid of repeating groups to bring a relation into conformance with the rules for first normal form — a right way and a wrong way. We will look first at the wrong way so you will know what *not* to do.

In Figure 5-3 you can see a relation that handles repeating groups by creating multiple columns for the multiple values. This particular example includes three pairs of columns for a child's name and birthdate.

Emp. ID	First	Last	Child Name 1	Child B_date 1	Child Name 2	Child B_date 2	Child Name 3	Child B_date 3
1001	Jane	Doe	Mary	1/1/92	Sam	5/15/94		
1002	John	Doe	Mary	1/1/92	Sam	5/15/94		
1003	Jane	Smith	John	10/5/94	Pat	10/12/90	Lee	6/6/96
1004	John	Smith	Michael	7/4/96				
1005	Jane	Jones	Edward	10/21/95	Martha	10/15/89		

Figure 5-3:   A relation handling repeating groups in the wrong way

The relation in Figure 5-3 does meet the criteria for first normal form: The repeating groups are gone and there is no problem identifying which birthdate belongs to which child. However, the design has introduced several problems of its own:

♦ The relation is limited to three children for any given employee. This means that there is no room to store Jane Smith's fourth child. Should you put another row for Jane Smith into the table? If so, then the primary key of this relation can no longer be just the employee ID. The primary key must include at least one child's name as well.

♦ The relation wastes space for people who have less than three children. Given that disk space is one of the least expensive elements of a database system, this is probably the least of the problems with this relation.

♦ Searching for a specific child becomes very clumsy. To answer the question "Does anyone have a child named Lee?" the DBMS must construct a query that includes a search of all three child name columns because there is no way to know in which column the name might be found.

The right way to handle repeating groups is to create another table (another entity) to handle multiple instances of the repeating group. In the example we have been using, we would create a second table for the children, producing something like Figure 5-4.

Neither of the two new tables contains any repeating groups, and this form of the design avoids all the problems of the preceding solution:

♦ There is no limit to the number of children that can be stored for a given employee. To add another child, you simply add another row to the table.

♦ There is no wasted space. The children table uses space only for data that are present.

♦ Searching for a specific child is much easier because the child's name is found in only one column.

Employees

Emp. ID	First	Last
1001	Jane	Doe
1002	John	Doe
1003	Jane	Smith
1004	John	Smith
1005	Jane	Jones

Children

Emp. ID	Child Name	Birthdate
1001	Mary	1/1/92
1001	Sam	5/15/94
1002	Mary	1/1/92
1002	Sam	5/15/94
1003	John	10/5/94
1003	Pat	10/12/90
1003	Lee	6/6/96
1003	Mary	8/21/94
1004	Michael	7/4/96
1005	Edward	10/21/95
1005	Martha	10/15/89

Figure 5-4:   The correct way to handle the repeating group

Problems with First Normal Form

Although first normal form relations have no repeating groups, they are full of other problems. To see what those problems are, we will look at the table underlying the data entry form in Chapter 1. (This table comes from Lasers Only's original data management system rather than the new and improved design you saw earlier in this chapter.) Expressed in the notation for relations that we have been using, the relation is:

```
orders (customer number, first name, last name, street, city, state,
    zip, phone, order date, item number, title, price, has shipped)
```

The first thing we need to do is determine the primary key for this table. The customer number alone will not be sufficient because the customer number repeats for every item ordered by the customer. The item number will also not suffice, because it is repeated for every order on which it appears. We cannot use the order number because it is repeated for every item on the order. The only solution is a concatenated key, in this example the combination of the order number and the item number.

Given that the primary key is made up of the order number and the item number, there are two important things we cannot do with this relation:

- ◆ We cannot add data about a customer until the customer places at least one order because without an order and an item on that order, we do not have a complete primary key.
- ◆ We cannot add data about a merchandise item we are carrying without that item being ordered. There must be an order number to complete the primary key.

The preceding are *insertion anomalies*, a situation that arises when you are prevented from inserting data into a relation because a complete primary key is not available. (Remember that no part of a primary key can be null.)

> Note: To be strictly correct, there is a third insertion anomaly in the orders relation: You cannot insert an order until you know one item on the order. In a practical sense, however, no one would enter an order without there being an item ordered.

Insertion anomalies are common in first normal form relations that are not also in any of the higher normal forms. In practical terms, they occur because there are data about more than one entity in the relation. The anomaly forces you to insert data about an unrelated entity (for example, a merchandise item) when you want to insert data about another entity (such as a customer).

First normal form relations can also give us problems when we delete data. Consider, for example, what happens if a customer cancels the order of a single item:

- ◆ In cases where the deleted item was the only item on the order, you lose all data about the order.
- ◆ In cases where the order was the only order on which the item appeared, you lose data about the item.
- ◆ In cases where the deleted item was the only item ordered by a customer, you lose all data about the customer.

These *deletion anomalies* occur because part of the primary key of a row becomes null when the merchandise item data are deleted, forcing you to remove the entire row. The result of a deletion anomaly is the loss of data that you would like to keep. In practical terms, you are forced to remove data about an unrelated entity when you delete data about another entity in the same table.

> Note: Moral to the story: More than one entity in a table is a very bad thing.

There is a final type of anomaly in the orders relation that is not related to the primary key: a *modification*, or *update*, anomaly. The orders relation has a great deal of unnecessary duplicated data, in particular information about customers. When a customer moves, then the customer's data must be changed in every row, for every item on every order ever placed by the customer. If every row is not changed correctly, then data that should be the same are no longer the same. The potential for these inconsistent data is the modification anomaly.

Second Normal Form

The solution to anomalies in a first normal form relation is to break the relation down so that there is one relation for each entity in the 1NF relation. The orders relation, for example, will break down into four relations (customers, merchandise items, orders, and line items). Such relations are in at least second normal form (2NF).

In theoretical terms, second normal form is defined as follows:

> The relation is in first normal form and all nonkey attributes are functionally dependent on the entire primary key.

The new term in the preceding is *functionally dependent*, a special relationship between attributes.

Understanding Functional Dependencies

A functional dependency is a one-way relationship between two attributes such that at any given time, for each unique value of attribute A, only one value of attribute B is associated with it through the relation. For example, assume that A is the customer number from the orders relation. Each customer number is associated with one customer first name, one last name, one street address, one city, one state, one zip code, and one phone number. Although the values for those attributes may change, at any moment, there is only one.

We therefore can say that first name, last name, street, city, state, zip, and phone are functionally dependent upon the customer number. This relationship is often written

```
customer number -> first name, last name, street, city, state, zip,
    phone
```

and read "customer number determines first name, last name, street, city, state, zip, and phone." In this relationship, customer number is known as the *determinant* (an attribute that determines the value of other attributes).

Notice that the functional dependency does not necessarily hold in the reverse direction. For example, any given first or last name may be associated with more than one customer number. (It would be unusual to have a customer table of any size without some repetition of names.)

The functional dependencies in the orders table are:

```
customer number -> first name, last name, street, city, state, zip,
    phone
item number -> title, price
order number -> customer number, order date
item number + order number -> has shipped
```

Notice first that there is one determinant for each entity in the relation and that the determinant is what we have chosen as the entity identifier. Notice also that when an entity has a concatenated identifier, the determinant is also concatenated. In this example, whether an item has shipped depends on the combination of the item and the order.

Using Functional Dependencies to Reach 2NF

If you have correctly identified the functional dependencies among the attributes in a database environment, then you can use them to create second normal form relations. Each determinant becomes the primary key of a relation. All the attributes that are functionally dependent upon it become nonkey attributes in the relation.

The four relations into which the original orders relation should be broken are:

```
customers (customer number, first name, last name, street, city,
    state, zip, phone)
items (item number, title, price)
orders (order number, customer number, order date)
line items (order number, item number, has shipped)
```

Each of these should in turn correspond to a single entity in your ER diagram.

> *Note: When it comes to deciding what is driving database design — functional dependencies or entities — it is really a "chicken and egg" situation. What is most important is that*

there is consistency between the ER diagram and the functional dependencies you identify in your relations. It makes no difference whether you design by looking for functional dependencies or for entities. In most cases, database design is an iterative process in which you create an intial design, check it, modify it, and check it again. You can look at either functional dependencies and/or entities at any stage in the process, checking one against the other for consistency.

The relations we have created from the original orders relation have eliminated the anomalies present in the original:

◆ It is now possible to insert data about a customer before the customer places an order.

◆ It is now possible to insert data about an order before we know an item on the order.

◆ It is now possible to store data about merchandise items before they are ordered.

◆ Line items can be deleted from an order without affecting data describing that item, the order itself, or the merchandise item.

◆ Data describing the customer are stored only once and therefore any change to those data need to be made only once. A modification anomaly cannot occur.

Problems with 2NF Relations

Although second normal form eliminates problems from many relations, you will occasionally run into relations that are in second normal form yet still exhibit anomalies. Assume, for example, that each laser disc title that Lasers Only carries comes from one distributor and that each distributor has only one warehouse, which has only one phone number. The following relation is therefore in second normal form:

```
items (item number, title, distributor, warehouse phone number)
```

For each item number, there is only one value for the item's title, distributor, and warehouse phone number. However, there is one insertion anomaly—you cannot insert data about a distributor until you have an item from that distributor—and a deletion anomaly—if you delete the only item from a distributor, you lose data about the distributor. There is also a modification anomaly: The distributor's warehouse phone number is duplicated for every item the company gets from that distributor. The relation is in second normal form, but not third.

Third Normal Form

Third normal form is designed to handle situations like the one you just read about in the preceding section. In terms of entities, the items relation does contain two entities: the merchandise item and the distributor. That alone should convince you that the relation needs to broken down into two smaller relations, both of which are now in third normal form:

```
items (item number, distributor)
distributors (distributor, warehouse phone number)
```

The theoretical definition of third normal form says:

> The relation is in second normal form and there are no transitive dependencies.

The functional dependencies found in the original relation are an example of a *transitive dependency*.

Transitive Dependencies

A transitive dependency exists when you have the following functional dependency pattern:

```
A -> B and B - > C therefore A -> C
```

This is precisely the case with the original items relation. The only reason that the warehouse phone number is functionally dependent on the item number is because the distributor is functionally

dependent on the item number and the phone number is functionally dependent on the distributor. The functional dependencies are
really:

```
item number -> distributor
distributor -> warehouse phone number
```

> *Note: Transitive dependencies take their name from the transi-*
> *tive property in mathematics, which states that if a > b and b >*
> *c, then a > c.*

There are two determinants in the original items relation, each of
which should be the primary key of its own relation. However, it is
not merely the presence of the second determinant that creates the
transitive dependency. What really matters is that the second determinant is not a candidate key for the relation.

Consider, for example, this relation:

```
items (item number, UPC code, distributor, price)
```

The item number is an arbitrary value that Lasers Only assigns to
each merchandise item. The UPC code is an industry-wide code
that is unique to each item as well. The functional dependencies in
this relation are:

```
item number -> UPC code, distributor, price
UPC code -> item number, distributor, price
```

Is there a transitive dependency here? No, because the second determinant is a candidate key. (Lasers Only could just as easily have
used the UPC code as the primary key.) There are no insertion, deletion, or modification anomalies in this relation; it describes only
one entity — the merchandise item.

A transitive dependency therefore exists only when the determinant
that is not the primary key is not a candidate key for the relation. For
example, in the items table we have been using as an example, the
distributor is a determinant but not a candidate key for the table.
(There can be more than one item coming from a single distributor.)

When you have a transitive dependency in a 2NF relation, you should break the relation into two smaller relations, each of which has one of the determinants in the transitive dependency as its primary key. The attributes determined by the determinants become the nonkey attributes in each relation. This removes the transitive dependency—and its associated anomalies—and places the relations in third normal form.

> *Note: A second normal form relation that has no transitive dependencies is, of course, automatically in third normal form.*

Boyce–Codd Normal Form

For most relations, third normal form is a good design objective. Relations in that state are free of most anomalies. However, occasionally you run across relations that exhibit special characteristics where anomalies still occur. Boyce–Codd normal form (BCNF) and fourth normal form (4NF) were created to handle such special situations.

> *Note: If your relations are in third normal form and do not exhibit the special characteristics that BCNF and 4NF were designed to handle, then they are automatically in 4NF. As mentioned earlier in this chapter, it is extremely difficult to determine if a relation is in fifth normal form without the aid of a computer to do the analyses, and therefore we rarely use 5NF in practice.*

The easiest way to understand BCNF is to start with an example. Assume that Lasers Only decides to add a relation to its database to handle employee work scheduling. Each employee works one or two 4-hour shifts a day at the store. During each shift, an employee is assigned to one station (a place in the store, such as the front desk or the stockroom). Only one employee works a station during a given shift.

A relation to handle the schedule might be designed as the following:

```
schedule (employee ID, date, shift, station, worked shift?)
```

Given the rules for the scheduling (one person per station per shift), there are two possible primary keys for this relation: employee ID + date + shift or date + shift + station. The functional dependencies in the relation are:

```
employee ID + date + shift -> station, worked shift?
date + shift + station -> employee ID, worked shift?
```

Keep in mind that this holds true only because there is only one person working each station during each shift.

> *Note: There is very little difference between the two candidate keys as far as the choice of a primary key is concerned. In cases like this, you can choose either one.*

This schedule relation exhibits overlapping concatenated candidate keys. (Both candidate keys have date and shift in common.) Boyce–Codd normal form was designed to deal with relations that exhibit this characteristic.

To be in Boyce–Codd normal form, a relation must meet the following rule:

> The relation is in third normal form and all determinants are candidate keys.

BCNF is considered to be a more general way of looking at 3NF because it includes those relations with the overlapping candidate keys. The sample schedule relation we have been considering does meet the criteria for BCNF because the two determinants are indeed candidate keys.

Fourth Normal Form

Like BCNF, fourth normal form was designed to handle relations that exhibit a special characteristic that does not arise too often. In this case, the special characteristic is something known as a *multivalued dependency.*

As an example, consider the following relation:

```
movie info (title, star, producer)
```

A given movie can have more than one star; it can also have more than one producer. The same star can appear in more than one movie; the producer can also work on more than one movie (for example, see the instance in Figure 5-5). The relation must therefore include all columns in its key.

Title	Star	Producer
Great Film	Lovely Lady	Money Bags
Great Film	Handsome Man	Money Bags
Great Film	Lovely Lady	Helen Pursestrings
Great Film	Handsome Man	Helen Pursestrings
Boring Movie	Lovely Lady	Helen Pursestrings
Boring Movie	Precocious Child	Helen Pursestrings

Figure 5-5:   A relation with a multivalued dependency

Because there are no nonkey attributes, this relation is in BCNF. Nonetheless, the relation exhibits anomalies:

- ◆ You cannot insert the stars of a movie without knowing at least one producer.
- ◆ You cannot insert the producer of a movie without knowing at least one star.
- ◆ If you delete the only producer from a movie, you lose information about its stars.
- ◆ If you delete the only star from a movie, you lose information about its producers.

♦ Each producer's name is duplicated for every star in the move. By the same token, each star's name is duplicated for each producer of the movie. This unnecessary duplication forms the basis of a modification anomaly.

There are at least two unrelated entities in this relation, one that handles the relationship between a movie and its stars and another that handles the relationship between a movie and its producers. In a practical sense, that is the cause of the anomalies. (Arguably, there are also movie, star, and producer entities involved.)

However, in theoretical terms, the anomalies are caused by the presence of a multivalued dependency in the same relation, which must be eliminated to go to fourth normal form. The rule for fourth normal form is:

The relation is in Boyce–Codd normal form and there are no multivalued dependencies.

Multivalued Dependencies

A multivalued dependency exists when for each value of attribute A, there exists a finite set of values of attribute B that are associated with it and a finite set of values of attribute C that are also associated with it. Attributes B and C are independent of each other.

In the example we have been using, there is just such a dependency. First, for each movie title, there is a group of actors (the stars) who are associated with the movie. For each title, there is also a group of producers who are associated with it. However, the actors and the producers are independent of one another.

Note: At this point, do not let semantics get in the way of database theory. Yes, it is true that producers fund the movies in which the actors are starring, but in terms of database relationships, there is no direct connection between the two.

The multivalued dependency can be written:

```
title ->> star
title ->> producer
```

and read "title multidetermines star and title multidetermines producer."

> *Note: To be strictly accurate, a functional dependency is a special case of a multivalued dependency where what is being determined is one value rather than a group of values.*

To eliminate the multivalued dependency and bring this relation into fourth normal form, you split the relation, placing each part of the dependency in its own relation:

```
movie stars (title, star)
movie producers (title, producer)
```

With this design, you can independently insert and remove stars and producers without affecting the other. Star and producer names also appear only once for each movie with which they are involved.

Normalized Relations and Database Performance

Normalizing the relations in a database separates entities into their own relations and makes it possible for you to enter, modify, and delete data without disturbing entities other than the one directly being modified. However, normalization is not without its downside.

When you split relations so that relationships are represented by matching primary and foreign keys, you force the DBMS to perform matching operations between relations whenever a query requires data from more than one table. For example, in a normalized database you store data about an order in one relation, data about a customer in a second relation, and data about the order lines in yet a third relation. The operation typically used to bring the data into a single table so you can prepare an output such as an invoice is known as a *join*.

In theory, a join looks for rows with matching values between two tables and creates a new row in a result table every time it finds a match. In practice, however, performing a join involves manipulating more data than the simple combination of the two tables being joined would suggest. Joins of large tables (those of more than a few hundred rows) can significantly slow down the performance of a DBMS.

To understand what can happen, you need to know something about the relational algebra join operation. As with all relational algebra operations, the result of a join is a new table.

> *Note: Relational algebra is a set of operations used to manipulate and extract data from relations. Each operation performs a single manipulation of one or two tables. To complete a query, a DBMS uses a sequence of relational algebra operations; relational algebra is therefore procedural. SQL, on the other hand, is based on the relational calculus, which is nonprocedural, allowing you to specify what you want rather than how to get it. A sinlge SQL retrieval command can require a DBMS to perform any or all of the operations in the relational algebra.*

Equi-Joins

In its most common form, a join forms new rows when data in the two source tables match. Because we are looking for rows with equal values, this type of join is known as an *equi-join* (or a *natural equi-join*). As an example, consider the two tables in Figure 5-6.

Notice that the ID number column is the primary key of the customers table and that the same column is a foreign key in the orders table. The ID number column in orders therefore serves to relate orders to the customers to which they belong.

```
customers

ID number  first name    last name

001        Jane          Doe
002        John          Doe
003        Jane          Smith
004        John          Smith
005        Jane          Jones
006        John          Jones


orders

order number   ID number   order date     order total

001            002          10/10/99         250.65
002            002           2/21/00         125.89
003            003          11/15/99        1567.99
004            004          11/22/99         180.92
005            004          12/15/99         565.00
006            006          10/8/99           25.00
007            006          11/12/99          85.00
008            006          12/29/99         109.12
```

Figure 5-6:   Two tables with a primary key–foreign key relationship

Assume that you want to see the names of the customers who placed each order. To do so, you must join the two tables, creating combined rows wherever there is a matching ID number. In database terminology, we are joining the two tables *over* ID number. The result table can be found in Figure 5-7.

```
result_table

ID number  first_name   last_name    order_numb   order_date    order_total

002        John         Doe          001          10/10/99         250.65
002        John         Doe          002           2/21/00         125.89
003        Jane         Smith        003          11/15/99        1597.99
004        John         Smith        004          11/22/99         180.92
004        John         Smith        005          12/15/99         565.00
006        John         Jones        006          10/8/99           25.00
006        John         Jones        007          11/12/99          85.00
006        John         Jones        008          12/29/99         109.12
```

Figure 5-7:   The joined table

An equi-join can begin with either source table. (The result should be the same regardless of the direction in which the join is performed.) The join compares each row in one source table with the rows in the second. For each row in the first source table that matches data in the second source table in the column or columns over which the join is being performed, a new row is placed in the result table.

Assuming that we are using the customers table as the first source table, producing the result table in Figure 5-7 might therefore proceed conceptually as follows:

1. Search orders for rows with an ID number of 001. Because there are no matching rows in orders, do not place a row in the result table.
2. Search orders for rows with an ID number of 002. There are two matching rows in orders. Create two new rows in the result table, placing the same customer information at the end of each row in orders.
3. Search orders for rows with an ID number of 003. There is one matching row in orders. Place one new row in the result table.
4. Search orders for rows with an ID number of 004. There are two matching rows in orders. Place two rows in the result table.
5. Search orders for rows with an ID number of 005. There are no matching rows in orders. Therefore do not place a row in the result table.
6. Search orders for rows with an ID number of 006. There are three matching rows in orders. Place three rows in the result table.

Notice that if an ID number does not appear in both tables, then no row is placed in the result table. This behavior categorizes this type of join as an *inner join*.

What's Really Going On: PRODUCT and RESTRICT

From a relational algebra point of view, a join can be implemented using two other operations: product and restrict. As you will see, this sequence of operations requires the manipulation of a great deal of data and, if implemented by a DBMS, can result in very slow query performance.

The restrict operation retrieves rows from a table by matching each row against logical criteria (a *predicate*). Those rows that meet the criteria are placed in the result table; those that do not meet the criteria are omitted.

The product operation (the mathematical Cartesian product) makes every possible pairing of rows from two source tables. In Figure 5-8, for example, the product of the customers and orders tables produces a result table with 48 rows (the six customers times the eight orders). The ID number column appears twice because it is a part of both source tables.

> *Note: Although 48 rows may not seem like a lot, consider the size of a product table created from tables with 100 and 1000 rows! The manipulation of a table of this size can tie up a lot of disk I/O and CPU time.*

In some rows, the ID number is the same. These are the rows that would have been included in a join. We can therefore apply a restrict predicate to the product table to end up with the same table provided by the join you saw earlier. The predicate's logical condition can be written:

```
customers.id_numb = orders.id_numb
```

The rows that are selected by this predicate appear in black in Figure 5-9; those eliminated by the predicate are in gray. Notice that the black rows are exactly the same as those in the result table of the join (Figure 5-7).

> *Note: Although this may seem like a highly inefficient way to implement a join, it is actually quite flexible, in particular be-*

product_table

ID number (Customers)	first name	last name	ID number (Orders)	order number	order date	order total
001	Jane	Doe	002	001	10/10/99	250.65
001	Jane	Doe	002	002	2/21/00	125.89
001	Jane	Doe	003	003	11/15/99	1597.99
001	Jane	Doe	004	004	11/22/99	180.92
001	Jane	Doe	004	005	12/15/99	565.00
001	Jane	Doe	006	006	10/8/99	25.00
001	Jane	Doe	006	007	11/12/99	85.00
001	Jane	Doe	006	008	12/29/99	109.12
002	John	Doe	002	001	10/10/99	250.65
002	John	Doe	002	002	2/21/00	125.89
002	John	Doe	003	003	11/15/99	1597.99
002	John	Doe	004	004	11/22/99	180.92
002	John	Doe	004	005	12/15/99	565.00
002	John	Doe	006	006	10/8/99	25.00
002	John	Doe	006	007	11/12/99	85.00
002	John	Doe	006	008	12/29/99	109.12
003	Jane	Smith	002	001	10/10/99	250.65
003	Jane	Smith	002	002	2/21/00	125.89
003	Jane	Smith	003	003	11/15/99	1597.99
003	Jane	Smith	004	004	11/22/99	180.92
003	Jane	Smith	004	005	12/15/99	565.00
003	Jane	Smith	006	006	10/8/99	25.00
003	Jane	Smith	006	007	11/12/99	85.00
003	Jane	Smith	006	008	12/29/99	109.12
004	John	Smith	002	001	10/10/99	250.65
004	John	Smith	002	002	2/21/00	125.89
004	John	Smith	003	003	11/15/99	1597.99
004	John	Smith	004	004	11/22/99	180.92
004	John	Smith	004	005	12/15/99	565.00
004	John	Smith	006	006	10/8/99	25.00
004	John	Smith	006	006	10/8/99	25.00
004	John	Smith	006	008	12/29/99	109.12
006	John	Jones	002	001	10/10/99	250.65
006	John	Jones	002	002	2/21/00	125.89
006	John	Jones	003	003	11/15/99	1597.99
006	John	Jones	004	004	11/22/99	180.92
006	John	Jones	004	005	12/15/99	565.00
006	John	Jones	006	006	10/8/99	25.00
006	John	Jones	006	006	10/8/99	25.00
006	John	Jones	006	008	12/29/99	109.12

Figure 5-8: The PRODUCT of the customers and orders tables

joined_table

ID number (Customers)	first name	last name	ID number (Orders)	order number	order date	order total
001	Jane	Doe	002	001	10/10/99	250.65
001	Jane	Doe	002	002	2/21/00	125.89
001	Jane	Doe	003	003	11/15/99	1597.99
001	Jane	Doe	004	004	11/22/99	180.92
001	Jane	Doe	004	005	12/15/99	565.00
001	Jane	Doe	006	006	10/8/99	25.00
001	Jane	Doe	006	007	11/12/99	85.00
001	Jane	Doe	006	008	12/29/99	109.12
002	**John**	**Doe**	**002**	**001**	**10/10/99**	**250.65**
002	**John**	**Doe**	**002**	**002**	**2/21/00**	**125.89**
002	John	Doe	003	003	11/15/99	1597.99
002	John	Doe	004	004	11/22/99	180.92
002	John	Doe	004	005	12/15/99	565.00
002	John	Doe	006	006	10/8/99	25.00
002	John	Doe	006	007	11/12/99	85.00
002	John	Doe	006	008	12/29/99	109.12
003	Jane	Smith	002	001	10/10/99	250.65
003	Jane	Smith	002	002	2/21/00	125.89
003	**Jane**	**Smith**	**003**	**003**	**11/15/99**	**1597.99**
003	Jane	Smith	004	004	11/22/99	180.92
003	Jane	Smith	004	005	12/15/99	565.00
003	Jane	Smith	006	006	10/8/99	25.00
003	Jane	Smith	006	007	11/12/99	85.00
003	Jane	Smith	006	008	12/29/99	109.12
004	John	Smith	002	001	10/10/99	250.65
004	John	Smith	002	002	2/21/00	125.89
004	John	Smith	003	003	11/15/99	1597.99
004	**John**	**Smith**	**004**	**004**	**11/22/99**	**180.92**
004	**John**	**Smith**	**004**	**005**	**12/15/99**	**565.00**
004	John	Smith	006	006	10/8/99	25.00
004	John	Smith	006	006	10/8/99	25.00
004	John	Smith	006	008	12/29/99	109.12
006	John	Jones	002	001	10/10/99	250.65
006	John	Jones	002	002	2/21/00	125.89
006	John	Jones	003	003	11/15/99	1597.99
006	John	Jones	004	004	11/22/99	180.92
006	John	Jones	004	005	12/15/99	565.00
006	**John**	**Jones**	**006**	**006**	**10/8/99**	**25.00**
006	**John**	**Jones**	**006**	**006**	**10/8/99**	**25.00**
006	**John**	**Jones**	**006**	**008**	**12/29/99**	**109.12**

Figure 5-9:   The PRODUCT of the Customers and Orders tables after applying a RESTRICT predicate

cause the relationship between the columns over which the join is being performed doesn't have to be equality. A user could just as easily request a join where the value in table A was greater than the value in table B, and so on.

The Bottom Line

Because of the processing overhead created when performing a join, some database designers make a conscious decision to leave tables unnormalized. For example, if Lasers Only always accessed the line items at the same time it accessed order information, then a designer might choose to combine the line item and order data into one table, knowing full well that the unnormalized relation exhibits anomalies. The benefit is that retrieval of order information will be faster than if it were split into two tables.

Should you leave unnormalized relations in your database to achieve better retrieval performance? In this author's opinion, there is rarely any need to do so. Assuming that you are working with a relatively standard DBMS that supports SQL as its query language, there are SQL syntaxes that you can use when writing queries that avoid joins. That being the case, it does not seem worth the problems that unnormalized relations present to leave them in the database. Careful writing of retrieval queries can provide performance that is nearly as good as that of retrieval from unnormalized relations.

Note: For a complete discussion of writing SQL queries to avoid joins, see the author's book SQL Clearly Explained, also published by Morgan-Kaufmann.

For Further Reading

There are many books available that deal with the theory of relational databases. You can find useful supplementary information in the following:

Stanczyk, Stefan, Champion, Bob, and Leton, Richard. *Theory and Practice of Relational Databases*. Taylor & Rances, 2001.

6

Database Structure and Performance Tuning

How long are you willing to wait for a computer to respond to your request for information? 30 seconds? 10 seconds? 5 seconds? In truth, we humans aren't very patient at all. Even five seconds can feel like an eternity when you're waiting for something to appear on the screen. A database that has a slow response time to user queries usually means that you will have dissatisfied users.

Slow response times can be the result of any number of problems. You might be dealing with a client workstation that isn't properly configured, a poorly written application program, a query involving multiple join operations, a query that requires reading large amounts of data from disk, a congested network, or even a DBMS that isn't robust enough to handle the volume of queries submitted to it.

One of the duties of a *database administrator* (DBA) is to optimize database performance (also known as *performance tuning*). This includes modifying the design—where possible—to avoid performance bottlenecks, especially those involving queries.

For the most part, a DBMS takes care of storing and retrieving data based on a user's commands without human intervention. The strategy used to process a data manipulation request is handled by the DBMS's *query optimizer*, a portion of the program that determines the most efficient sequence of relational algebra operations to perform a query.

Although most of the query optimizer's choices are out of the hands of a database designer or application developer, you can influence the behavior of the query optimizer and also optimize database performance to some extent with database design elements. In this chapter you will be introduced to three such techniques: indexing, clustering, and partitioning.

Indexing

Indexing is a way of providing a fast access path to the values in a column or a concatenation of columns. New rows are typically added to the bottom of a table, resulting in a relatively random ordering of the values in any given column. Without some way of ordering the data, the only way a DBMS can search a column is by sequentially scanning each row from top to bottom. The larger a table becomes, the slower a sequential search will be.

The conceptual operation of an index is diagrammed in Figure 6-1. (The different weights of the lines have no significance other than to make it easier for you to follow the crossed lines.) In this illustration, you are looking at Lasers Only's merchandise item relation and an index that provides fast access to rows in the table based on the item's title. The index itself contains an ordered list of keys (the titles) along with the locations of the associated rows in the merchandise item table. The rows in the merchandise item table are in relatively random order. However, because the index is in alphabet-ical order by title, it can be searched quickly to locate a specific title. Then the DBMS can use the information in the index to go directly to a correct row or rows in the merchandise item table, thus avoid-ing a slow sequential scan of the base table's rows.

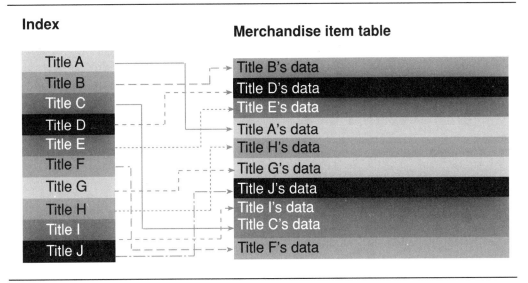

Figure 6-1:   Indexing

Once you have created an index, the DBMS's query optimizer will use the index whenever it determines that using the index will speed up data retrieval. You never need to access the index again yourself unless you want to delete it.

When you create a primary key for a table, the DBMS automatically creates an index for that table using the primary key column or col-umns as the index key. The first step in inserting a new row into a table is therefore verification that the index key (the primary key of the table) is unique to the index. In fact, uniqueness is enforced by requiring the index entries to be unique, rather than by actually searching the base table. This is much faster than attempting to ver-ify uniqueness directly on the base table because the ordered index can be searched much more rapidly than the unordered base table.

Deciding Which Indexes to Create

You have no choice as to whether the DBMS creates indexes for your primary keys; you get them whether you want them or not. In addition, you can create indexes to provide fast access to any column or combination of columns you want. However, before you jump headfirst into creating indexes on every column in every table, there are some trade-offs to consider:

♦ Indexes take up space in the database. Given that disk space is inexpensive today, this is usually not a major drawback.

♦ When you insert, modify, or delete data in indexed columns, the DBMS must update the index as well as the base table. This may slow down data modification operations, especially if the tables have a lot of rows.

♦ Indexes definitely speed up access to data.

The trade-off is therefore generally between update speed and retrieval speed. A good rule of thumb is to create indexes for foreign keys and for other columns that are used frequently in queries that apply logical criteria to data. If you find that update speed is severely affected, you may choose at a later time to delete some of the indexes you created.

Clustering

The slowest part of a DBMS's actions is retrieving data from or writing data to a disk. If you can cut down on the number of times the DBMS must read from or write to a disk, you can speed up overall database performance.

The trick to doing this is understanding that a database must retrieve an entire disk *page* of data at one time. The size of a page varies from one operating system to another—it can be anywhere from 512 bytes to 4K, with 1K being typical on a PC—but data always travel to and from disk in page-sized units. Therefore, if you can get data that are often accessed together stored on the same disk page (or on pages that are physically close together), you can speed up data access. This process is known as *clustering* and is available with many DBMSs (for example, Oracle).

> *Note: The term "clustering" has another meaning in the SQL-92 standard. It refers to a group of catalogs (which in turn are groups of schemas) manipulated by the same DBMS. The use of the term in this section, however, is totally distinct from the SQL-92 meaning.*

In practice, a cluster is designed to keep rows related by matching primary and foreign keys together. To define the cluster, you specify a column or columns on which the DBMS should form the cluster and the tables that should be included. Then, all rows that share the same value of the column or columns on which the cluster is based are stored as physically close together as possible. As a result, the rows in a table may be scattered across several disk pages, but matching primary and foreign keys are usually on the same disk page.

Clustering can significantly speed up join performance. However, just as with indexes, there are some trade-offs to consider when contemplating creating clusters:

- ♦ Because clustering involves physical placement of data in a file, a table can be clustered on only one column or combination of columns.
- ♦ Clustering can slow down performance of operations that require a scan of the entire table because clustering may mean that the rows of any given table are scattered throughout many disk pages.
- ♦ Clustering can slow down inserting data.
- ♦ Clustering can slow down modifying data in the columns on which clustering is based.

Partitioning

Partitioning is the opposite of clustering: It involves the splitting of large tables into smaller ones so that the DBMS does not need to retrieve as much data at any one time. Consider, for example, what happens to Lasers Only's orders and order lines tables over time. Assuming that the business is reasonably successful, those tables (especially order lines) will become very large. Retrieval of data from those tables will therefore begin to slow down.

There are two ways to partition a table: horizontally and vertically. *Horizontal partitioning* involves splitting the rows of a table between two or more tables with the identical structure. *Vertical partitioning* involves splitting the columns of a table, placing them into two or more tables linked by the table's primary key. As you might expect, there are benefits and drawbacks to both.

Horizontal Partitioning

Horizontal partitioning involves creating two or more tables with exactly the same structure and splitting rows between those tables. Lasers Only might use this technique, for example, to solve problems with the orders and line items tables becoming increasingly large. The database design might be modified as follows:

```
open orders (order number, customer number, order date)
open order lines (order number, item number, quantity, shipped?)
filled orders (order number, customer number, order date)
filled order lines (order number, item number, quantity, shipped?)
```

Whenever all items in an open order have shipped, an application program deletes rows from the open orders and open order lines tables and inserts them into the filled orders and filled order lines tables. The open order and open order lines tables remain relatively small, speeding up both retrieval and modification performance. Although retrieval from filled orders and filled order lines will be slower, Lasers Only uses those tables much less frequently.

The drawback to this solution occurs when Lasers Only needs to access all of the orders and/or order lines at the same time. A query whose result table includes data from both sets of open and filled tables must actually be two queries connected by the UNION operator. Performance of such a query will be worse than that of a query of either set of tables individually. Nonetheless, if an analysis of Lasers Only's data access patterns reveals that such queries occur rarely and that most retrieval involves the open set of tables, then the horizontal partitioning is worth doing.

The only way you can determine whether horizontal partitioning will increase performance is to examine the ways in which your database applications access data. If there is a group of rows that are accessed together significantly more frequently than the rest of the rows in a table, then horizontal partitioning may make sense.

Vertical Partitioning

Vertical partitioning involves creating two or more tables with selected columns and all rows of a table. For example, if Lasers Only accesses the titles and prices of their merchandise items more frequently than the other columns in the merchandise item table, the merchandise item table might be partitioned as follows:

```
item titles (item number, title, price)
item details (item number, distributor, release date, …)
```

The benefit of this design is that the rows in the smaller item titles table will be physically closer together; the smaller table will take up fewer disk pages and thus support faster retrieval.

Queries that require data from both item tables must join the tables over the item number. Like most joins, this will be a relatively slow operation. Therefore, vertical partitioning makes sense only when there is a highly skewed access pattern for the columns of a table. The more often a small, specific group of columns is accessed together, the more vertical partitioning will help.

For Further Reference

Most of the publications dealing with database performance tuning focus on a single product, as, for example, in the following:

Harrison, Guy. *Oracle SQL High-Performance Tuning*. Prentice Hall PTR, 2000.

Whalen, Ed. *Microsoft SQL Server2000 Performance Tuning Technical Reference*. Microsoft Press, 2001.

To find materials related to your specific DBMS, go to any major on-line bookstore and search on "database performance" and the name of the product.

7

Codd's Rules

In October of 1985, E. F. Codd published a series of two articles in the computer industry weekly called *Computerworld*. The first article laid out 12 criteria to which a "fully relational" database should adhere. The second article compared current mainframe products to those 12 rules, producing a flurry of controversy over whether it was important that DBMSs be theoretically rigorous or that they simply work effectively.

> *Note: If you read Chapter 3, then you will be aware of a product based on the simple network data model called IDMS/R. When Codd rated IDMS/R—which was then being marketed as a relational DBMS—it met none (0) of the 12 rules. DB/2, IBM's flagship relational product, met 10 of the rules.*

To help you understand the issues raised and why Codd's rules for relational databases for the most part make sense, in this chapter we will look at those criteria along with the implications of their implementation. Should you then choose not to adhere to one or more of the rules, you will be doing so with full understanding of the consequences. (In some cases, the consequences are minimal; in others they may significantly affect the integrity of the data in a database.)

Note: The complete citation for Codd's original articles can be found in the bibliography at the end of Chapter 3.

Rule 1: The Information Rule

The first criterion for relational databases deals with the data structures that are used to store data and represent data relationships:

"All information in a relational database is represented explicitly at the logical level in exactly one way — by values in tables."

The purpose of this rule is to require that relations (two-dimensional tables) be the *only* data structure used in a relational database. Therefore, products that require hard-coded links between tables are not relational.

At the time Codd's article was published, one of the most widely used mainframe products was IDMS/R, a version of IDMS that placed a relational-style query language on top of a simple network database. The simple network data model requires data structures such as pointers or indexes to represent data relationships. Therefore, IDMS/R, although being marketed as relational, was not relational according to the very first rule of a relational database. It was this product that was at the heart of the "who cares about rules if my product works" controversy.

Regardless of which side you take in this particular argument, there are two very good reasons why creating a database from nothing but tables is a good idea:

♦ Logical relationships are very flexible. In a simple network or hierarchical database, the only relationships that can be used for retrieval are those that have been predetermined by the database designer who wrote the schema. However, because a relational database represents its relationships through matching data values, the join operation can be used to implement relations on the fly, even those that a database designer may not have anticipated.

♦ Relational database schemas are very flexible. You can add, modify, and remove individual relations without disturbing the rest of the schema. In fact, as long as you are not changing the structure of tables currently being used, you can modify the schema of a live database. However, to modify the schema of a simple network or hierarchical database you must stop all processing of the database and regenerate the entire schema. In many cases, modifying the database design also means recreating all the physical files (using a dump and load process) to correspond to the new design.

Note: DBMSs that require you to specify "relationships between files" when you design a database fail this first rule. If you read Chapter 3, then you know that a number of PC-only products work in this way and that although they are marketed as relational, they really use the simple network data model. Keep in mind that the ER diagrams for simple networks and 3NF relational databases are identical. The differences come in how the relationships between the entities are represented. In a simple network, it is with hard-coded relationships; in a relational database, it is with primary key–foreign key pairs.

When Codd originally wrote his rules, databases couldn't store images. Today, many DBMSs give you the choice of storing images as BLOBs (binary large objects) inside the database or as path names or URLs to image files that are stored outside the database. Technically, path names or URLs to external files are pointers to something other than tables and therefore would seem to cause a DBMS to violate this rule. However, the spirit of the rule is that relationships between entities—the logical relationships in the database—are represented by matching data values, without the use of pointers of any kind to indicate entity connections.

> *Note: This is not the only rule that needs to be stretched a bit to accommodate graphics in a database environment. See also rule 5 later in this chapter.*

Rule 2: The Guaranteed Access Rule

Given that the entire reason we put data into a database is to get the data out again, we must be certain that we can retrieve every single piece of data:

> "Each and every datum (atomic value) in a relational database is guaranteed to be logically accessible by resorting to a combination of table name, primary key value and column name."

This rule states that you should need to know only three things to locate a specific piece of data: the name of the table, the name of the column, and the primary key of the row.

> *Note: With today's DBMSs, the definition of a table name can mean many things. For example, if you are working with IBM's DB/2, a table name is the table creator's loginName.tableName. If you are working with Oracle, then a complete table name may include a catalog name, schema name, and Oracle owner name, as well as the name of the individual table.*

There is no rule in this set of 12 rules that specifically states that each row in a relation must have a unique primary key. However, a relation cannot adhere to the guaranteed access rule unless it does have unique primary keys. Without unique primary keys, you will retrieve some row with the primary key value used in a search, but not necessarily the exact row you want. Some data may therefore be inaccessible without the ability to uniquely identify rows.

Early relational databases did not require primary keys at all. You could create and use tables without primary key constraints. Today, however, SQL will allow you to create a table without a primary key specification, but most DBMSs will not permit you to enter data into that table.

> *Note: A DBMS that requires "relationships between files" cannot adhere to this rule because you must specify the file in which data reside to locate data.*

Rule 3: Systematic Treatment of Null Values

As you know, null is a special database value that means "unknown." Its presence in a database brings special problems during data retrieval. Consider, for example, what happens if you have an employees relation that contains a column for salary. Assume that the salary is null for some portion of the rows. What, then, should happen if someone queries the table for all people who make more than 60,000? Should the rows with null be retrieved or should they be left out?

When the DBMS evaluates a null against the logical criterion of salary value greater than 60,000, it cannot state whether the row containing the null meets the criteria. Maybe it does; maybe it does not. For this reason, we say that relational databases use *three-valued logic*. The result of the evaluation of a logical expression is either true, false, or maybe.

Codd's third rule deals with the issue of nulls:

> "Null values (distinct from the empty character string or a string of blank characters or any other number) are supported in the fully relational DBMS for representing missing information in a systematic way, independent of data type."

First, a relational DBMS must store the same value of null in all columns and rows where the user does not explicitly enter data values. The value used for null must be the same, regardless of the data type of the column. Note that null is not the same as a space character; it has its own, distinct ASCII or UNICODE value. However, in most cases when you see a query's result table on the screen, nulls do appear as blank.

Second, the DBMS must have some consistent, known way of handling those nulls when performing queries. Typically, you will find that rows with nulls are not retrieved by a query such as the salary greater than 60,000 example unless the user explicitly asks for rows with a value of null. Most relational DBMSs today adhere to a three-valued logic truth table to determine retrieval behavior when they encounter nulls.

The inclusion of nulls in a relation can be extremely important. They provide a consistent way to distinguish between valid data such as a 0 and missing data. For example, it makes a great deal of difference to know that the balance in an account payable is 0 instead of unknown. The account with 0 is something we like to see; the account with an unknown balance could be a significant problem.

> *Note: The concept of unknown values is not unique to relational databases. Regardless of the data model it uses, a DBMS must contend with the problem of how to behave when querying against a null.*

Rule 4: Dynamic Online Catalog Based on the Relational Model

Earlier in this book you read about relational database data dictionaries. Codd very clearly specifies that those dictionaries (which he calls *catalogs*) should be made up of nothing but relations:

"The data base description is represented at the logical level in the same way as ordinary data, so that authorized users can apply the same relational language to its interrogation as they apply to regular data."

One advantage of using the same data structures for the data dictionary as you do for data tables is that you have a consistent way to access all elements of the database. You need to learn only one query language. This also simplifies the DBMS itself, since it can use the same mechanism for handling data about the database (*metadata*) as it can data about the organization.

When you purchase a DBMS, it comes with its own way of handling a data dictionary. There is rarely anything you can do to change it. Therefore, the major implication of this particular rule comes in selecting relational software: You want to look for something that has a data dictionary that is made up of nothing but tables.

> Note: Because of they way in which their schemas were implemented, it was rare for a prerelational DBMS to have an online data dictionary.

Rule 5: The Comprehensive Data Sublanguage Rule

A relational database must have some language that can maintain database structural elements, modify data, and retrieve data. Codd included the following rule that describes his ideas about what such a language should do:

"A relational system may support several languages and various modes of terminal use (for example, fill-in-the-blanks mode). However, there must be at least one language whose statements are expressible, per some well-defined syntax, as character strings and that is comprehensive in supporting <u>all</u> of the following items:

- ◆ Data definition
- ◆ View definition
- ◆ Data manipulation (interactive and by program)
- ◆ Integrity constraints
- ◆ Transaction boundaries (begin, commit and rollback)"

The SQL-92 language does meet all of these rules. (Earlier versions did not include complete support for primary keys and referential integrity.) Given that most of today's relational DBMSs use SQL as their primary data manipulation language, there would seem to be no issue here.

However, a DBMS that does not support SQL, but uses a graphic language, would technically not meet this rule. Nonetheless, there are several products today whose graphic language can perform all the tasks Codd has listed without a command-line syntax. Such DBMSs might not be theoretically "fully relational," but since they can perform all the necessary relational tasks, you lose nothing by not having the command-line language.

> *Note: Keep in mind the time frame in which Codd was writing. In 1985, the Macintosh—whose operating system legitimized the graphic user interface — was barely a year old. Most people still considered the GUI-equipped computers to be little more than toys.*

Rule 6: The View Updating Rule

As you will read in more depth in Chapter 9, some views can be used to update data. Others—those that are created from more than one base table or view, those that do not contain the primary keys of their base tables, and so on—cannot be used for updating. Codd's sixth rule speaks only about those that meet the criteria for updatability:

"All views that are theoretically updatable are also updatable by the system."

This rule simply means that if a view meets the criteria for updatability, a DBMS must be able to handle that update and propagate the updates back to the base tables.

> *Note: DBMSs that used prerelational data models included constructs similar in concept to views. For example, CODA-SYL DBMSs included "subschemas," which allowed an application programmer to construct a subset of a schema to be used by a specific end user or by an application program.*

Rule 7: High-Level Insert, Update, and Delete

Codd wanted to ensure that a DBMS could handle multiple rows of data at a time, especially when data were modified. Therefore, the seventh rule insists that a DBMS's data manipulation language be able to insert, update, and delete more than one row with a single command:

"The capability of handling a base relation or a derived relation as a single operand applies not only to the retrieval of data but also to the insertion, update and deletion of data."

SQL provides this capability for today's relational DBMSs. What does it bring you? Being able to modify more than one row with a single command simplifies data manipulation logic. Rather than needing to scan a relation row by row to locate rows for modification, for example, you can specify logical criteria that identify rows to be affected and let the DBMS find the rows for you.

Rule 8: Physical Data Independence

One of the benefits of using a database system rather than a file processing system is that a DBMS isolates the user from physical storage details. The physical data independence rule speaks to that issue:

> "Applications programs and terminal activities remain logically unimpaired whenever any changes are made in either storage representation or access methods."

This means you should be able to move the database from one disk volume to another, change the physical layout of the files, and so on, without any impact on the way in which application programs and end users interact with the tables in the database.

Most of today's DBMSs give you little control over the file structures used to store data on disk. (Only the very largest mainframe systems allow systems programmers to determine physical storage structures.) Therefore, in a practical sense, physical data independence means that you should be able to move the database from one disk volume or directory to another without affecting application programs or interactive users. With a few exceptions—in particular, end-user DBMSs based on the dBase model—most of today's DBMSs do provide physical data independence.

> *Note: Prerelational DBMSs generally fail this rule to a greater or lesser degree. The older the data model, the closer it was tied to its physical storage structures. The tradeoff, however, is performance. Hierarchical systems are much faster than relational systems when processing data in tree traversal order. The same can be said for a CODASYL database: When traversing in set order, access will be faster than row-by-row access with a relational database. The tradeoff is flexibility to perform ad hoc queries, something at which relational systems excel.*

Rule 9: Logical Data Independence

Logical data independence is a bit more subtle than physical data independence. In essence, it means that if you change the schema—perhaps adding or removing a table or adding a column to a table—then other parts of the schema that should not be affected by the change remain unaffected:

> "Application programs and terminal activities remain logically unimpaired when information-preserving changes of any kind that theoretically permit unimpairment are made to the base tables."

As an example, consider what happens when you add a table to a database. Since relations are logically independent of one another, adding a table should have absolutely no impact on any other table. To adhere to the logical data independence rule, a DBMS must ensure that there is indeed no impact on other tables.

On the other hand, if you delete a table from the database, such a modification is not "information-preserving." Data will almost certainly be lost when the table is removed. Therefore, it is not necessary that application programs and interactive users be unaffected by the change.

Rule 10: Integrity Independence

Although the requirement for unique primary keys is a corollary to an earlier rule, the requirement for nonnull primary keys and for referential integrity is very explicit:

> "Integrity constraints specific to a particular relational data base must be definable in the relational data sublanguage and storable in the catalog, not in the application programs.

"A minimum of the following two integrity constraints must be supported:

"1. Entity integrity: No component of a primary key is allowed to have a null value.

"2. Referential integrity: For each distinct nonnull foreign key value in a relational data base, there must exist a matching primary key value from the same domain."

Notice that this rule requires that the declaration of integrity constraints must be a part of whatever language is used to define database structure. In addition, integrity constraints of any kind must be stored in a data dictionary that can be accessed while the database is being used.

When IBM released its flagship relational database — DB/2 — one of the two things users complained about was the lack of referential integrity support. IBM, and other DBMS vendors for that matter, omitted referential integrity because it slows down performance. Each time you modify a row of data, the DBMS must go to the data dictionary, search for an integrity rule, and perform the test indicated by the rule, all before performing an update. A referential integrity check of a single column can involve two or more disk accesses, all of which takes more time than simply making the modification directly to the base table.

However, without referential integrity, the relationships in a relational database very quickly become inconsistent. Retrieval queries therefore do not necessarily retrieve all data because missing cross-references cause joins to omit data. In that case, the database is unreliable and virtually unusable. (Yes, IBM added referential integrity to DB/2 fairly quickly!)

> Note: One solution to the problem of a DBMS not supporting referential integrity was to have application programmers perform the referential integrity checks within application programs. This certainly works, but it puts the burden of integrity

checking in the wrong place. It should be an integral part of the database, rather than left up to an application programmer.

Note: Most DBMSs using prerelational data models provided some types of integrity constraints, including domain constraints, unique entity identifiers, and required values (nonnull). CODASYL could also enforce manditory relationships, something akin to referential integrity.

Rule 11: Distribution Independence

A distributed database is a database where the data themselves are stored on more than one computer. The database is therefore the union of all its parts. In practice, the parts are not unique but contain a great deal of duplicated data.

Nonetheless, according to rule 11:

"A relational DBMS has distribution independence."

In other words, a distributed database must look to the user like a centralized database. Application programs and interactive users should not be required to know where data are stored, including the location of multiple copies of the same data.

DBMS vendors have been working on distributed DBMS software since the late 1970s. However, at the time this book was written, no relational DBMS truly met this rule. Even the most sophisticated distributed DBMS software requires that the user indicate some location information when retrieving data.

Rule 12: Nonsubversion Rule

The final rule might be subtitled the "no cheating rule":

> "If a relational system has a low-level (single-record-at-a-time) language, that low-level language cannot be used to subvert or bypass the integrity rules or constraints expressed in the higher level relational language (multiple-records-at-a-time)."

Many DBMS products during the 1980s had languages that could directly access rows in tables, separate from SQL, which operates on multiple rows at a time. This rule states that there must be no way to use that direct-access language to get around the integrity constraints stored in the data dictionary. The integrity rules must be observed without exceptions.

8

Integrating Objects

The relational data model has been a mainstay of business data processing for nearly 30 years. Nothing has superseded it the way the relational data model superseded the simple network data model. However, a newer data model—the object-oriented data model—has come into use as an alternative for some types of navigational data processing.

Classes—definitions of entities and procedures that operate on entity data—can be used to model a complete data environment. This provides a total alternative to a relational design. Relational DBMSs, however, have embraced classes in a different way: Classes become domains, making it possible to store an entire *object* (an incident of a class) in a column. Such DBMSs are often known as *hybrid object-relational* DBMSs or *post-relational* DBMSs. Products providing support for objects as domains include Oracle and DB/2.

*Note: For in-depth information on the object-oriented data model,
including designing object-oriented databases, see the author's
book* Object-Oriented Database Design Clearly Explained, *
also from Morgan-Kaufmann.*

This chapter presents an overview of some object-oriented concepts
for readers who aren't familiar with the object-oriented paradigm.
It then looks at how classes can be integrated into a relational database.

An Introduction to Object-Oriented Concepts

The object-oriented paradigm was the brainchild of Dr. Kristen
Nygarrd, a Norwegian who was attempting to write a computer
program to model the behavior of ships, tides, and fjords. He found
that the interactions were extremely complex and realized that it
would be easier to write the program if he separated the three types
of program elements and let each one model its own behavior
against each of the others.

The object-oriented programming languages in use today (most no-
tably C++, SmallTalk, and Java) are a direct outgrowth of Nygarrd's
early work. The way in which objects are used in relational databases today is an extension of object-oriented programming.

*Note: This is in direct contrast to the relational data model,
which was designed specifically to model data relationships, although much of its theoretical foundations are found in mathematical set theory.*

To understand the role of objects in relational databases, you therefore must first understand the object-oriented paradigm as it is used
in object-oriented programming. In this chapter, you will read
about the fundamental concepts of that paradigm. Do not worry if
you cannot program: You *do not* need to be a programmer to understand this material. If you *are* fluent in an object-oriented programming language, however, you can skip the portion of this chapter

that deals with object-oriented concepts and just read the section titled "Integrating Objects into a Relational Database" at the end of the chapter.

The easiest way to understand what object-oriented programming is all about is to begin with an example that has absolutely nothing to do with programming at all.

Writing Instructions

Assume that you have a 16-year-old daughter (or sister, whichever is more appropriate) named Jane and that your family is going to take a long car trip. Like most 16-year-olds, Jane is less than thrilled about a trip with the family and in particular with spending so much time with her 12-year-old brother. In self-defense, Jane needs something to keep her 12-year-old brother busy so he won't bother her as she reads while her parents are driving. She therefore decides to write up some instructions for playing solitaire card games for him.

The first set of instructions is for the most common solitaire game, Klondike. As you can see in Figure 8-1, the deal involves seven piles of cards of increasing depth, with the top card turned over. The rest of the deck remains in the draw pile. Jane decides to break the written instructions into two main parts: information about the game and questions her brother might ask. She therefore produces instructions that look something like Figure 8-2. She also attaches the illustration of the game's deal.

The next game she tackles is Canfield. Like Klondike, it is played with one deck, but the deal and play are slightly different (see Figure 8-3). Jane uses the same pattern for the instructions as she did for Klondike because it cuts down the amount of writing she has to do (see Figure 8-4).

And finally, just to make sure her brother doesn't get too bored, Jane prepares instructions for Forty Thieves (see Figure 8-5). This game uses two decks of cards and plays in a very different way from the

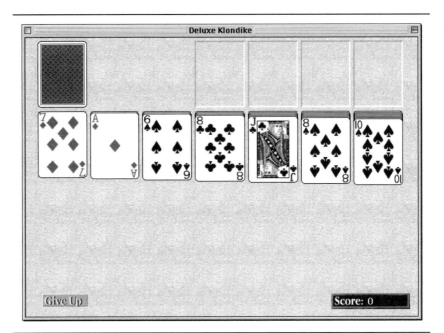

Figure 8-1:   The initial deal for Klondike

other two games (see Figure 8-6). Nonetheless, preparing the in-structions for the third game is fairly easy, because she has the tem-plate for the instructions down pat.

After completing three sets of instructions, it becomes clear to Jane that having the template for the instructions makes the process extremely easy. Jane can use the template to organize any number of sets of in-structions for playing solitaire. All she has to do is photocopy the tem-plate and fill in the values for the information about the game.

Objects

If someone were writing an object-oriented computer program to manage the instructions for playing solitaire, each game would be known as an *object*. It is a self-contained element used by the program. It has things that it knows about itself: its name, an illustration of its layout, the number of decks needed to play, how to deal, how to play,

---

Information about the Game
    Name: Klondike
    Illustration: See next page
    Decks: One
    Dealing: Deal from left to right.
        First pass: First card face up, six cards down.
        Second pass: First card face up on top of card #2, five cards down.
        Third pass: First card face up on top of card #3, four cards down.
        ... repeat pattern for total of seven passes ...
    Playing: One or three cards can be turned at a time.
        As encountered, put aces on top. Build up in suits.
        Build down from deal, opposite suit colors.
        Can move cards from the middle of a stack, moving card and all cards
    built below it.
        Move kings only into empty spots.
        If turning one card, make only one pass through the deck.
        If turning three cards, make as many passes as you like through the
    deck.
    Winning: All cards built on top of their aces.
Questions to Ask
    What is the name of the game?
        Read **Name** section.
    How many decks do I need?
        Read **Decks** section.
    What does the layout look like?
        Read **Illustration** section.
    How do I deal the game?
        Read the **Dealing** section.
    How do I play the game?
        Read the **Playing** section.
    How do I know when I've won?
        Read the **Winning** section.

Figure 8-2:   Instructions for playing Klondike

and how to determine when the game is won. In object-oriented terms, the values that an object stores about itself are known as *attributes* or *variables* or occasionally, *properties*.

The solitaire game object also has some things it knows how to do: explain how to deal, explain how to play, explain how to identify a win, and so on. In object-oriented programming terminology, actions that objects know how to perform are called *methods*, *services*, *functions*, *procedures*, or *operations*.

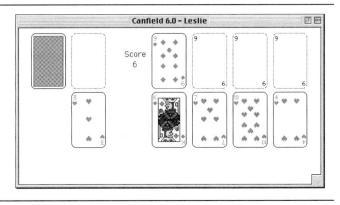

Figure 8-3:   The initial Canfield deal

Information about the Game
    Name: Canfield
    Illustration: See next page
    Decks: One
    Dealing: Deal four cards face up.
        Place on additional card face up above the first four as the starting card for building suits.
        The remaining cards stay in the draw pile.
    Playing: Turn one card at a time, going through the deck as many times as desired.
        Build down from deal, opposite suit colors.
        Can move cards from the middle of a stack, moving card and all cards built below it.
        Place cards of the same value as the initial foundation card above the deal as encountered.
        Build up in suits from the foundation cards.
        Any card can be placed in an empty slot.
    Winning: All cards built on top of the foundation cards.
Questions to Ask
    What is the name of the game?
        Read **Name** section.
    How many decks do I need?
        Read **Decks** section.
    What does the layout look like?
        Read **Illustration** section.
    How do I deal the game?
        Read the **Dealing** section.
    How do I play the game?
        Read the **Playing** section.
    How do I know when I've won?
        Read the **Winning** section.

Figure 8-4   The instructions for playing Canfield

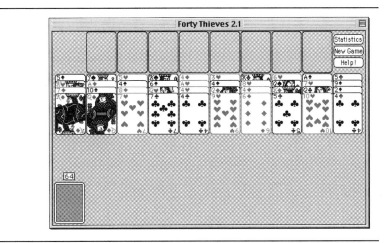

Figure 8-5: The initial deal for Forty Thieves

Information about the Game
   Name: Forty Thieves
   Illustration: See next page
   Decks: Two
   Dealing: Make ten piles of four cards, all face up.
      Jog cards so that the values of all cards can be seen.
      Remaining cards stay in the deck.
   Playing: Turn one card at a time. Make only one pass through the deck.
      Build down in suits.
      Only the top card of a stack can be moved.
      As aces are encountered, place at top of deal and build up in suits
   from the aces.
      Any card can be moved into any open space in the deal.
   Winning: All cards built on top of their aces.
Questions to Ask
   What is the name of the game?
      Read **Name** section.
   How many decks do I need?
      Read **Decks** section.
   What does the layout look like?
      Read **Illustration** section.
   How do I deal the game?
      Read the **Dealing** section.
   How do I play the game?
      Read the **Playing** section.
   How do I know when I've won?
      Read the **Winning** section.

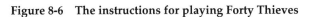

Figure 8-6   The instructions for playing Forty Thieves

Note: It is unfortunate, but there is no single accepted terminology for the object-oriented paradigm. Each programming language or DBMS chooses which terms it will use. You therefore need to recognize all of the terms that might be used to describe the same thing.

An object is very security minded. It typically keeps the things it knows about itself private and releases that information only through a method whose purpose is to share data values. For example, a user or program using the Klondike game object cannot access the contents of the Dealing variable directly. Instead, the user or program must execute the How Do I Deal the Game? method to see that data.

Objects also keep private the details of the procedures for the things they know how to do, but they make it easy for someone to ask them to perform those actions. Users or programs cannot see what is inside any of the methods. They see only the result of executing the method. This characteristic of objects is known as *information hiding* or *data encapsulation*.

An object presents a public interface to other objects that might use it. This provides other objects with a way to ask for data values or for actions to be performed. In the example of the solitaire games, the questions that Jane's little brother can ask are the game's public interface. The instructions below each question represent the procedure to be used to answer the question. A major benefit of data encapsulation is that as long as the object's public interface remains the same, you can change the details of the object's methods without needing to inform any other objects that might be using those methods. For example, the card game objects currently tell the user to "read" the contents of an attribute. However, there is no reason that the methods couldn't be changed to tell the user to "print" the contents of an attribute. The user would still access the method in the same way, but the way in which the method operates would be slightly different.

An object requests data or an action by sending a *message* to another object. For example, if you were writing a computer program to manage the instructions for solitaire games, the program (an object in its own right) could send a message to the game object asking the game object to display the instructions for dealing the game. Because the actual procedures of the method are hidden, your program would ask for the instruction display and then you would see the instructions on the screen. However, you would not need to worry about the details of how the screen display was produced. That is the job of the game object rather than the object that is asking the game to do something.

An object-oriented program is made up of a collection of objects, each of which has attributes and methods. The objects interact by sending messages to one another. The trick, of course, is figuring out exactly which objects a program needs and the attributes and methods those objects should have.

Classes

The template on which the solitaire game instructions are based is the same for each game. Without data, it might be represented as in Figure 8-7. The nice thing about this template is that it provides a consistent way of organizing all the characteristics of a game. When you want to create the instructions for another game, you make a copy of the template and "fill in the blanks": You write the data values for the attributes. The procedures that make up the answers to the questions someone might ask about the game have already been completed.

In object-oriented terminology, the template on which similar objects like the solitaire game instructions are based is known as a *class*. When a program creates an object from a class, it provides data for the object's variables. The object can then use the methods that have been written for its class. All of the objects created from the same class share the same procedures for their methods. They also have the same types of data, but the values for the data may differ, for example, just as the names of the solitaire games are different.

```
Information about the Game (Variables)
    Name:
    Illustration:
    Decks:
    Dealing:
    Playing:
    Winning:
Questions to Ask (Methods)
    What is the name of the game?
        Read Name section.
    How many decks do I need?
        Read Decks section.
    What does the layout look like?
        Read Illustration section.
    How do I deal the game?
        Read the Dealing section.
    How do I play the game?
        Read the Playing section.
    How do I know when I've won?
        Read the Winning section.
```

Figure 8-7:   The solitaire game instruction template

A class is also a data type. In fact, a class is an implementation of what is known as an *abstract data type*, which is just another term for a user-defined data type. The implication of a class being a data type is that you can use a class as the data type of an attribute.

Suppose, for example, you were developing a class to handle data about the employees in your organization. The attributes of the class might include the employee ID, the first name, the last name, and the address. The address itself is made up of a street, city, state, and zip. Therefore, you would probably create an address class with those attributes and then, rather than duplicating those attributes in the employee class, simply indicate that an object of the employee class will include an object created from the address class to contain the employee's address.

Types of Classes

There are three major types of classes used in an object-oriented program:

- ◆ *Control classes:* Control classes neither manage data nor have visible output. Instead, they control the operational flow of a program. For example, *application classes* represent the program itself. In most cases, each program creates only one object from an application class. The application class's job includes starting the execution of the program, detecting menu selections, and executing the correct program code to satisfy the user's requests.
- ◆ *Entity classes:* Entity classes are used to create objects that manage data. The solitaire game class, for example, is an entity class. Classes for people, tangible objects, and events (for example, business meetings) are entity classes. Most object-oriented programs have at least one entity class from which many objects are created. In fact, in its simplest sense, the object-oriented data model is built from the representation of relationships between objects created from entity objects.
- ◆ *Interface classes:* Interface classes handle the input and output of information. For example, if you are working with a graphic user interface, then each window and menu used by the program is an object created from an interface class.

In an object-oriented program, entity classes do not do their own input and output (I/O). Keyboard input is handled by interface objects that collect data and send it to entity objects for storage and processing. Screen and printed output is formatted by interface objects that get data for display from entity objects. When entity objects become part of a database, the DBMS takes care of file I/O; the rest of the I/O is handled by application programs or DBMS utilities.

Why is it so important to keep data manipulation separate from I/O? Wouldn't it be simpler to let the entity object manage its own I/O? It might be simpler, but if you decided to change a screen layout, you would need to modify the entity class. If you keep them separate, then data manipulation procedures are independent of data display. You can change one without affecting the other. In a large program, this can not only save you a lot of time but also help you avoid programming errors. In a database environment, the separation of I/O and data storage becomes especially critical, because you do not want to modify data storage each time you decide to modify the look and feel of an application program.

Many object-oriented programs also use a fourth type of class: a *container class*. Container classes exist to "contain," or manage, multiple objects created from the same type of class. Because they gather objects together, they are also known as *aggregations*. For example, if you had a program that handled the instructions for playing solitaire, then that program would probably have a container class that organized all the individual card game objects. The container class would keep the objects in some order, list them for you, and probably search through them as well. As you will see, many pure object-oriented DBMSs require container classes, known as *extents*, to provide access to all objects created from the same class.

Types of Methods

Several types of methods are common to most classes, including the following:

- ◆ *Constructors:* A constructor is a method that has the same name as the class. It is executed whenever an object is created from a class. A constructor therefore usually contains instructions to initialize an object's variables in some way.
- ◆ *Destructors:* A destructor is a method that is executed when an object is destroyed. Not all object-oriented languages support destructors, which are usually used to release system resources (for example, main memory) allocated by the object.

◆ *Accessors:* An accessor, also known as a *get method*, returns the value of a private attribute to another object. This is the typical way in which external objects gain access to encapsulated data.

◆ *Mutators:* A mutator, or *set method*, stores a new value in an attribute. This is the typical way in which external objects can modify encapsulated data.

The remaining methods defined for a class depend on the specific type of class and the specific behaviors it needs to perform.

Method Overloading

One of the characteristics of a class is its ability to contain *overloaded* methods, methods that have the same name but require different data to operate. Because the data are different, the public interfaces of the methods are distinct.

As an example, assume that a human relations program has a container class named AllEmployees that aggregates all objects created from the Employees class. Programs that use the AllEmployees class create one object from the class and then relate all employee objects to the container using some form of program data structure (for example, an array, linked list, or binary tree).

To make the container class useful, there must be some way to locate specific employee objects. You might want to search by the employee ID number, by first and last name, or by telephone number. The AllEmployees class therefore contains three methods named find. One of the three requires an integer (the employee number) as input, the second requires two strings (the first and last name), and the third requires a single string (the phone number). Although the methods have the same name, their public interfaces are different because the combination of the name and the required input data is distinct.

Many classes have overloaded constructors. One might accept interactive input, another might read input from a file, and a third might get its data by copying the data in another object (a *copy constructor*). For example, most object-oriented environments have a Date class that supports initializing a date object with a string, three integers (day, month, year), the current system date, another Date object, and so on.

The benefit of method overloading is that the methods present a consistent interface to the programmer. Whenever a programmer wants to locate an employee, he or she knows to use a method named `find`. Then, the programmer just uses whichever of the three types of data he or she happens to have. The object-oriented program locates the correct method by using its entire public interface (its *signature*), made up of the name and the required input data.

Naming Classes, Attributes, and Methods

There are a few naming conventions used throughout the object-oriented world. Although there is absolutely nothing that says you have to name your classes, attributes, and methods in this way, you will be consistent with other programmers and database designers if you do so.

- Class names start with uppercase letters, followed by lowercase letters. If a class name is more than one word, it either uses an underscore (_) to separate the words — as in Merchandise_item—or uses embedded uppercase letters, as in MerchandiseItem.
- Attribute and method names start with lowercase letters and contain uppercase letters, lowercase letters, and numbers. If an attribute or method name is more than one word, it either uses an underscore to separate the words (for example, product_numb or display_label) or uses embedded uppercase letters, as in productNumb or displayLabel.
- Accessor method names begin with the word *get* followed by the name of the attribute whose value is to be retrieved. For example, a method to retrieve a product number would be *getProductNumb*.

◆ Mutator method names begin with the word *set* followed by the name of the attribute whose value is to be modified, as in *setProductNumb*.

Class Relationships

The classes in an object-oriented environment aren't always independent. The basic object-oriented paradigm has two major ways to relate objects, distinct from any logical data relationships that might be included in a pure object-oriented database: inheritance and composition.

Inheritance

As you are developing an object-oriented program or an object-oriented database, you will run into situations where you need to use similar—but not identical—classes. If these classes are related in general to specific relationships, then you can take advantage of one of the major features of the object-oriented paradigm known as *inheritance*.

Inheriting Attributes. To see how inheritance works, assume that you are writing a program to manage a pet shop. One of the entity classes you will use is Animal, which will describe the living creatures sold by the shop. The data that describe objects created from the Animal class include the English and Latin names of the animal, the animal's age, and the animal's gender. However, the rest of the data depends on what type of animal is being represented. For example, for reptiles, you want to know the length of the animal, but for mammals, you want to know the weight. And for fish, you don't care about the weight or length, but you do want to know the color. All the animals sold by the pet shop share some data, yet have pieces of data that are specific to certain subgroups.

You could diagram the relationship as in Figure 8-8. The Animal class provides the data common to all types of animals. The subgroups—Mammals, Reptiles, and Fish—*add* the data specific to themselves. They don't need to repeat the common data because they *inherit* them from Animals. In other words, Mammals, Reptiles, and Fish all include the four pieces of data that are part of Animal.

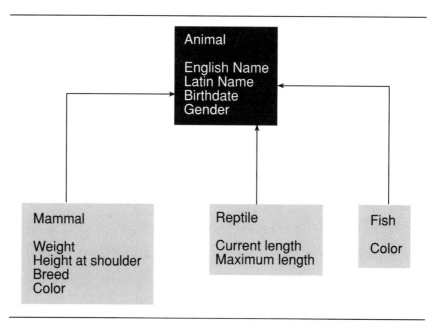

Figure 8-8:   The relationship of classes for a program for a pet shop

If you look closely at Figure 8-8, you'll notice that the lines on the arrows go from the subgroups up to Animal. This is actually contrary to what is happening: The data from Animal are flowing down the lines into the subgroups. Unfortunately, the direction of the arrows is dictated by convention, even though it may seem counterintuitive.

In object-oriented terminology, the subgroups are known as *subclasses* or *derived* classes. The Animal class is a *superclass* or *base* class.

The trick to understanding inheritance is to remember that subclasses represent a more specific occurrence of their superclass. The relationships between a base class and its derived classes therefore can be expressed using the phrase "is a":

- ♦ A mammal is an animal.
- ♦ A reptile is an animal.
- ♦ A fish is an animal.

If the "is a" phrasing does not make sense in a given situation, then you are not looking at inheritance. As an example, assume that you are writing a program to handle the rentals of equipment at a ski shop. You create a class for a generic merchandise item and then subclasses for the specific types of items being rented, as in the top four rectangles in Figure 8-9. Inheritance works properly here because skis are a specific type of merchandise item, as well as boots and poles.

However, you run into trouble when you begin to consider the specific items being rented and the customer doing the renting (the renter). Although there is a logical database-style relationship between a renter and an item being rented, inheritance does not work because the "is a" test fails. A rented item is not a renter!

The situation with merchandise items and rental inventory is more complex. The Merchandise Item, Skis, Boots, and Poles classes represent descriptions of types of merchandise but not physical inventory. For example, the ski shop may have many pairs of one type of ski in inventory and many pairs of boots of the same type, size, and width. Therefore, what is being rented is individual inventory items, represented by the Item Rented class. A given inventory item is either skis, boots, or poles. It can only be *one*, not all three as shown in Figure 8-9. Therefore, an item rented is not a pair of skis, a pair of boots, and a set of poles. (You also have the problem of having no class that can store the size or length of an item.)

One solution to the problem is to create a separate rented item class for each type of merchandise, as in Figure 8-10. When you are looking at this diagram, be sure to pay attention to the direction of the arrows. The physical layout of the diagram does not correspond to the direction of the inheritance. Remember that by convention, the arrows point from the derived class to the base class.

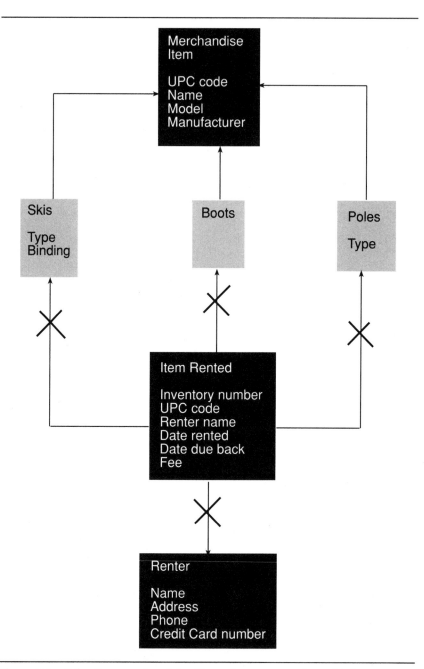

Figure 8-9:   Inheritance and no inheritance in a program for a ski shop

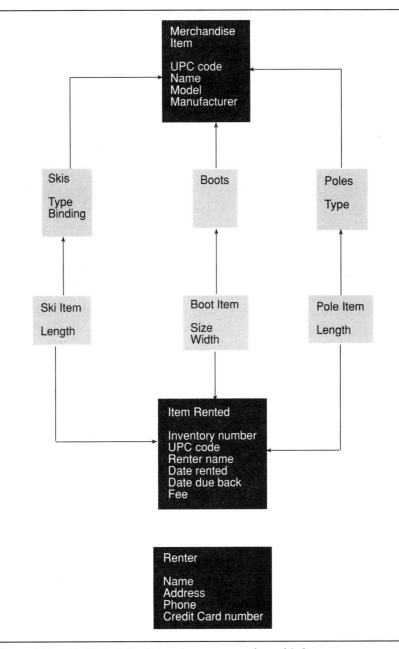

Figure 8-10:   Multiple inheritance in a program for a ski shop

The Ski Item class inherits information about the type of item it is from the Skis class. It also inherits information about an item being rented from the Item Rented class. A ski item "is a" pair of skis; a ski item "is a" rented item as well. Now the design of the classes passes the "is a" test for appropriate inheritance. (Note that this also gives you a class that can contain information such as the length and size of a specific inventory item.) The Renter class does not participate in the inheritance hierarchy at all.

Multiple Inheritance. When a class inherits from more than one base class, you have *multiple inheritance*. The extent to which multiple inheritance is supported in programming languages and by DBMSs varies considerably from one product to another. You will read much more about this concept throughout this book.

Not every class in an inheritance hierarchy is necessarily used to create objects. For example, in Figure 8-10 it is unlikely that any objects are ever created from the Merchandise Item or Item Rented classes. These classes are present simply to provide the common attributes and methods that their derived classes share.

Such classes are known as *abstract*, or *virtual*, classes. In contrast, classes from which objects are created are known as *concrete* classes.

> Note: Many computer scientists use the verb "instantiate" to mean "creating an object from a class." For example, you could say that abstract classes are never instantiated. However, this author finds that term rather contrived (although not quite as bad as saying "we now will motivate the code" to mean "we will now explain the code") and prefers to use the more direct "create an object from a class."

Inheriting Methods: Polymorphism. In general, methods are inherited by subclasses from their superclass. A subclass can use its base class's methods as its own. However, in some cases it may not be possible to write a generic method that can be used by all subclasses. For example, assume that the ski rental shop's Merchandise Item class has a method named printCatalogEntry, the intent of which is to print a properly formatted catalog entry for each distinct type of merchandise item. The subclasses of Merchandise Item, however, have attributes not shared by all subclasses, and the printCatalog-Entry method therefore must work somewhat differently for each subclass.

To solve the problem, the ski rental shop can take advantage of *polymorphism*, the ability to write different bodies for methods of the same name that belong to classes in the same inheritance hierarchy. The Merchandise Item class includes a *prototype* for the print-CatalogEntry method, indicating just the method's public interface. There is no body for the method, no specifications of how the method is to perform its work (a *virtual method*). Each subclass then redefines the method, adding the program instructions necessary to execute the method.

The beauty of polymorphism is that a programmer can expect methods of the same name and same type of output for all the subclasses of the same base class. However, each subclass can perform the method according to its own needs. Encapsulation hides the details from all objects outside the class hierarchy.

> *Note: It is very easy to confuse polymorphism and overloading. Just keep in mind that overloading applies to methods of the same class that have the same name but different signatures, whereas polymorphism applies to several subclasses of the same base class that have methods with the same signature but different implementations.*

Composition

Inheritance can be described as a general–specific relationship. In contrast, *composition* is a whole-part relationship. It specifies that one class is a component of another and is often read as "has a."

To help you understand how composition can be used, let's look at another version of the ski shop classes (see Figure 8-11). Notice that the diagram is considerably simpler. Not only has the multiple inheritance been eliminated, but there are only three classes.

Figure 8-11: Composition

The Renter class continues to stand alone. However, the inheritance hierarchy for the types of merchandise and items that are rented is now made up of two classes, each of which contains an object of another class. A merchandise item has an object of the Merchandise Type class to classify it as either a ski, boot, or pole. By the same token, an item rented has an object of the Rental Item class to contain descriptive information (size, width, and length, as appropriate).

Some pure object-oriented DBMSs take composition to the extreme. They provide simple data types such as integers, real numbers, characters, and Booleans. Everything else in the database—even strings—is built by creating classes from those simple data types and using those classes to build more complex classes, and so on.

Benefits of Object Orientation

There are several reasons why the object-oriented paradigm has become so pervasive in programming. Among the perceived benefits are the following:

- ◆ An object-oriented program consists of modular units that are independent of one another. These units can therefore be reused in multiple programs, saving development time. For example, if you have a well-debugged employee class, you can use it in any of your business programs that require data about employees.
- ◆ As long as a class's public interface remains unchanged, the internals of the class can be modified as needed without requiring any changes to the programs that use the class. This can significantly speed up program modification. It can also make program modification more reliable, as it cuts down on many unexpected side effects of program changes.
- ◆ An object-oriented program separates the user interface from data handling, making it possible to modify one independent of the other.
- ◆ Inheritance adds logical structure to a program by relating classes in a general to specific manner, making the

program easier to understand and therefore easier to maintain.

However, the object-oriented paradigm merely provides a framework for organizing the elements in a database. It does not eliminate the need to perform a good database design that identifies entities and the relationship between entities.

Integrating Objects into a Relational Database

In the pure object-oriented data model, a class is an entity, the element that is involved in data relationships. However, when we look at merging objects into the relational data model, a class takes on an entirely different role. As mentioned at the beginning of this chapter, it becomes a domain, acting as the data type for a column.

There are two very important implications of using a class as a domain:

♦ It becomes possible to store multiple values in the same column in the same row because an object usually contains multiple values. However, if a class is a domain assigned to a column, then any given intersection of a column and row can contain only one object created from that class. The relation therefore still conforms to the relational constraint of there being no multivalued attributes.

♦ It becomes possible to store procedures in a relation, because an object is linked to the program code for the processes that it knows how to do.

There are, however, a few limitations to the implementation of object-oriented structures in a relational database. First and foremost, current implementations do not support inheritance. You will therefore be unable to relate classes in that way. However, because a class is essentially a user-defined data type, you can use composition to build complex classes from simpler classes.

Second, although a DBMS may support objects as domains, application development tools (both those provided by the DBMS vendor and third-parties) may not recognize columns with classes as domains. This means that application development must be done in a high-level language such as C++ or COBOL to take advantage of the objects until such time as the tools catch up with the DBMS.

Some database designers have attempted to make a relational database act like an object-oriented database by creating a class that corresponds to an entity and then creating a table with one column for the object and one or more columns for the primary key. The problem with this approach is that a relational database doesn't represent relationships like an object-oriented database, which uses pointers much like a simple network database. No matter what you do, you will still need columns for foreign keys. The result is a design that is clumsy and hard to maintain. This is therefore not a recommended approach for relational database design. If you need an object-oriented database, then that's what you should be using rather than trying to force a relational database to behave like one.

ER Diagrams for Object-Relational Designs

The Information Engineering style of ER diagramming does not lend itself to the inclusion of objects because it has no way to represent a class. Therefore, when we add objects to a relational database, we have to use another ERD style.

Although there are many techniques for object-oriented ERDs, one of the most commonly used is the Unified Modeling Language (UML). When used to depict a post-relational database design, UML looks a great deal like the IE style, but indicates relationships in a different way.

An example of an ER diagram using UML can be found in Figure 8-12. This design is of a purely object-oriented database and includes some elements that therefore won't appear in a hybrid design. It has been included here to give you an overview of UML so that you can better understand the portions of the modeling tool that we will be using.

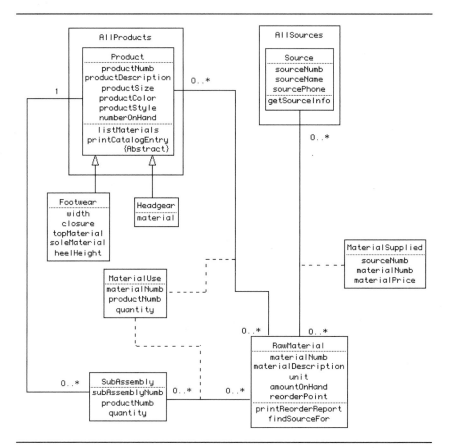

Figure 8-12:   **An object-oriented database design using UML notation**

The basic features of UML include the following:

♦ A regular class is represented by a rectangle, divided into the three parts (name, attributes, procedures).

♦ An aggregate class—a class that collects all objects of a given class (i.e., an extent)—is represented by a rectangle containing its name and the rectangles of the classes whose objects it aggregates. For example, in Figure 8-12, the Product and Source classes are within their aggregate classes, AllProducts and AllSources, respectively.

Note: The purpose of an aggregate class is the same as a system set in a CODASYL database. It provides access to all objects created from a single class.

♦ Relationships between entities are shown with lines with plain ends. The cardinality of a relationship is expressed as n, n..n, or n..*. For example, if the cardinality is 1, it is simply written as 1. If the cardinality is 0 or 1, it is written as 0..1. If the cardinality is 0 or more, it appears as 0..*; 1 or more appears as 1..*. Notice in Figure 8-12 that there are several direct many-to-many relationships, shown with 0..* at either end of the association line.

Note: The object-oriented data model can handle direct many-to-many relationships. However, as mentioned in Chapter 3, a designer must be very careful when including them to avoid losing meaning in the database.

♦ Inheritance is shown by a line with an open arrow pointing toward the base class. In Figure 8-12, the Footwear and Headgear classes have such arrows pointing toward Product.

♦ What we call composite entities in a relational database are known as *association classes*. They are connected to the relationship to which they apply with a dashed line. As you can see in Figure 8-12, the MaterialSupplied and MaterialUse classes are each connected to at least one many-to-many relationship by the required dashed line.

In addition to the basic features shown in Figure 8-12, UML diagrams can include any of the following:

♦ An attribute can include information about its visibility (public, protected, or private), data type, default value, and domain. In Figure 8-13, for example, you can see four classes and the data types of their attributes. Keep in mind that in an object-oriented environment, data types can be other classes. Therefore, the Source class uses an object of the TelephoneNumber class for its phoneNumber attribute and an object of the Address class for its sourceAddress attribute. In turn, Source, Address, and Telephone number all contain attributes that are objects of the String class.

Figure 8-13:   UML classes showing their data types

   ♦ Procedures (officially called *operations* in UML) can include their complete program signature and return data type. If you look at Figure 8-13, for example, you can see each operation's name followed by the types of data that it requires to perform its job (*parameters*). Together, the procedure's name and its parameters make up the procedure's signature. If data are returned by the operation, then the operation's signature is followed by a colon and the data type of the return value, which may be an object of another class or a simple data type such as an integer.

Note: Because classes take on the role of data types within a relational database, the classes you will be seeing in the case studies in Chapters 11 through 13 will appear generally like those in Figure 8-13. They will be connected to the entities that use them with gray dashed lines with arrows on one end.

◆ Solid arrows can be used at the end of associations to indicate the directions in which a relationship can be navigated.

Note: As mentioned earlier in this chapter, pure object-oriented databases, like simple network databases, are navigational, meaning that traversal through the database is limited to following predefined relationships. Because of this characteristic, some theorists feel that the object-oriented data model is a step backward rather than forward and that the relational data model continues to have significant advantages over any navigational data model.

There are three possible ways to use the arrows:
- Use arrows on the ends of all associations where navigation is possible. If an association has a plain end, then navigation is not possible in that direction. This would indicate, for example, a relationship between two objects that is not an inverse relationship, where only one of the two objects in a relationship contains the object identifier of a related object.
- Show no arrows at all, as was done in Figure 8-13. In that case, the diagram provides no information about how the database design can be navigated.
- Show no arrows on associations that can be navigated in both directions, but use arrows on associations that can be navigated in only one direction. The drawback to this approach is that you cannot differentiate associations that can be navigated in both directions from associations that cannot be navigated at all.

♦ An association that ends in a filled diamond indicates a whole–part relationship. For example, if you were representing a spreadsheet in a database, the relationship between the spreadsheet and its cells could be diagrammed as in Figure 8-14. The filled diamond can also be used to show aggregation instead of placing one object within another, as was done in Figure 8-12.

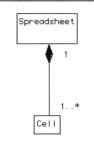

Figure 8-14:   Using UML to diagram a whole–part relationship

♦ When an association is between more than two objects, UML uses a diamond to represent the relationship. If an association class is present, it will be connected to the diamond, as in Figure 8-15. The four classes in the illustration represent entities from a poetry reading society's database. A "reading" occurs when a single person reads a single poem that was written by one or more poets. The association entity indicates when and where the reading took place.

For Further Reading

The equivalent of Codd's rules for the integration of objects into a relational database can be found in the following book, which provides a complete (but opinionated) discussion of the topic:

Date, C. J. and Darwen, H. *Foundation for Object/Relational Databases: The Third Manifesto*. Addison-Wesley, 1998.

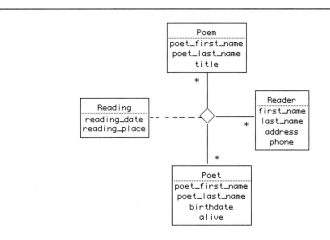

Figure 8-15: **Using UML to diagram a relationship between more than two classes**

For a broader and more thorough treatment of object-oriented analysis and design, see:

Booch, Grady. *Object-Oriented Analysis and Design with Applications.* Addison-Wesley, 1994.

Part Two

Practice

In this part of the book you will read about some of the practical techniques we use when working with relational database designs. You will be introduced to the SQL language statements needed to create relational schemas and their contents. You will also see how a CASE tool can help design and document a database. In addition, this part contains two complete relational design case studies to provide further examples of the database design process.

9

Using SQL to Implement a Relational Design

As a complete data manipulation language, SQL contains statements that allow you to insert, modify, delete, and retrieve data. However, to a database designer, the portions of SQL that support the creation of database structural elements are of utmost importance. In this chapter you will be introduced to the SQL commands that you will use to create and maintain the tables, views, indexes, and other structures that make up a relational database.

The actual file structure of a database is implementation dependent, as is the procedure needed to create database files. Therefore, the discussion in this chapter assumes that the necessary database files are already in place.

You will see examples of the use of the syntax presented in this chapter at the end of each of the three case studies that follow in this book.

Database Object Hierarchy

The objects in a database maintained by a SQL-92–compliant DBMS are arranged in a hierarchy, diagrammed in Figure 9-1. The smallest units with which a database works—the columns and rows— appear in the center. These in turn are grouped into tables and views.

The tables and views that comprise a single logical database are collected into a schema. Multiple schemas are grouped into catalogs, which can then be grouped into clusters. A catalog usually contains information describing all the schemas handled by one DBMS. Catalog creation is implementation dependent and therefore not part of the SQL-92 standard.

Prior to SQL-92, clusters often represented database files, and the clustering of objects into files was a way to increase database performance by placing objects accessed together in the same physical file. The SQL-92 concept of a cluster, however, is a group of catalogs that are accessible using the same connection to a database server.

Under SQL-92, none of the groupings of database objects are related to physical storage structures. If you are working with a centralized mainframe DBMS, you may find multiple catalogs stored in the database file. However, on smaller or distributed systems, you are just as likely to find one catalog or schema per database file or to find a catalog or schema split between multiple files.

Clusters, catalogs, and schemas are not required elements of a database environment. In a small installation where there is one collection of tables serving a single purpose, for example, it may not even be necessary to create a schema to hold them.

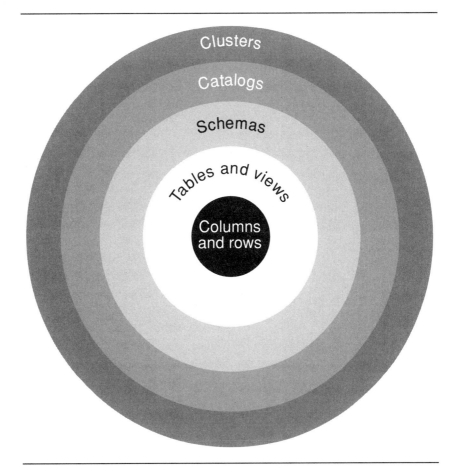

Figure 9-1:   The SQL-92 database object hierarchy

Naming and Identifying Objects

The way in which you name and identify database objects is in some measure dictated by the object hierarchy:

- ◆ Column names must be unique within the table.
- ◆ Table names must be unique within the schema.
- ◆ Schema names must be unique within their catalog.
- ◆ Catalog names must be unique within their cluster.

When a column name appears in more than one table in a query, a user must specify the table from which a column should be taken (even if it makes no difference which table is used). The general form for qualifying duplicate names is:

```
table_name.column_name
```

If an installation has more than one schema, then a user must also indicate the schema in which a table resides:

```
schema_name.table_name.column_name
```

This naming convention means that two different schemas can include tables with the same name.

By the same token, if an installation has multiple catalogs, a user will need to indicate the catalog from which an object comes:

```
catalog_name.schema_name.table_name.column_name
```

The names that you assign to database elements can include the following:

- ♦ Letters
- ♦ Numbers
- ♦ Underscores (_)

Names can be up to 128 characters long. They are not case-sensitive. (In fact, many SQL command processors convert names to all upper- or lowercase characters before submitting a SQL statement to a DBMS for processing.)

> *Note: Some DBMSs also allow pound signs (#) and dollar signs ($) in element names, but neither is recognized by SQL queries so their use should be avoided.*

Schemas

To a database designer, a schema represents the overall, logical design of a complete database. As far as SQL is concerned, however, a schema is nothing more than a container for tables, views, and other structural elements. It is up to the database designer to place a meaningful group of elements within each schema.

A schema is not required to create tables and views. In fact, if you are installing a database for an environment in which there is likely to be only one logical database, then you can just as easily do without one. However, if more than one database will be sharing the same DBMS and the same server, then organizing database elements into schemas can greatly simplify the maintenance of the individual databases.

Creating a Schema

To create a schema, you use the CREATE SCHEMA statement. In its simplest form, it has the syntax

```
CREATE SCHEMA schema_name
```

as in

```
CREATE SCHEMA lasers_only
```

By default, a schema belongs to the user who created it (the user ID under which the schema was created). The owner of the schema is the only user ID that can modify the schema unless the owner grants that ability to other users.

To assign a different owner to a schema, you add an AUTHORIZATION clause:

```
CREATE SCHEMA schema_name AUTHORIZATION owner_user_ID
```

For example, to assign the lasers_only schema to the user ID DBA, someone could use:

```
CREATE SCHEMA lasers_only AUTHORIZATION dba
```

When creating a schema, you can also create additional database elements at the same time. To do so, you use braces to group the CREATE statements for the other elements, as in:

```
CREATE SCHEMA schema_name AUTHORIZATION owner_user_ID
{
    other create statements go here
}
```

This automatically assigns the elements within the braces to the schema.

Identifying the Schema You Want to Use

One of the nicest things about a relational database is that you can add or delete database structure elements at any time. There must therefore be a way to specify a current schema for new database elements after the schema has been created initially with the CREATE SCHEMA statement.

One way to do this is with the SET SCHEMA statement:

```
SET SCHEMA schema_name
```

To use SET SCHEMA, the user ID under which you are working must have authorization to work with that schema.

Alternatively, you can qualify the name of a database element with the name of the schema. For example, if you are creating a table, then you would use something like

```
CREATE TABLE schema_name.table_name
```

For those DBMSs that do not support SET SCHEMA, this is the only way to attach new database elements to a schema after the schema has been created.

Domains

As you know, a domain is an expression of the permitted values for a column in a relation. When you define a table, you assign each column a data type (for example, character or integer) that provides a broad domain. A DBMS will not store data that violate that constraint.

The SQL-92 standard introduced the concept of user-defined domains, which can be viewed as user-defined data types that can be applied to columns in tables. (This means you have to create a domain before you can assign it to a column!)

Domains can be created as part of a CREATE SCHEMA statement or, if your DBMS supports SET SCHEMA, at any time after a schema has been defined.

To create a domain, use the CREATE DOMAIN statement, which has the following general syntax:

```
CREATE DOMAIN domain_name data_type
CHECK (expression_to_validate_values)
```

The CHECK clause is actually a generic way of expressing a condition that data must meet. It can include a SELECT to validate data against other data stored in the database or it can include a simple logical expression. In that expression, the keyword VALUE represents the data being checked.

For example, if Lasers Only wanted to validate the price of a disc, someone might create the following domain:

```
CREATE DOMAIN price numeric (6,2)
CHECK (VALUE >= 19.95)
```

After creating this domain, a column in a table can be given the data type of price. The DBMS will then check to be certain that the value in that column is always greater than or equal to 19.95. (We will leave a discussion of the data type used in the preceding SQL statement until we cover creating tables in the next section of this chapter.)

The domain mechanism is very flexible. Assume, for example, that you want to ensure that telephone numbers are always stored in the format XXX-XXX-XXXX. A domain to validate that format might be created as:

```
CREATE DOMAIN telephone char (12)
CHECK (SUBSTRING (VALUE FROM 4 FOR 1 = '-') AND
    SUBSTRING (VALUE FROM 8 FOR 1 = '-'))
```

You can use the CREATE DOMAIN statement to give a column a default value. For example, the following statement sets up a domain that holds either Y or N and defaults to Y:

```
CREATE DOMAIN boolean char (1)
DEFAULT 'Y'
CHECK (UPPER(VALUE) = 'Y' OR UPPER(VALUE) = 'N')
```

Tables

The most important structure within a relational database is the table. As you know, tables contain just about everything, including business data and the data dictionary.

The SQL-92 standard divides tables into three categories:

♦ Permanent base tables: Permanent base tables are tables whose contents are stored in the database and remain permanently in the database unless they are explicitly deleted.

♦ Global temporary tables: Global temporary tables are tables used for working storage that are destroyed at the end of a SQL session. The definitions of the tables are stored in the data dictionary, but their data are not. The tables must be loaded with data each time they are going to be used. Global temporary tables can be used only by the current user, but they are visible to an entire SQL session (either an application program or a user working with an interactive query facility).

♦ Local temporary tables: Local temporary tables are similar to global temporary tables. However, they are visible only to the specific program module in which they are created.

Temporary base tables are subtly different from views, which assemble their data by executing a SQL query. You will read more about this difference and how temporary tables are created and used later in this chapter.

Most of the tables in a relational database are permanent base tables. You create them with the CREATE TABLE statement:

```
CREATE TABLE table_name
(   column1_name column1_data_type
    column_constraints,
    column2_name column2_data_type
    column_constraints, …
    table_constraints)
```

The constraints on a table include declarations of primary and foreign keys. The constraints on a column include whether values in the column are mandatory as well as other constraints you may decide to include in a CHECK clause.

Column Data Types

Each column in a table must be given a data type. Although data types are somewhat implementation dependent, you can expect to find most of the following:

♦ INTEGER (abbreviated INT): A positive or negative whole number. The number of bits occupied by the value is implementation dependent. On today's desktop computers, an integer is either 16 or 32 bits. Large computers use only 32-bit integers.

♦ SMALLINT: A positive or negative whole number. A small integer is usually half the size of a standard integer.

Using small integers when you know you will need to store only small values can save space in the database.

♦ NUMERIC: A fixed-point positive or negative number. A numeric value has a whole number portion and a fractional portion. When you create it, you must specify the total length of the number (including the decimal point) and how many of those digits will be to the right of the decimal point (its precision). For example:

```
NUMERIC (6,2)
```

creates a number in the format XXX.XX. The DBMS will store exactly two digits to the right of the decimal point.

♦ DECIMAL: A fixed-point positive or negative number. A decimal number is similar to a numeric value. However, the DBMS may store more digits to the right of the decimal than you specify. Although there is no guarantee that you will get the extra precision, its presence can provide more accurate results in computations.

♦ REAL: A "single-precision" floating point value. A floating point number is expressed in the format:

```
±X.XXXXX * 10YY
```

where YY is the power to which 10 is raised. Because of the way in which computers store floating point numbers, a real number may not be an exact representation of a value, but only a close approximation. The range of values that can be stored is implementation dependent, as is the precision. You therefore cannot specify a size for a real number column.

♦ DOUBLE PRECISION (abbreviated DOUBLE): A "double-precision" floating point number. The range and precision of double precision values are implementation dependent, but generally both will be greater than with single-precision real numbers.

♦ FLOAT: A floating point number for which you can specify the precision. The DBMS will maintain at least the precision that you specify. (It may be more.)

- BIT: Storage for a fixed number of individual bits. You must indicate the number of bits, as in

```
BIT (n)
```

where n is the number of bits. (If you do not, you will have room for only one bit.)
- BIT VARYING: Storage for a varying number of bits, up to a specified maximum, as in

```
BIT VARYING (n)
```

where n is the maximum number of bits. In some DBMSs, columns of this type can be used to store graphic images.
- DATE: A date.
- TIME: A time.
- TIMESTAMP: The combination of a date and a time.
- CHARACTER (abbreviated CHAR): A fixed-length space to hold a string of characters. When declaring a CHAR column, you need to indicate the width of the column:

```
CHAR (n)
```

where n is the amount of space that will be allocated for the column in every row. Even if you store less than n characters, the column will always take up n bytes and the column will be padded with blanks to fill up empty space. The maximum number of characters allowed is implementation dependent.
- CHARACTER VARYING (abbreviated VARCHAR): A variable length space to hold a string of characters. You must indicate the maximum width of the column—

```
VARCHAR (n)
```

—but the DBMS stores only as many characters as you insert, up to the maximum n. The overall maximum number of characters allowed is implementation dependent.
- INTERVAL: A date or time interval. An interval data type is followed by a qualifier that specifies the size of the interval and optionally the number of digits. For example:

```
INTERVAL YEAR
INTERVAL YEAR (n)
INTERVAL MONTH
INTERVAL MONTH (n)
INTERVAL YEAR TO MONTH
INTERVAL YEAR (n) TO MONTH
INTERVAL DAY
INTERVAL DAY (n)
INTERVAL DAY TO HOUR
INTERVAL DAY (n) TO HOUR
INTERVAL DAY TO MINUTE
INTERVAL DAY (n) TO MINUTE
INTERVAL MINUTE
INTERVAL MINUTE (n)
```

In the preceding examples, n specifies the number of digits. When the interval covers more than one date–time
unit, such as YEAR TO MONTH, you can specify a size
for only the first unit. Year–month intervals can include
years, months, or both. Time intervals can include days,
hours, minutes, and/or seconds.

Many DBMSs also support a *BLOB* (*binary large object*) data type. A
BLOB is usually the contents of a file containing text and/or graphics that cannot be interpreted by the DBMS (although the BLOB is
readable by the application that created it). BLOBs use a great deal
of space in the database. In addition, they cannot be used for searches. Identifying information about the contents of a BLOB must be
contained in other columns of the table using data types that can be
understood by the DBMS.

Notice that there is no specification for a Boolean (true–false) data
type. This means that if you need to use a column as a flag, the best
solution is to create a boolean domain like the one you saw earlier
in this chapter in the section on domains.

In Figure 9-2 you will find bare-bones CREATE TABLE statements
for the Lasers Only database. These statements include only column names and data types. SQL will create tables from statements
in this format, but because the tables have no primary keys, many
DBMSs will not let you enter data.

```
CREATE TABLE customer
    (customer_numb int,
    customer_first_name varchar (15),
    customer_last_name varchar (15),
    customer_street varchar (30),
    customer_city varchar (15),
    customer_state char (2),
    customer_zip char (5),
    customer_phone char (12),
    credit_card_numb varchar (15),
    card_exp_date date)

CREATE TABLE item
    (item_numb integer,
    title varchar (60),
    distributor_numb int,
    retail_price numeric (6,2),
    release_date date,
    genre char (15))

CREATE TABLE order
    (order_numb integer,
    customer_numb integer,
    order_date date,
    order_filled char (1))

CREATE TABLE order_line
    (order_numb int,
    item_numb int,
    quantity integer,
    discount_applied numeric (6,2),
    selling_price numeric (6,2),
    shipped char (1))

CREATE TABLE distributor
    (distributor_numb int,
    distributor_name varchar (15),
    distributor_street varchar (30),
    distributor_city varchar (15),
    distributor_state char (2),
    distributor_zip char (5),
    distributor_phone char (12),
    distributor_contact_person varchar (30),
    contact_person_ext varchar (5))
```

Continued next page

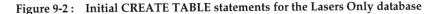

Figure 9-2 :   Initial CREATE TABLE statements for the Lasers Only database

```
CREATE TABLE actor
    (actor_numb int,
    actor_name varchar (30)

CREATE TABLE performance
    (actor_numb int,
    item_numb int,
    role varchar (30))

CREATE TABLE producer
    (producer_name varchar (30),
    studio varchar (30))

CREATE TABLE production
    (producer_name varchar (30),
    item_numb int)
```

Figure 9-2 (Continued):   Initial CREATE TABLE statements for the Lasers Only database

Default Values

As you are defining columns, you can designate a default value for individual columns. To indicate a default value, you add a DEFAULT keyword to the column definition, followed by the default value. For example, in the Orders relation the order_date column defaults to the current system date. The column declaration is therefore written:

```
order_date date DEFAULT CURRENT_DATE
```

Notice that this particular declaration is using the SQL value CURRENT_DATE. However, you can place any value after DEFAULT that is a valid instance of the column's data type.

NOT NULL Constraints

The values in primary key columns must be unique and not null. In addition, there may be columns for which you want to require a value. You can specify such columns by adding NOT NULL after the column declaration. Since the online bookstore wants to ensure that an order date is always entered, the complete declaration for that column in the Orders table is:

```
order_date date NOT NULL DEFAULT CURRENT_DATE
```

Primary Keys

To specify a table's primary key, you add a PRIMARY KEY clause to a CREATE TABLE statement. The keywords PRIMARY KEY are followed by the names of the primary key column or columns, surrounded by parentheses.

In Figure 9-3 you will find the CREATE TABLE statements for the Lasers Only database including primary key declarations. Notice that in the order_line, performance, and production tables, all of which have a concatenated primary key, both primary key columns have been included in the PRIMARY KEY clause.

Foreign Keys

As you know, a foreign key is a column (or concatenation of columns) that is exactly the same as the primary key of some table. When a foreign key value matches a primary key value, we know that there is a logical relationship between the database objects represented by the matching rows.

One of the major constraints on a relation is referential integrity, which states that every nonnull foreign key value must reference an existing primary key value. To maintain the integrity of the database, it is vital that foreign key constraints be stored within the database's data dictionary so that the DBMS can be responsible for enforcing those constraints.

To specify a foreign key for a table, you add a FOREIGN KEY clause:

```
FOREIGN KEY foreign_key_name (foreign_key_columns)
REFERENCES primary_key_table (primary_key_columns)
```

```
CREATE TABLE customer
    (customer_numb int,
    customer_first_name varchar (15),
    customer_last_name varchar (15),
    customer_street varchar (30),
    customer_city varchar (15),
    customer_state char (2),
    customer_zip char (5),
    customer_phone char (12) NOT NULL,
    credit_card_numb varchar (15),
    card_exp_date date
    PRIMARY KEY (customer_numb))

CREATE TABLE item
    (item_numb integer,
    title varchar (60),
    distributor_numb int,
    retail_price numeric (6,2),
    release_date date,
    genre char (15)
    PRIMARY KEY (item_numb))

CREATE TABLE order
    (order_numb integer,
    customer_numb integer,
    order_date date,
    order_filled char (1)
    PRIMARY KEY (order_numb))

CREATE TABLE order_line
    (order_numb int,
    item_numb int,
    quantity integer,
    discount_applied numeric (6,2),
    selling_price numeric (6,2),
    shipped char (1)
    PRIMARY KEY (order_numb, item_numb))
```

Continued next page

Figure 9-3 :   **CREATE TABLE statements for the Lasers Only database
including primary key declarations**

```
CREATE TABLE distributor
    (distributor_numb int,
    distributor_name varchar (15),
    distributor_street varchar (30),
    distributor_city varchar (15),
    distributor_state char (2),
    distributor_zip char (5),
    distributor_phone char (12),
    distributor_contact_person varchar (30),
    contact_person_ext varchar (5)
    PRIMARY KEY (distributor_numb))

CREATE TABLE actor
    (actor_numb int,
    actor_name varchar (30)
    PRIMARY KEY (actor_numb))

CREATE TABLE performance
    (actor_numb int,
    item_numb int,
    role varchar (30)
    PRIMARY KEY (actor_numb, item_numb))

CREATE TABLE producer
    (producer_name varchar (30),
    studio varchar (30)
    PRIMARY KEY (producer_name))

CREATE TABLE production
    (producer_name varchar (30),
    item_numb int)
    PRIMARY KEY (producer_name, item_numb))
```

Figure 9-3 (Continued): CREATE TABLE statements for the Lasers Only database including primary key declarations

```
ON UPDATE update_action
ON DELETE delete_action
```

Each foreign key–primary key reference is given a name. This makes it possible to identify the reference at a later time, in particular, so you can remove the reference if necessary.

> *Note: Some DBMSs, such as Oracle, do not support the naming of foreign keys, in which case you would use the preceding syntax without the name.*

The names of the foreign key columns follow the name of the foreign key. The REFERENCES clause contains the name of the primary key table being referenced. If the primary key columns are named in the PRIMARY KEY clause of their table, then you don't need to list the column names. However, if the columns aren't part of a PRIMARY KEY clause, you must list the primary key columns in the REFERENCES clause.

The final part of the FOREIGN KEY specification indicates what should happen when a primary key value being referenced by the foreign key is deleted or updated. There are three options that apply to both updates and deletions and one additional option for each:

- ◆ SET NULL: Replace the foreign key value with null. This isn't possible when the foreign key is part of the primary key of its table.
- ◆ SET DEFAULT: Replace the foreign key value with the column's default value.
- ◆ CASCADE: Delete or update all foreign key rows.
- ◆ NO ACTION: On update, make no modification of foreign key values.
- ◆ RESTRICT: Do not allow deletion of the primary key row.

The complete declarations for the Lasers Only database tables, which includes foreign key constraints, can be found in Figure 9-4. Notice that although there are no restrictions on how to name foreign keys, the foreign keys in this database have been named to indicate the tables involved. This makes them easier to identify if you need to delete or modify a foreign key at a later date.

Additional Column Constraints

There are additional constraints that you can place on columns in a table beyond primary and foreign key constraints. These include requiring unique values and predicates in CHECK clauses.

```
CREATE TABLE customer
    (customer_numb int,
    customer_first_name varchar (15),
    customer_last_name varchar (15),
    customer_street varchar (30),
    customer_city varchar (15),
    customer_state char (2),
    customer_zip char (5),
    customer_phone char (12) NOT NULL,
    credit_card_numb varchar (15),
    card_exp_date date
    PRIMARY KEY (customer_numb))

CREATE TABLE item
    (item_numb integer,
    title varchar (60),
    distributor_numb int,
    retail_price numeric (6,2),
    release_date date,
    genre char (15)
    PRIMARY KEY (item_numb)
    FOREIGN KEY (item2distributor)
    REFERENCES distributor (distributor_numb)
        ON UPDATE CASCADE
        ON DELETE RESTRICT)

CREATE TABLE order
    (order_numb integer,
    customer_numb integer,
    order_date date,
    order_filled char (1)
    PRIMARY KEY (order_numb)
    FOREIGN KEY (order2customer)
    REFERENCES customer (customer_numb)
        ON UPDATE CASCADE
        ON DELETE RESTRICT)

CREATE TABLE actor
    (actor_numb int,
    actor_name varchar (30)
    PRIMARY KEY (actor_numb))

CREATE TABLE producer
    (producer_name varchar (30),
    studio varchar (30)
    PRIMARY KEY (producer_name))
```

Continued next page

Figure 9-4 :   Complete CREATE TABLE statements for the Lasers Only database including primary and foreign key declarations

```
CREATE TABLE order_line
    (order_numb int,
    item_numb int,
    quantity integer,
    discount_applied numeric (6,2),
    selling_price numeric (6,2),
    shipped char (1)
    PRIMARY KEY (order_numb, item_numb)
    FOREIGN KEY (order_line2order)
    REFERENCES order (order_numb)
        ON UPDATE CASCADE
        ON DELETE RESTRICT
    FOREIGN KEY (order_line2item)
    REFERENCES item (item_numb)
        ON UPDATE CASCADE
        ON DELETE RESTRICT)

CREATE TABLE performance
    (actor_numb int,
    item_numb int,
    role varchar (30)
    PRIMARY KEY actor_numb, item_numb)
    FOREIGN KEY (performance2actor)
    REFERENCES actor (actor_numb)
        ON UPDATE CASCADE
        ON DELETE CASCADE
    FOREIGN KEY (performance2item)
    REFERENCES item (item_numb)
        ON UPDATE CASCADE
        ON DELETE CASCADE)

CREATE TABLE production
    (producer_name varchar (30),
    item_numb int)
    PRIMARY KEY (producer_name, item_numb)
    FOREIGN KEY (production2producer)
    REFERENCES producer (producer_name)
        ON UPDATE CASCADE
        ON DELETE CASCADE
    FOREIGN KEY (production2item)
    REFERENCES item (item_numb)
        ON UPDATE CASCADE
        ON DELETE CASCADE)
```

Continued next page

Figure 9-4 (Continued):   Complete CREATE TABLE statements for the Lasers Only database including primary and foreign key declarations

```
CREATE TABLE distributor
    (distributor_numb int,
    distributor_name varchar (15),
    distributor_street varchar (30),
    distributor_city varchar (15),
    distributor_state char (2),
    distributor_zip char (5),
    distributor_phone char (12),
    distributor_contact_person varchar (30),
    contact_person_ext varchar (5)
    PRIMARY KEY distributor_numb)
```

Figure 9-4 (Continued):   Complete CREATE TABLE statements for the Lasers Only database including primary and foreign key declarations

Requiring Unique Values

If you want to ensure that the values in a non–primary key column are unique, then you can use the UNIQUE keyword. UNIQUE verifies that all nonnull values are unique. For example, if you were storing social security numbers in an employees table that used an employee ID as the primary key, you could also enforce unique social security numbers with:

```
ssn char (11) UNIQUE
```

The UNIQUE clause can also be placed at the end of the CREATE TABLE statement, along with the primary key and foreign key specifications. In that case, it takes the form:

```
UNIQUE (column_names)
```

Check Clauses

The CHECK clause to which you were introduced earlier in this chapter in the "Domains" section can also be used with individual columns to declare column-specific constraints. To add a constraint, you place a CHECK clause after the column declaration, using the keyword VALUE in a predicate to indicate the value being checked.

For example, to verify that a column used to hold true–false values is limited to T and F, you could write a CHECK clause as:

```
CHECK (UPPER(VALUE) = 'T' OR UPPER(VALUE) = 'F')
```

Views

As you first read in Chapter 3, views provide a way to give users a specific portion of a larger schema with which they can work. Before you actually can create views, there are two things you should consider: which views you really need and whether the views can be used for updating data.

Deciding Which Views to Create

Views take up very little space in a database, occupying only a few rows in a data dictionary table. That being the case, you can feel free to create views as needed.

A typical database might include the following views:

- ♦ One view for every base table that is exactly the same as the base table, but with a different name. Then, you prevent end users from seeing the base tables and do not tell the end users the table names; you give end users access only to the views. This makes it harder for end users to attempt to gain access to the stored tables because they do not know their names. However, as you will see in the next section, it is essential for updating that there be views that do match the base tables.
- ♦ One view for each primary key–foreign key relationship over which you join frequently. If the tables are large, the actual syntax of the query may include methods for avoiding the join operation but still combining the tables.
- ♦ One view for each complex query that you issue frequently.
- ♦ Views as needed to restrict user access to specific columns and rows. For example, you might recreate a view for a receptionist that shows employee office numbers and telephone extensions, but leaves off home address, telephone number, and salary.

View Updatability Issues

A database query can apply any operations supported by the DBMS's query language to a view, just as it can to base tables. However, using views for updates is a much more complicated issue. Given that views exist only in main memory, any updates made to a view must be stored in the underlying base tables if the updates are to have any effect on the database.

Not every view is updatable, however. Although the rules for view updatability vary from one DBMS to another, you will find that most DBMSs share the following restrictions:

- ♦ A view must be created from no more than one base table or view.
- ♦ If the source of the view is another view, then the source view must also adhere to the rules for updatability.
- ♦ A view must be created from only one query. Two or more queries cannot be assembled into a single view table using operations such as union.
- ♦ The view must include the primary key columns of the base table.
- ♦ The view must include all columns specified as not null (columns requiring mandatory values).
- ♦ The view must not include any groups of data. It must include the original rows of data from the base table, rather than rows based on values common to groups of data.
- ♦ The view must not remove duplicate rows.

Creating Views

To create a view whose columns have the same name as the columns in the base tables from which it is derived, you give the view a name and include the SQL query that defines its contents:

```
CREATE VIEW view_name AS
    SELECT …
```

For example, if Lasers Only wanted to create a view that included action films, the SQL is written:

```
CREATE VIEW action AS
    SELECT title_numb, title
    FROM item
    WHERE genre = 'action'
```

If you want to rename the columns in the view, you include the new column names in the CREATE VIEW statement:

```
CREATE VIEW action
    (identifier, name)
AS
    SELECT title_numb, title
    FROM item
    WHERE genre = 'action'
```

The preceding statement will produce a view with two columns named Identifier and Name. Note that if you want to change even one column name, you must include *all* the column names in the parentheses following the view name. The DBMS will match the columns following SELECT with the view column names by their position in the list.

Views can be created from any SQL query, including those that perform joins, unions, and grouping. For example, to simplify looking at sales figures, Lasers Only might create a view like the following:

```
CREATE VIEW sales_summary AS
    SELECT customer_numb, orders.order_numb, orders.order_date,
        SUM (selling_price)
    FROM order_line JOIN order
    GROUP BY customer_numb, orders.order_date, orders.order_numb
```

The view table will then contain grouped data along with a computed column.

Temporary Tables

A temporary table is a base table that is not stored in the database but instead exists only while the database session in which it was created is active. At first glance, this may sound like a view, but views and temporary tables are rather different:

- ◆ A view exists only for a single query. Each time you use the name of a view, its table is recreated from existing data.
- ◆ A temporary table exists for the entire database session in which it was created.
- ◆ A view is automatically populated with the data retrieved by the query that defines it.
- ◆ You must add data to a temporary table with SQL INSERT commands.
- ◆ Only views that meet the criteria for view updatability can be used for data modification.
- ◆ Because temporary tables are base tables, all of them can be updated.
- ◆ Because the contents of a view are generated each time the view's name is used, a view's data are always current.
- ◆ The data in a temporary table reflect the state of the database at the time the table was loaded with data. If the data from which the temporary table was loaded are modified after the temporary table has received its data, then the contents of the temporary table may be out of sync with other parts of the database.

If the contents of a temporary table become outdated when source data change, why use a temporary table at all? Wouldn't it be better simply to use a view whose contents are continually regenerated? The answer lies in performance. It takes processing time to create a view table. If you are going to use data only once during a database session, then a view will actually perform better than a temporary table because you don't need to create a structure for it. However, if you are going to be using the data repeatedly during a session, then a temporary table provides better performance because it needs to be created only once. The decision therefore results in a trade-off: Using a view repeatedly takes more time but provides continually updated data; using a temporary table repeatedly saves time, but you run the risk that the table's contents may be out of date.

Creating Temporary Tables

Creating a temporary table is very similar to creating a permanent base table. You do, however, need to decide on the *scope* of the table. A temporary table can be *global*, in which case it is accessible to the entire application program that created it. Alternatively, it can be *local*, in which case it is accessible only to the program module in which it was created.

To create a global temporary table, you add the keywords GLOBAL TEMPORARY to the CREATE TABLE statement:

```
CREATE GLOBAL TEMPORARY TABLE
    (remainder of CREATE statement)
```

By the same token, you create a local temporary table with:

```
CREATE LOCAL TEMPORARY TABLE
    (remainder of CREATE statement)
```

For example, if Lasers Only was going to use the sales summary information repeatedly, it might create the following temporary table instead of using a view:

```
CREATE GLOBAL TEMPORARY TABLE sales_summary
(customer_numb INTEGER,
order_numb INTEGER,
order_date DATE,
order_total NUMERIC (6,2),
PRIMARY KEY (customer_numb,order_numb))
```

Loading Temporary Tables with Data

To place data in a temporary table, you use one or more SQL IN-SERT statements. For example, to load the Sales_summary table created in the preceding section, you could write:

```
INSERT INTO sales_summary
    SELECT customer_numb, orders.order_numb, orders.order_date,
        SUM (selling_price)
    FROM order_line JOIN order
    GROUP BY customer_numb, orders.order_date, orders.order_numb
```

You can now query and manipulate the Sales_summary table just as you would a permanent base table.

Disposition of Temporary Table Rows

When you write *embedded SQL* (SQL statements coded as part of a program written in a high-level language such as C++ or Java), you have control over the amount of work that the DBMS considers to be a unit (a *transaction*). To understand what happened to the rows in a temporary table, you do need to know that a transaction can end in one of two ways: It can be *committed* (its changes made permanent) or it can be *rolled back* (its changes undone).

By default, the rows in a temporary table are purged whenever a transaction is committed. You can, however, instruct the DBMS to retain the rows by including ON COMMIT PRESERVE ROWS to the end of the table creation statement:

```
CREATE GLOBAL TEMPORARY TABLE sales_summary
(customer_numb INTEGER,
order_numb INTEGER,
order_date DATE,
order_total NUMERIC (6,2),
PRIMARY KEY (customer_numb,order_numb),
ON COMMIT PRESERVE ROWS)
```

Because a rollback returns the database to the state it was in before the transaction began, a temporary table will also be restored to its previous state (with or without rows).

Creating Indexes

As you read in Chapter 5, an index is a data structure that provides a fast access path to rows in a table based on the values in one or more columns (the index key). Because an index stores key values in order, the DBMS can use a fast search technique to find the values rather than being forced to search each row in an unordered table sequentially.

You create indexes with the CREATE INDEX statement:

```
CREATE INDEX index_name
ON table_name (index_key_columns)
```

For example, to create an index on the title column in the Item table, the online bookstore would use:

```
CREATE INDEX title
ON item (title)
```

By default, the index will allow duplicate entries and sorts the entries in ascending order. To require unique index entries, add the keyword UNIQUE after CREATE:

```
CREATE UNIQUE INDEX title
ON item (title)
```

To sort in descending order, insert DESC after the column whose sort order you want to change. For example, Lasers Only might want to create an index on order_date in the Order relation in descending order so that the most recent orders are first:

```
CREATE INDEX order_date
ON order (order_date DESC)
```

If you want to create an index on a concatenated key, you include all the columns that should be part of the index key in the column list. For example, the following creates an index organized by actor and item number:

```
CREATE INDEX actor_item
ON performance (actor_numb, item_numb)
```

Although you do not need to access an index directly unless you want to delete it from the database, it helps to give indexes names that tell you something about their keys. This makes it easier to remember them should you need to get rid of the indexes.

Modifying Database Elements

With the exception of tables, database elements are largely unchangeable. When you want to modify them, you must delete them from the database and create them from scratch. In contrast, just about every characteristic of a table can be modified without deleting the table using the ALTER TABLE statement.

Adding New Columns

To add a new column to a table, use the ALTER TABLE statement with the following syntax:

```
ALTER TABLE table_name
ADD column_name column_data_type column_constraints
```

For example, if Lasers Only wanted to add a telephone number column to the Producer table they would use:

```
ALTER TABLE producer
ADD phone CHAR (12)
```

To add more than one column at the same time, simply separate the clauses with commas:

```
ALTER TABLE producer
ADD phone CHAR (12),
ADD producer_street VARCHAR (30),
ADD producer_city VARCHAR (30),
ADD producer_state CHAR (2),
ADD producer_zip CHAR (5)
```

Adding Table Constraints

You can add table constraints such as foreign keys at any time. To do so, include the new constraint in the ADD clause of an ALTER TABLE statement:

```
ALTER TABLE table_name
ADD table_constraint
```

Assume, for example, that Lasers Only created a new table named States and included in it all the two-character U.S. state abbreviations. The company would then need to add references to that table from the Customer, Distributor, and Producer tables:

```
ALTER TABLE customer
ADD FOREIGN KEY customers2states (customer_state)
   REFERENCES states (state_name)

ALTER TABLE distributor
ADD FOREIGN KEY distributor2states (distributor_state)
   REFERENCES states (state_name)

ALTER TABLE publisher
ADD FOREIGN KEY publishers2states (publisher_state)
   REFERENCES states (state_name)
```

When you add a foreign key constraint to a table, the DBMS verifies that all existing data in the table meet that constraint. If they do not, the ALTER TABLE will fail.

Modifying Columns

You can modify columns by changing any characteristic of the column, including its data type, size, and constraints:

♦ To replace a complete column definition, use the MODIFY command with the current column name and the new column characteristics. For example, to change the customer number in the Customer table from an integer to a character column, the online bookstore could use:

```
ALTER TABLE customers
MODIFY customer_numb CHAR (4)
```

♦ To add or change a default value only (without changing the data type or size of the column), include the DEFAULT keyword:

```
ALTER TABLE customers
MODIFY customer_numb DEFAULT 0
```

♦ To switch between allowing nulls and not allowing nulls without changing any other column characteristics, add NULL or NOT NULL as appropriate:

```
ALTER TABLE customers
MODIFY customer_zip NOT NULL
```

or

```
ALTER TABLE customers
MODIFY customer_phone NULL
```

♦ To modify a column constraint without changing any other column characteristics, include a CHECK clause:

```
ALTER TABLE item
MODIFY retail_price
    CHECK (VALUE >= 19.95)
```

When you change the data type of a column, the DBMS will attempt to convert any existing values to the new data type. If the current values cannot be converted, then the table modification will not be performed. In general, most columns can be converted to character. However, conversions from a character data type to numbers or datetimes require that existing data represent legal values in the new data type.

Deleting Elements

You can also delete structural elements from a table as needed:

♦ To delete a column:

```
ALTER TABLE order_line
DELETE line_cost
```

♦ To delete a CHECK table constraint (a CHECK that has been applied to an entire table rather than to a specific column):

```
ALTER TABLE customer
DELETE CHECK
```

♦ To remove the UNIQUE constraint from one or more columns:

```
ALTER TABLE item
DELETE UNIQUE (title)
```

♦ To remove a table's PRIMARY KEY:

```
ALTER TABLE customer
DELETE PRIMARY KEY
```

Although you can delete a table's primary key, keep in mind that if you do not add a new one, you will not be able to modify any data in that table.

♦ To delete a foreign key:

```
ALTER TABLE item
DELETE FOREIGN KEY item2distributor
```

Renaming Elements

You can rename both tables and columns:

♦ To rename a table, place the new table name after the RENAME keyword:

```
ALTER TABLE order_line
RENAME line_item
```

♦ To rename a column, include both the old and new column names separated by the keyword TO:

```
ALTER TABLE item
RENAME title TO item_title
```

Deleting Database Elements

To delete a structural element from a database, you *drop* the element. For example, to delete a table, you would type:

```
DROP TABLE table_name
```

Dropping a table is irreversible. In most cases, the DBMS will not bother to ask you "are you sure?" but will immediately delete the structure of the table and all of its data.

You can remove the following elements from a database with the DROP statement:

- ◆ Tables
- ◆ Views

  ```
  DROP VIEW view_name
  ```

- ◆ Indexes

  ```
  DROP INDEX index_name
  ```

- ◆ Domains

  ```
  DROP DOMAIN domain_name
  ```

A DROP of a table or view will fail if the element being dropped is currently in use by another user.

Granting and Revoking Access Rights

When you create an element of database structure, the user name under which you are working becomes that element's owner. The owner has the right to do anything to that element; all other users have no rights at all. This means that if tables and views are going to be accessible to other users, you must *grant* them access rights.

Types of Access Rights

There are six types of access rights that you can grant:

- ♦ SELECT: Allows a user to retrieve data from a table or view.
- ♦ INSERT: Allows a user to insert new rows into a table or updatable view. Permission may be granted to specific columns rather than the entire database element.
- ♦ UPDATE: Allows a user to modify rows in a table or updatable view. Permission may be granted to specific columns rather than the entire database element.
- ♦ DELETE: Allows a user to delete rows from a table or updatable view.
- ♦ REFERENCES: Allows a user to reference a table as a foreign key in a table he or she creates. Permission may be granted to specific columns rather than the entire table.
- ♦ ALL PRIVILEGES: Gives a user all of the preceding rights to a table or view.

By default, granting access rights to another user does not give that user the right to pass on those rights to others. If, however, you add a WITH GRANT OPTION clause, you give the user the ability to grant the rights that he or she has to another user.

Storing Access Rights

Access rights to tables and views are stored in the data dictionary. Although the details of the data dictionary tables vary from one DBMS to another, you will usually find access rights split between two system tables named something like Systableperm and Syscolperm. The first table is used when access rights are granted to entire tables or views; the second is used when rights are granted to specific columns within a table or view.

A Systableperm table has a structure similar to the following:

```
systableperm (table_id, grantee, grantor, selectauth, insertauth,
    deleteauth, updateauth, updatecols, referenceauth)
```

The columns represent:

- ◆ table_id: An identifier for the table or view.
- ◆ grantee: The user ID to which rights have been granted.
- ◆ grantor: The user ID granting the rights.
- ◆ selectauth: The grantee's SELECT rights.
- ◆ insertauth: The grantee's INSERT rights.
- ◆ deleteauth: The grantee's DELETE rights.
- ◆ updateauth: The grantee's UPDATE rights.
- ◆ updatecols: Indicates whether rights have been granted to specific columns within the table or view. When this value is Y (yes), the DBMS must also look in Syscolperm to determine whether a user has the rights to perform a specific action against the database.
- ◆ referenceauth: The grantee's REFERENCE rights.

The columns that hold the access rights take one of three values: Y (yes), N (no), or G (Yes with grant option).

Whenever a user makes a request to the DBMS to manipulate data, the DBMS first consults the data dictionary to determine whether the user has the rights to perform the requested action. If the DBMS cannot find a row with a matching user ID and table identifier, then the user has no rights at all to the table or view. If a row with a matching user ID and table identifier exist, then the DBMS checks for the specific rights that the user has to the table or view and— based on the presence of Y, N, or G in the appropriate column— either permits or disallows the requested database access.

Granting Rights

To grant rights to another user, a user that either created the database element (and therefore has all rights to it) or has GRANT rights issues a GRANT statement:

```
GRANT type_of_rights
ON table_or_view_name TO user_ID
```

For example, if the DBA of Lasers Only wants to allow the accounting manager (who has a user ID of acctg_mgr) to access the sales summary view, the DBA would type:

```
GRANT SELECT
ON sales_summary TO acctg_mgr
```

To allow the accounting manager to pass those rights on to other users, the DBA would need to add one line to the SQL:

```
GRANT SELECT
ON sales_summary TO acctg_mgr
WITH GRANT OPTION
```

If Lasers Only wants to give some student interns limited rights to some of the base tables, the GRANT might be written:

```
GRANT SELECT, UPDATE (retail_price, distributor_numb)
ON item TO intern1, intern2, intern3
```

The preceding example grants SELECT rights to the entire table but gives UPDATE rights only on two specific columns. Notice also that you can grant multiple rights in the same command as well as give the same group of rights to more than one user. However, a single GRANT applies to only one table or view.

In most cases, rights are granted to specific user IDs. You can, however, make database elements accessible to anyone by granting rights to the special user ID PUBLIC. For example, the following statement gives every authorized user the rights to see the sales_summary view:

```
GRANT SELECT
ON sales_summary TO PUBLIC
```

Revoking Rights

To remove previously granted rights, use the REVOKE statement, whose syntax is almost the opposite of GRANT:

```
REVOKE access_rights
FROM table_or_view_name FROM user_ID
```

For example, if Lasers Only's summer interns have finished their work, the DBA might want to remove their access from the database:

```
REVOKE SELECT, UPDATE (retail_price, distributor_numb)
ON item FROM intern1, intern2, intern3
```

If the user from which you are revoking rights has the GRANT option for those rights, then you also need to make a decision about what to do if the user has passed on those rights. In the following case, the REVOKE will be disallowed if the acctg_mgr user has passed on his or her rights:

```
REVOKE SELECT
ON sales_summary FROM acctg_mgr
RESTRICT
```

In contrast, the syntax

```
REVOKE SELECT
ON sales_summary FROM acctg_mgr
CASCADE
```

will remove the rights from the acctg_mgr ID along with any user IDs to which acctg_mgr granted rights.

Object-Relational Extensions

SQL is a standard language that varies only minimally from one implementation to another. However, there is no standard for declaring objects as domains. The best that can be done is to show you how one major product—Oracle—has extended SQL to support a post-relational data model.

Oracle classes are defined as data types, using a CREATE TYPE statement with the following general syntax:

```
CREATE TYPE type_name AS OBJECT (
    attribute_name datatype[, attribute_name datatype]...
    MEMBER function_specification,]
    [ MEMBER {procedure_specification | function_specification} ])
```

In the preceding syntax, a MEMBER is an operation, what Oracle calls a "method." If it returns a value through the traditional programming return mechanism, it is declared as a function; it if does not return a value, it is declared as a procedure, although output and input–output parameters are supported.

For example, we could create a rental item class for the ski shop with:

```
CREATE TYPE Rental_Item AS OBJECT (
    size CHAR (6),
    width CHAR (4),
    length CHAR (6),
    MEMBER PROCEDURE initialize );
```

Once the data type for a class has been declared, you can then provide the implementation, written in a combination of extended SQL and PL/SQL (Oracle's Pascal-like language):

```
[CREATE TYPE BODY type_name {IS | AS}
{ {MAP | ORDER} MEMBER function_body;
| MEMBER {procedure_body | function_body};}
[MEMBER {procedure_body | function_body};]... END;]
```

Both the declaration of the class and its implementation are therefore stored in the database's data dictionary.

As an example, consider the following implementation of the initialization function for the rental item class declared earlier:

```
CREATE TYPE BODY Rental_Item AS
    MEMBER PROCEDURE initialize IS
    BEGN
        size := NULL;
        width := NULL;
        length := NULL;
    END initialize;
END;
```

Oracle supplies accessor and mutator methods as well as provides SQL extensions for searching the object. Therefore, a database implementer doesn't need to write them.

10

Using CASE Tools for Database Design

A CASE (computer-aided software engineering) tool is a software package that provides support for the design and implementation of information systems. By integrating many of the techniques used to document a system design—including the data dictionary, data flows, and entity relationships—CASE software can increase the consistency and accuracy of a database design.

> *Note: It is also true that CASE tools can save you a lot of time when it comes to drawing ER diagrams. At a guess, the complete Lasers Only ER diagram would have taken about 10 hours to draw using a graphics package but only about 2 hours using a CASE tool.*

There are many CASE tools on the market. The diagrams and screens you will see throughout this chapter come from MacA&D.

Although the exact "look" of the diagrams is specific to this one particular package, the software capabilities you will see are typical of most CASE tools.

A word of warning is in order about CASE tools before we proceed any further: A CASE tool is exactly that—a tool. It can document a database design and it can provide invaluable help in maintaining the consistency of a design. Although some current CASE tools can verify the integrity of a data model, they cannot design the database for you. There is no software in the world that can examine a database environment and identify the entities, attributes, and relationships that should be represented in a database. The model created with CASE software is therefore only as good as the analysis of the database environment performed by the people using the tool.

CASE Capabilities

Most CASE tools organize the documents pertaining to a single system into a "project." As you can see in Figure 10-1, by default a typical project supports the following types of documents:

- ♦ Data dictionary: In most CASE tools, the data dictionary forms the backbone of the project, providing a single repository for all processes, entities, attributes, and domains used anywhere throughout the project.
- ♦ Requirements: Requirements are usually text specifications of what individual parts of the system must do.
- ♦ Data flow diagrams: As you read in Chapter 2, data flow diagrams document the way in which data travel throughout an organization, indicating who handles the data. Although it isn't necessary to create data flow diagrams if your only goal with the project is to document a database design, data flow diagrams can often be useful in documenting the relationships between multiple organization units and the data they handle. Data flow diagrams can, for example, help you determine whether an

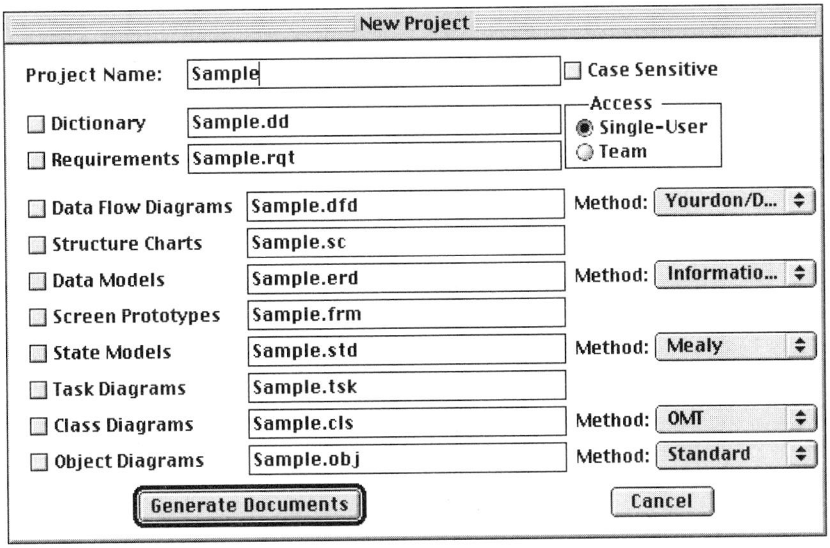

Figure 10-1:   CASE software project documents

organization needs a single database or a combination of databases.

♦ Structure charts: Structure charts are used to model the structure of application programs that will be developed using structured programming techniques. The charts show the relationship between program modules.

♦ Data models: Data models are the ER diagrams that you have been reading about.

♦ Screen prototypes: Drawings of sample screen layouts are typically most useful for documenting the user interface of application programs. However, they can also act as a cross-check to ensure that a database design is complete by allowing you to verify that everything needed to generate the sample screen designs is present in the database.

♦ State models: State models, documented in state transition diagrams, indicate the ways in which data change.

♦ Task diagrams: Task diagrams are used to help plan application programs in which multiple operations (tasks) must occur at the same time. They are therefore not particularly relevant to the database design process.

♦ Class diagrams: Class diagrams are used when performing object-oriented rather than structured analysis.

♦ Object diagrams: Object diagrams are used during object-oriented analysis to indicate how objects communicate with one another by passing messages.

Although object-oriented analysis can be used as the launching point for a relational database, it is better suited to the object-oriented data model and therefore will not be discussed in this book.

Many of the diagrams and reports that a CASE tool can provide are designed to follow a single theoretical model. For example, the ER diagrams that you have seen earlier in this book might be based on the Chen model or the Information Engineering model. Any given CASE tool will support some selection of diagramming models. You must therefore examine what a particular product supports before you purchase it to ensure that it provides exactly what you need.

ER Diagram Reports

In addition to providing tools for simplifying the creation of ER diagrams, many CASE tools can generate reports that document the contents of an ERD. For example, in Figure 10-2 you can see a portion of a report that provides a description of each entity and its attributes, including the attribute's data type. For many designers, this type of report actually constitutes a paper-based data dictionary.

A CASE tool can also translate the relationships in an ER diagram into a report such as that in Figure 10-3. The text in the report describes the *cardinality* of each relationship in the ERD (whether the relationship is one-to-one, one-to-many, or many-to-many) and can therefore be very useful for pinpointing errors that may have crept into the graphic version of the diagram.

```
ENTITY SPECIFICATION
DIAGRAMS IN DOCUMENT: Lasers Only

Entity: actor

Attributes:

...*actor_numb
DataType: INT

...actor_name
DataType: CHAR (40)


Entity: customer

Attributes:

...*customer_numb: int
DataType: INT

...customer_first_name: char (15)
DataType: CHAR (15)

...customer_last_name: char (15)
DataType: CHAR (15)

...customer_street: char (25)
DataType: CHAR (30)

...customer_city: char (15)
DataType: CHAR (30)

...customer_state: char (2)
DataType: CHAR (2)

...customer_zip: char (10)
DataType: CHAR (10)

...customer_phone: char (12)
DataType: CHAR (12)

...credit_card_numb: char (20)
DataType: CHAR (30)

...card_exp_date: date
DataType: DATE
```

Figure 10-2:   Part of an entity specifications report

```
RELATION SPECIFICATION
DIAGRAMS IN DOCUMENT: Lasers Only

customer is associated with zero or more instances of order.
order is associated with one and only one instance of customer.

distributors is associated with zero or more instances of items.
items is associated with one and only one instance of distributors.

order is associated with zero or more instances of order_lines.
order_lines is associated with one and only one instance of order.

items is associated with zero or more instances of order_lines.
order_lines is associated with one and only one instance of items.

actor is associated with zero or more instances of performance.
performance is associated with one and only one instance of actor.

items is associated with zero or more instances of performance.
performance is associated with one and only one instance of items.

producer is associated with zero or more instances of production.
production is associated with one and only one instance of
producer.

items is associated with zero or more instances of production.
production is associated with one and only one instance of items.
```

Figure 10-3:   A relation specification report

Data Flow Diagrams

There are two widely used styles for data flow diagrams (DFDs): Yourdon/DeMarco (which has been used throughout this book) and Gane & Sarson.

The Yourdon/Demarco style, which you can see in Figure 10-4, uses circles for processes. (This particular example is for a small taxi company that rents its cabs to drivers.) Data stores are represented by parallel lines. Data flows are curved or straight lines with labels that indicate the data that are moving along that pathway. External sources of data are represented by rectangles.

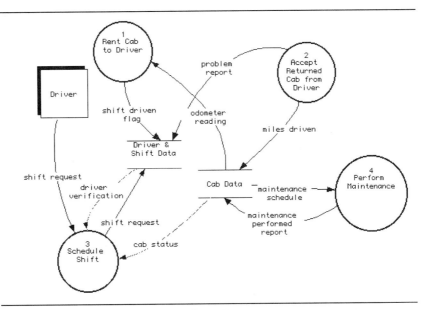

Figure 10-4: Yourdon/DeMarco style DFD

In concept, the Gane & Sarson style is very similar; it varies primarily in style. As you can see in Figure 10-5, the processes are round-cornered rectangles as opposed to circles. Data stores are open-ended rectangles rather than parallel lines. External sources of data remain as rectangles and data flows use only straight lines. However, the concepts of numbering the processes and exploding each process with a child diagram that shows further detail is the same, regardless of which diagramming style you use.

As mentioned earlier, DFDs are very useful in the database design process for helping a designer to determine whether an organization needs a single, integrated database or a collection of independent databases. For example, it is clear from the taxi company's DFDs that an integrated database is required. Of the four processes shown in the diagram, three use data from both the cab data store and the driver and shift data store. (Only the maintenance process uses just one data store.) You will see further examples of using DFDs in this way throughout the case studies in the rest of this book.

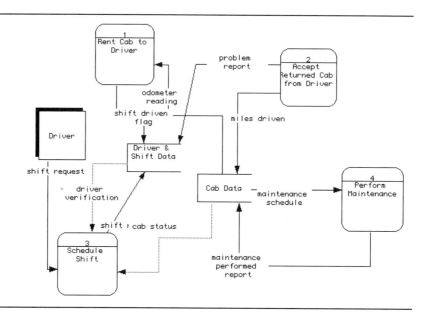

Figure 10-5:   Gane & Sarson style DFD

The Data Dictionary

From a database designer's point of view, the ER diagram and its associated data dictionary are the two most important parts of CASE software. Since you were introduced to several types of ER diagrams in Chapter 2, we will not repeat them here but instead focus on the interaction of the diagrams and the data dictionary.

A data dictionary provides a central repository for documenting entities, attributes, and domains. In addition, by linking entries in the ER diagram to the data dictionary, you can provide enough information for the CASE tool to generate the SQL CREATE statements needed to define the structure of the database.

The layout of a data dictionary varies with the specific CASE tool, as does the way in which entries are configured. With Mac A&D, for example, all attributes, entities, and domains appear in a single alphabetical list (see Figure 10-6). Domain names begin with a $, but there is no simple way when first viewing the dictionary to distinguish between entities and attributes.

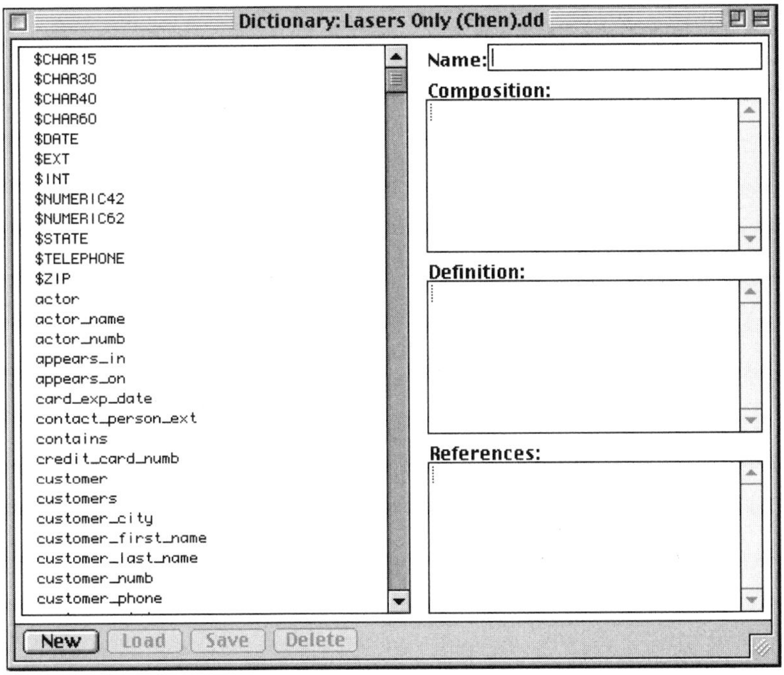

Figure 10-6:   A data dictionary window

However, if you double-click on an item, then its declaration appears in the dictionary window, as in Figure 10-7. Double-clicking on an entity displays the domain that has been assigned (see Figure 10-8).

As you look at the data dictionary, keep in mind that a data dictionary is not intended to show the actual design of a database. Many of the attributes listed in the data dictionary are used by more than one table. Maintaining a hierarchy of attributes and tables would therefore require duplicating data dictionary entries for each table in which an attribute appeared. Instead, a data dictionary typically provides an alphabetical list of elements in which you can look up the definition of an element, regardless of where it is used within

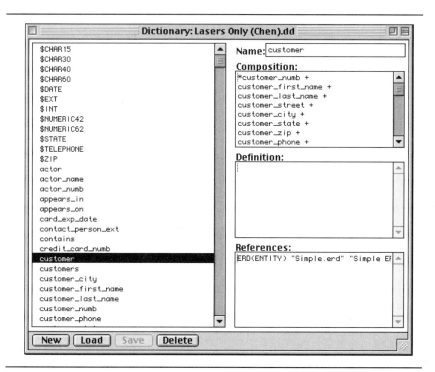

Figure 10-7:   The definition of an entity showing in a data dictionary window

the database. Its purpose is also to ensure that a given database element is defined consistently. For example, wherever the customer number is used in the Lasers Only database, it will be an integer.

Nonetheless, if you need a visual representation of the structure of an entity, most CASE tools will build some sort of tree diagram for you. For example, the diagram in Figure 10-9 shows the structure of the customer entity.

The linking of data dictionary entries to an ER diagram has one major benefit. Assuming that each attribute has a single entry in the data dictionary, then CASE software can examine an ER diagram and automatically identify foreign keys. This is yet another way in which the consistency of attribute definitions enforced by a CASE tool's data dictionary can support the database design process.

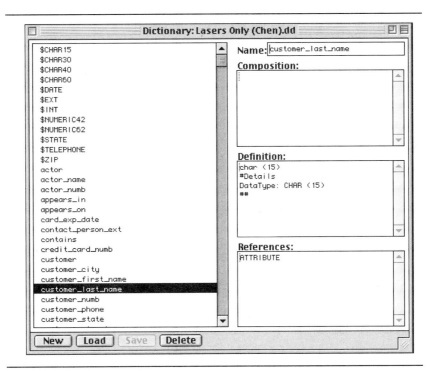

Figure 10-8: The definition of an attribute showing in a data dictionary window

Most CASE tools will provide a way for you to store the characteristics of an attribute in the data dictionary. For example, in Figure 10-10, you will find a window used to indicate an attribute's domain and any additional constraints that should be placed on the attribute (in this case, NOT NULL) and to enter a short description of the attribute. Once those details have been saved, they appear as part of the attribute's definition in the data dictionary (Figure 10-11).

Code Generation

The end product of most database design efforts is a set of SQL CREATE TABLE commands. If you are using CASE software and

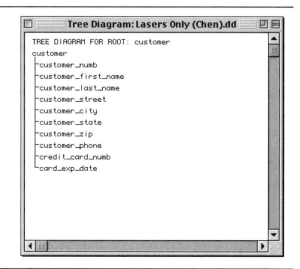

Figure 10-9: A tree diagram showing entity structure

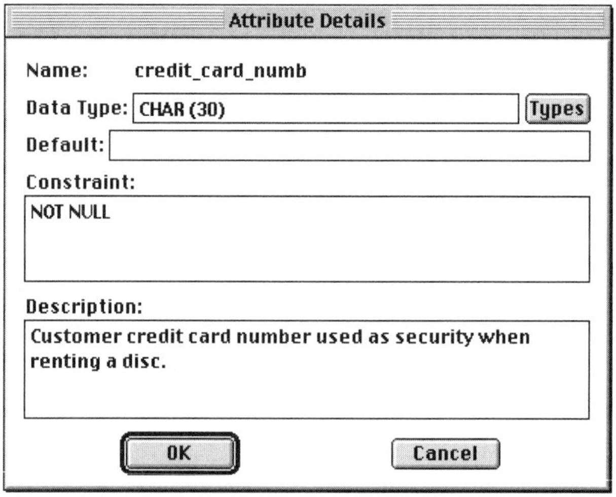

Figure 10-10: Storing attribute details

the software contains a complete data dictionary, then the software can generate the SQL for you. You will typically find that a given CASE tool can tailor the SQL syntax to a range of specific DBMSs.

```
┌──────────────────────────────────────────────────────────────────┐
│ ▫  ═══════════ Dictionary: Lasers Only (Chen).dd ═══════════  ▣▤   │
├──────────────────────────────────────────────────────────────────┤
│  $CHAR15        ▲   Name: credit_card_numb                         │
│  $CHAR30        ▨   Composition:                                    │
│  $CHAR40            ┌──────────────────────────────────────────┐▲ │
│  $CHAR60            │                                          │    │
│  $DATE              │                                          │    │
│  $EXT               │                                          │    │
│  $INT               │                                          │    │
│  $NUMERIC42         │                                          │    │
│  $NUMERIC62         └──────────────────────────────────────────┘▼ │
│  $STATE             Definition:                                    │
│  $TELEPHONE         ┌──────────────────────────────────────────┐▲ │
│  $ZIP               │#Details                                  │    │
│  actor              │DataType: CHAR (30)                       │    │
│  actor_name         │Describe: Customer credit card number used│    │
│  actor_numb         │as security when renting a disc.          │    │
│  appears_in         │Constraint: NOT NULL                      │    │
│  appears_on         │##                                        │▼  │
│  card_exp_date      └──────────────────────────────────────────┘   │
│  contact_person_ext References:                                    │
│  contains           ┌──────────────────────────────────────────┐▲ │
│ [credit_card_numb]  │ATTRIBUTE                                 │    │
│  customer           │                                          │    │
│  customers          │                                          │    │
│  customer_city  ▼   └──────────────────────────────────────────┘▼ │
├──────────────────────────────────────────────────────────────────┤
│  [ New ]  [ Load ]  [ Save ]  [ Delete ]                           │
└──────────────────────────────────────────────────────────────────┘
```

Figure 10-11:   A complete attribute definition stored in the data dictionary

In most cases, the code will be saved in a text file, which you can then use as input to a DBMS.

Note: If you are using UML as your ER diagramming model, then a CASE tool may also generate XML for you. XML schemas provide a template for interpreting the contents of files containing data and are therefore especially useful when you need to transfer data between DBMSs with different SQL implementations or between DBMSs that do not use SQL at all.

The effectiveness of the SQL that a CASE tool can produce, as you might expect, depends on the completeness of the data dictionary entries. To get truly usable SQL, the data dictionary must contain:

♦ Domains for every attribute
♦ Primary key definitions (created as attributes are added to entities in an ER diagram)
♦ Foreign key definitions (created by a CASE tool after the ER diagram is complete)

♦ Any additional constraints that are to be placed on individual attributes (created when adding attributes to entities in the ER diagram)

Sample Input and Output Designs

As mentioned in the first section of this chapter, sample screen designs are typically of most use to application programmers. However, they can also support the database designer by providing a way to double-check that the database can provide all the data needed by application programs. Most CASE tools therefore provide a way to draw and label sample screen and report layouts.

Most of today's CASE tools allow multiple users to interact with the same project. This means that interface designers can work with the same data dictionary that the database designers are building, ensuring that all the necessary data elements have been handled.

For example, one of the most important things that the person scheduling cab reservations for the taxi company needs to know is which cabs are not reserved for a given date and shift. A simple screen such as that in Figure 10-12 will do the trick. The diagram shows what data the user needs to enter (the shift date and the shift name). It also shows the output (cab numbers). The names of the fields on the sample screen design can be linked automatically to the data dictionary.

A CASE tool can be used to model an entire application program. The "browse" tool at the very bottom of the tool bar in Figure 10-12 switches into browse mode, in which buttons and menus become active. Users can make choices from pull-down menus that can be linked to other forms. Buttons can also trigger the opening of other forms. Users can click into data entry fields and tab between fields. Users can therefore not only see the layout of input and output screens and documents but also navigate through an application.

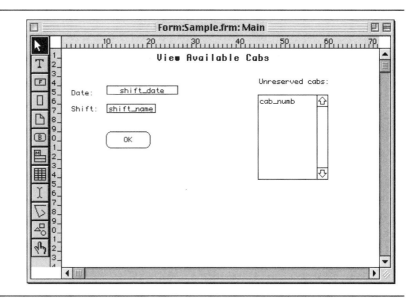

Figure 10-12:   Sample screen design

The Drawing Environment

To this point, you've been reading about the way in which the functions provided by CASE software can support the database design effort. In this last section we will briefly examine the tools you can expect to find as part of CASE software, tools with which you can create the types of documents you need.

Because most of the documents you create with CASE software are diagrams, the working environment of a CASE tool is primarily a specialized graphics environment. For example, in Figure 10-13 you can see the drawing tools provided by Mac A&D for creating ER diagrams. (Keep in mind that each CASE tool will differ somewhat in the precise layout of its drawing tool bar, but the basic capabilities will be the same.)

The important thing to note is that the major shapes needed for the diagrams are provided as individual tools. You therefore simply

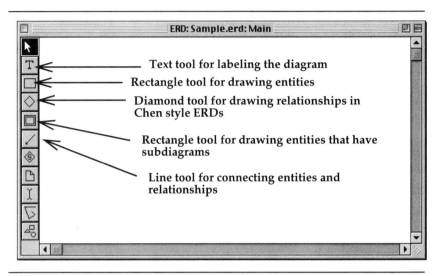

Figure 10-13:   Example CASE tool drawing environment for ER diagrams

click on the tool you want to use in the tool bar and draw the shape in the diagram, just as you would if you were working with a general-purpose graphics program.

For Further Reading

To learn more about the Yourdon/DeMarco method of structured analysis using data flow diagrams, see either of the following:

DeMarco, Tom and Plauger, P. J. *Structured Analysis and System Specification.* Prentice Hall, 1985.

Yourdon, Edward. *Modern Structured Analysis.* Prentice Hall PTR, 2000.

11

Database Design Case Study #1: Mighty-Mite Motors

It is not unusual for a database designer to be employed to reengineer the information systems of an established corporation. As you will see from the company described in this chapter, information systems in older companies have often grown haphazardly, with almost no planning and integration. The result is a hodgepodge of data repositories that cannot provide the information needed for the corporation to function because they are isolated from one another. In such a situation, it is the job of the database designer to examine the environment as a whole and to focus on the integration of data access across the corporation as well as the design of one or more databases that will meet individual department needs.

On the bright side, an organization such as Mighty-Mite Motors, which has a history of data processing of some kind, knows quite well what it needs in an information system, even if the employees are unable to articulate those needs immediately. There will almost certainly be a collection of paper forms and reports that the organization uses regularly. Such documents specify the input and output needs of the organization and can greatly simplify a database designer's task.

Corporate Overview

Mighty-Mite Motors, Inc. (MMM) is a closely held corporation, established in 1980, that designs, develops, manufactures, and markets miniature ridable motor vehicles for children. Products include several models of cars, trucks, all-terrain vehicles, and trains (see Figure 11-1). Vehicles are powered by car batteries and achieve top speeds of about 5 mph.

At this time, MMM is organized into three divisions: Product Development, Manufacturing, and Marketing & Sales. Each division is headed by a vice president who reports directly to the CEO. (An organization chart appears in Figure 11-2.) All three divisions are housed in a single location that the corporation owns outright.

Product Development Division

The Product Development division is responsible for designing and testing new products. The division employs design engineers who use computer-aided design (CAD) software to prepare initial designs for new vehicles. Once a design is completed, between 1 and 10 prototypes are built. The prototypes are first tested in house using robotic drivers–passengers. After refinement, the prototypes are tested by children in a variety of settings. Feedback from the testers is used to refine product designs and to make decisions about which designs should actually be manufactured for mass marketing.

Mighty-Mite Motors

Product Catalog

Winter Holiday Season 2003

Figure 11-1 :   Mighty-Mite Motors product catalog

Model #001

All Terrain Vehicle: Accelerator in the handlegrip lets young riders reach speeds of up to 5 miles per hour. Vehicle stops immediately when child removes his or her hand from the handlegrip. Can carry one passenger up to 65 lbs. **Suggested retail price: $124.95**

Model #002

4 Wheel Drive Cruiser: Two-pedal drive system lets vehicle move forward at $2\,^1/2$ mph on hard surfaces, plus reverse. Electronic speed reduction for beginners. Includes one 6v battery and one recharger. Ages 3–7 (can carry two passengers up to 65 lbs. each). **Suggested retail price: $249.99**

Figure 11-1 (Continued):   Mighty-Mite Motors product catalog

Model #003

Classic roadster: Sounds include engine start-up, rev, shifting gears, and idle. Two forward speeds—2 $\frac{1}{2}$ mph and 5 mph; reverses at 2 $\frac{1}{2}$ mph. High-speed lockout. On/off power pedal. Power-Lock electric brake. Includes two 6v batteries and recharger. Ages 3–7 (can carry two passengers up to 65 lbs. each). **Suggested retail price: $189.99**.

Model #004

Sports car #1: Two forward speeds, 2 $\frac{1}{2}$ and 5 mph. Reverses at 2 $\frac{1}{2}$ mph. High-speed lockout. Power-Lock electric brake. Includes two 6v batteries and one recharger. Ages 3–6 (can carry two passengers up to 90 lbs. combined). **Suggested retail price: $249.99.**

Model #005

Sports car #2: Phone lets child pretend to talk while he or she drives. Two forward speeds—2 $\frac{1}{2}$ and 5 mph; reverses at 2 $\frac{1}{2}$ mph. High-speed lockout. Power-Lock electric brake. Includes two 6v batteries and one recharger. Ages 3–6 (can carry two passengers up to 90 lbs. combined). **Suggested retail price: $249.99.**

Figure 11-1 (Continued): **Mighty-Mite Motors product catalog**

Model #006

Turbo Injected Porsche 911: Working stick shift—3 and 6 mph forward; 3 mph reverse. High-speed lockout. Adjustable seat. Doors, trunk, and hood open. Simulated car phone. Includes one 18v battery and recharger. Ages 3–8 (can carry two passengers up to 120 lbs combined). **Suggested retail price: $299.99.**

Model #007

Indy Car: Dual motors for cruising on a variety of surfaces, even up hills. Two forward speeds (2 $1/2$ and 5 mph), plus reverse (2 $1/2$ mph). Adjustable seat. Includes two 6v batteries and recharger. Ages 3–7 (can carry one passenger up to 80 lbs.). **Suggested retail price: $269.99.**

Model #008

2-Ton Pickup Truck: In metallic teal color. Simulated chrome engine covers and headlight with over-size wheels. 2 $1/2$ mph forward speed. Includes one 6v battery and recharger. Ages 3–7 (can carry one passenger up to 65 lbs.). **Suggested retail price: $189.99.**

Figure 11-1 (Continued):   Mighty-Mite Motors product catalog

Model #009

Santa Fe Train: Soundly engineered by a little guy or gal. A hand-operated on/off button controls the 6v battery-operated motor. Reaches speeds to 3 mph. Even includes a battery-powered "whoo whoo" whistle to greet passersby. Rides on 76" x 168" oval track (sold separately) or carpet or sidewalk, indoors or outdoors. Plastic body and floorboard; steel axles and coupling pins. Bright red, blue, and yellow body features a large lift-up seat and trailing car for storage. Includes battery and charger. Ages 3–6. **Suggested retail price: $159.90.**

Model #010

Oval Track: Measures 76" by 168". **Suggested retail price: $39.90.**

Model #011

Additional 6-Pc Straight Track: Six straight sections 19" each (total 105"). **Suggested retail price: $19.90.**

Figure 11-1 (Continued): Mighty-Mite Motors product catalog

Model #012

Rechargeable Batteries (6 volt): For use with 6 or 12 volt vehicles. For 12 volt vehicles, use two. To charge, use charger included with vehicle. **Suggested retail price: $27.99**.

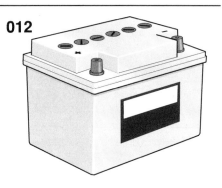

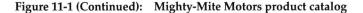

Figure 11-1 (Continued):   Mighty-Mite Motors product catalog

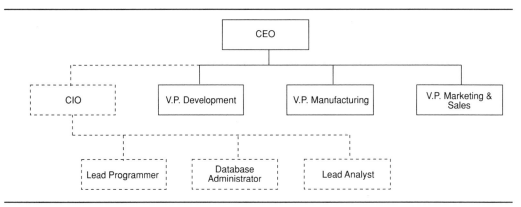

Figure 11-2:   Mighty-Mite Motors organization chart

Manufacturing Division

The Manufacturing division is responsible for producing products for mass market sales. Manufacturing procures its own raw materials and manages its own operations, including personnel (hiring, firing, scheduling) and assembly line management. Manufacturing maintains the inventory of products ready for sale. It also handles shipping of products to resellers, based on sales information received from Marketing & Sales.

Marketing & Sales Division

MMM sells directly to toy stores and catalog houses; the corporation has never used distributors. Marketing & Sales employs a staff of 25 salespeople who make personal contacts with resellers. Salespeople are responsible for distributing catalogs in their territories, visiting and/or calling potential resellers, and taking reseller orders. Order accounting is handled by Marketing & Sales. As noted earlier, Marketing & Sales transmits shipping information to Manufacturing, which takes care of actual product delivery.

Current Information Systems

MMM's information systems are a hodgepodge of computers and applications that have grown up with little corporate planning. The Product Development division relies primarily on stand-alone CAD workstations. In contrast to the sophistication of the CAD workstations, testing records are kept and analyzed manually. Product Development employs product designers (some of whom function as project leaders) and clerical support staff, but no information systems personnel. Attempts to have clerical staff develop simple database applications to store data about children who test new products and the results of those tests have proved futile. It has become evident that Product Development needs information systems professionals, and although the division is willing to hire IS staff, corporate management has decided to centralize the IS staff, rather than add to a decentralized model.

Manufacturing uses a stand-alone minicomputer to track purchases and inventory levels of raw materials, personnel scheduling, manufacturing line scheduling, and finished product inventory. Each of these applications was written in COBOL in the early 1980s, shortly after the corporation was established. The data used by a Manufacturing application are contained in files that do not share information with any of the other applications. Manufacturing employs a data processing staff of five, most of whom are COBOL maintenance programmers. Although these programmers are talented, the basic applications no longer meet the needs of the Manufacturing division and management has determined that it isn't cost effective to rewrite them from scratch.

> *Note: Minicomputers, which were smaller versions of main-frames, have almost entirely disappeared from the computing scene. The closest thing to a minicomputer you can buy today is probably an IBM AS/400. In general, today's high-end personal computers and LAN servers are more powerful than most mini-computers.*

Marketing & Sales, which wasn't computerized until 1987, has a local area network consisting of one server and 15 workstations. The server provides shared applications such as word processing and spreadsheets. It also maintains a marketing and sales database, which has been developed using dBase III Plus. The database suffers from several problems, including a limit of 10 users at one time and concurrency control problems that lead to severe data inconsistencies. The marketing and sales database was developed by one member of the division's three-person IS staff. However, that individual left the company in 1992 and no current staff member totally understands the software. Regardless of the amount of time spent trying to maintain the database, inaccurate data continue to be introduced.

The Marketing & Sales LAN has no data communications capabilities. Salespeople therefore must transmit hard copies of their orders to the central office, where the orders are manually keyed into the existing database. (Some of the salespeople do have laptop computers, but because the LAN has no modems, the salespeople cannot connect to it.)

Reengineering Project

Because MMM seems to have lost its strategic advantage in the marketplace, the CEO has decided to undertake a major systems reengineering project. The overall thrust of the project is to provide an integrated information system that will support better evaluation of product testing, better analysis of sales patterns, and better control of the manufacturing process. New information systems will be based on a client–server model and include one or more databases running on a network of servers, workstations, and PCs.

New Information Systems Division

The first step in the reengineering project is to establish an Information Systems division. This new division will also be housed in the corporate headquarters, along with the three existing divisions. To accommodate the new division, MMM will be constructing a 10,000 square foot addition to its building.

MMM is in the process of searching for a Chief Information Officer (CIO). This individual, who will report directly to the CEO, will manage the new division and be responsible for overseeing the reengineering of computer-based information systems that will handle all of the corporation's operations.

All current IS personnel (those who work for the Manufacturing and Marketing & Sales divisions) will be transferred to the new IS division. The division will hire (either internally or externally) three management-level professionals: a Lead Programmer (responsible for overseeing application development), a Database Administrator (responsible for database design and management), and a Lead Analyst (responsible for overseeing systems analysis and design efforts). Retraining in the client–server model and client–server development tools will be provided for all current employees who are willing to make the transition. Those who are unwilling to move to the new development environment will be laid off.

Basic System Goals

The CEO has defined the following goals for the reengineering project:

   ◆ Develop a corporation-wide data administration plan that documents all databases to be developed for the corporation. This documentation will include ER diagrams, schemas, and data dictionaries.

♦ Provide an application road map that documents all application programs that will be needed to provide access to corporate databases.

♦ Create a timeline for the installation of corporate databases and the development of application programs.

♦ Specify hardware changes and/or acquisitions that will be necessary to support access to the databases from within the headquarters building and by salespeople who are traveling. Although not every employee will have access to every database, the equipment should nonetheless make universal access possible, providing maximum flexibility for future growth.

♦ Develop and implement a security plan that supports access restrictions to the corporate databases.

♦ Install the databases and develop application programs.

♦ Acquire and install necessary hardware upgrades.

Current Business Processes

To aid the systems analysts in their assessment of MMM's information systems needs, the CEO of MMM asked all existing division heads to document the way in which information is currently processed. This documentation, which also includes some information about what an improved system should do, provides a starting point for the redesign of both business and IS processes.

The Sales and Ordering Processes

MMM receives orders at its plant in two ways: either by telephone directly from customers or from members of the sales staff who have visited customers in person. Orders from the remote sales staff usually arrive by fax or overnight courier.

Each order is taken on a standard order form (Figure 11-3). If the order arrives by fax, it will already be on the correct form. Telephone orders are written directly onto the form. Several times a day a clerk enters the orders into the dBase III database application. Unfortunately, if the sales office is particularly busy, order entry may be delayed. This backup has a major impact on production line scheduling and thus on the company's ability to fill orders. The new information system must streamline the order-entry process, including the electronic transmission of orders from the field and the direct entry of in-house orders into electronic form.

The in-house sales staff has no access to the computer files that show the current finished-goods inventory. They are therefore unable to tell customers when their orders will ship. They can, however, tell customers how many orders are ahead of theirs to be filled and, based on general manufacturing timetables, come up with an approximation of how long it will take to ship a given order. One of the goals of the information systems reengineering project is to provide better company-wide knowledge of how long it will take to fill customer orders.

The Manufacturing, Inventory, and Shipping Processes

The MMM Manufacturing division occupies a large portion of the MMM facility. The division controls the actual manufacturing lines (three assembly lines), a storage area for finished goods, a storage area for raw materials, and several offices for supervisory and clerical staff.

The manufacturing process is triggered when a batch of order forms is received each morning by the manufacturing office. (The batch consists of all orders that were entered into the sales database the previous working day.) A secretary takes the individual order forms and compiles a report summarizing the number ordered by model (Figure 11-4). This report is then given to the Manufacturing Supervisor, whose responsibility it is to schedule which model will be produced on each manufacturing line each day.

The scheduling process is somewhat complex, because the Manufacturing Supervisor must take into account previously placed orders, which have determined the current manufacturing schedule, and current inventory levels as well as the new orders when

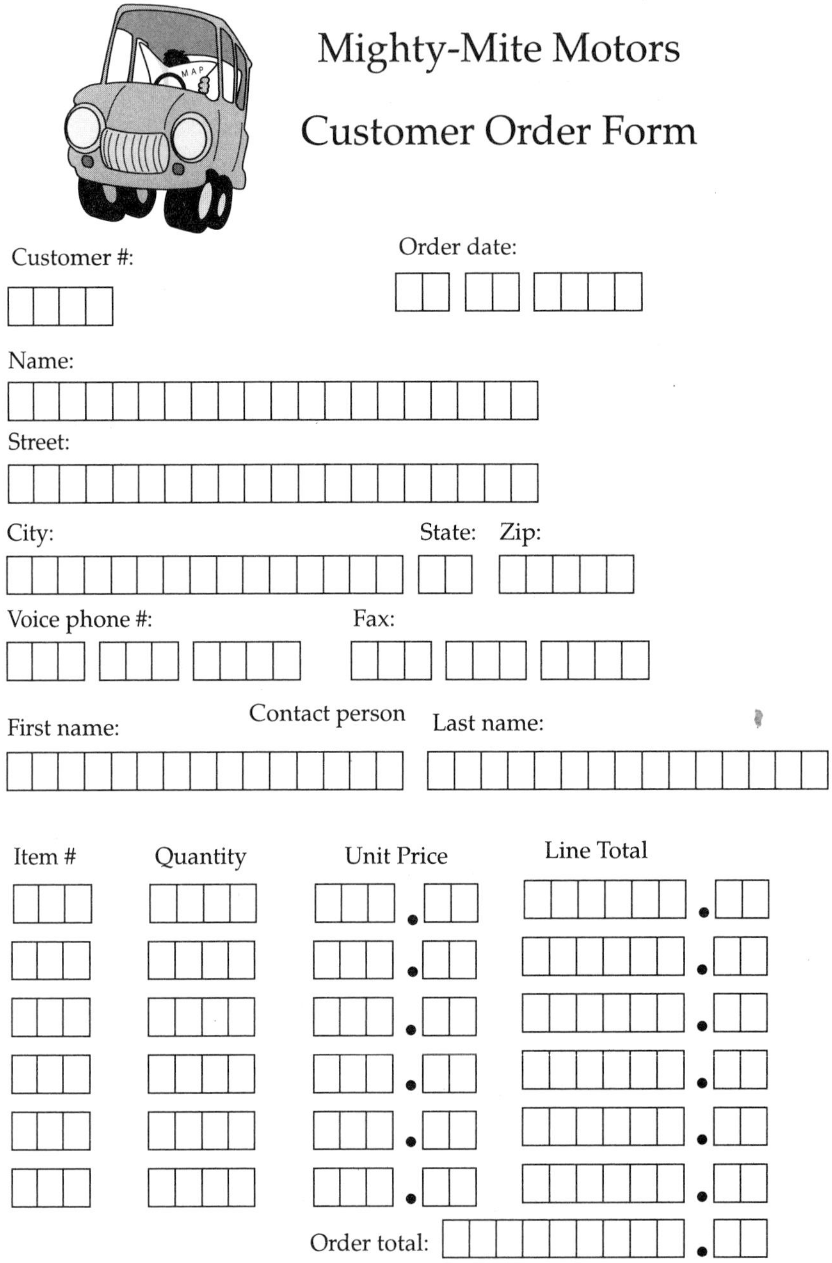

Mighty-Mite Motors

Customer Order Form

Customer #:

Order date:

Name:

Street:

City: State: Zip:

Voice phone #:   Fax:

Contact person

First name: Last name:

Item #	Quantity	Unit Price	Line Total

Order total:

Figure 11-3:   Mighty-Mite Motors order form

Mighty-Mite Motors
Order Summary

mm/dd/yyyy

Model #	Quantity Ordered
001	75
002	150
004	80
005	35
008	115
009	25
010	25
011	15

Figure 11-4:   Mighty-Mite Motors order summary report format

adjusting the schedule. The availability of raw materials and the time it takes to modify a manufacturing line to produce a different model also enter into the scheduling decision. This is one function that MMM's management understands will be almost impossible to automate; there is too much human expertise involved to translate it into an automatic process. However, it is vital that the Manufacturing Supervisor have access to accurate, up-to-date information about orders, inventory, and the current line schedule so that judgements can be made based on as much hard data as possible.

As finished vehicles come off the assembly line, they are packed for shipping, labeled, and sent to finished goods storage. Each shipping carton contains one vehicle, which is marked with its model number, serial number, and date of manufacturing. The Shipping Manager, who oversees finished goods storage and shipping, ensures that newly manufactured items are entered into the existing inventory files.

The Shipping Manager receives customer order forms after the order report has been completed. (Photocopies of the order forms are kept in the Marketing & Sales office as backup.) The orders are placed in a box in reverse chronological order so that the oldest orders can be filled first. The Shipping Manager checks orders against inventory levels by looking at the inventory level output screen (Figure 11-5). If the manager sees that there is enough inventory to fill an order, then the order is given to a shipping clerk for processing. If there isn't enough inventory, then the order is put back in the box, where it will be checked again the following day. Under this system, no partial orders are filled because they would be extremely difficult to track. (The reengineered information system should allow handling of partial shipments.)

Current Finished Goods Inventory Levels
mm/dd/yy

INV#	NUMBER ON HAND
001	215
002	35
003	180
004	312
005	82
006	5
007	212
008	189
009	37
010	111
011	195
012	22

Figure 11-5:   Mighty-Mite Motors inventory screen layout

Shipping clerks are given orders to fill. They create shipping labels for all vehicles that are part of a shipment. The cartons are labeled and set aside for pickup by UPS. The shipping clerks create UPS manifests (which also serve as packing slips), ensure that the items being shipped are removed from the inventory file, and return the filled orders to the Shipping Manager. The orders are then marked as filled and returned to Marketing & Sales. The reengineered information system should automate the generation of pick-lists, packing slips, and updating of finished-goods inventory.

MMM's raw materials inventory is maintained on a just-in-time basis. The Manufacturing Supervisor checks the line schedule (Figure 11-6) and the current raw materials inventory (Figure 11-7) daily to determine what raw materials need to be ordered. This process relies heavily on the Manufacturing Supervisor's knowledge of which materials are needed for which model vehicle. MMM's CEO is very concerned about this process because the Manufacturing Supervisor, while accurate in scheduling the manufacturing line, is nowhere near as accurate in judging raw materials needs. The result is that occasionally manufacturing must stop because raw materials have run out. The CEO would therefore like to see ordering of raw materials triggered automatically. The new information system should keep track of the raw materials needed to produce each model and, based on the line schedule and a reorder point established for each item, generate orders for items when needed.

Raw materials are taken from inventory each morning as each manufacturing line is being set up for the day's production run. The inventory files are modified immediately after all raw materials have been removed for a given manufacturing line. There is no way to automate the reduction of inventory; however, the new information system should make it easy for nontechnical users to update inventory levels.

The Product Testing and Support Function

MMM's top management makes decisions about which model vehicles to produce based on data from three sources: product testing, customer registrations, and problem reports.

Customer registrations are received on cards packaged with sold vehicles (Figure 11-8). Currently, the registration cards are filed by customer name. However, MMM would also like access to these data by model and serial number to make it easier to notify customers if a recall occurs. Management would also like summaries of the data by model purchased, age of primary user, gender of primary user, and who purchased the vehicle for the child.

Line Schedule
mm/dd/yy

mm/dd/yy
                Line #1: Model 005   100 units
                Line #2: Model 007   150 units
                Line #3: Model 010   100 units

mm/dd/yy
                Line #1: Model 003   200 units
                Line #2: Model 005   150 units
                Line #3: Model 008   300 units

mm/dd/yy
                Line #1: Model 006   150 units
                Line #2: Model 008   100 units
                Line #3: Model 002   300 units

                        :
                        :
                        :

Total production scheduled:

                Model 002   300 units
                Model 003   200 units
                Model 005   250 units
                Model 006   150 units
                Model 007   150 units
                Model 008   400 units
                Model 010   100 units

Figure 11-6:   Mighty-Mite Motors line schedule report format

Problem reports (Figure 11-9) are taken by customer support representatives who work within the product testing division. These reports include the serial number and model experiencing problems along with the date and type of problem. Currently, the problem descriptions are nonstandard, written in whatever language the customer support representative happens to use. It is therefore difficult

Current Raw Materials Inventory Levels
mm/dd/yy

ITEM#	ITEM	QUANTITY ON HAND
001	Plastic #3	95 lbs
002	Red dye 109	25 gals
003	Wheel 12"	120 each
004	Plastic #4	300 lbs
005	Yellow dye 110	5 gals
006	Yellow dye 65	30 gals
007	Strut 15"	99 each
008	Axle 18"	250 each
009	Blue dye 25	18 gals
010	Plastic #8	350 lbs
011	Cotter pin small	515 each
012	Cotter pin medium	109 each

Figure 11-7:   Mighty-Mite Motors raw materials inventory screen layout

to summarize problem reports to get an accurate picture of which models are experiencing design problems that should be corrected. MMM would therefore like to introduce a standardized method for describing problems, probably through a set of problem codes. The result should be regular reports on the problems reported for each model that can be used to help make decisions about which models to continue, which to discontinue, which to redesign, and which to recall.

MMM does not repair its own products. When a problem report is received, the customer is either directed to return the product to the store where it was purchased for an exchange (during the first 30 days after purchase) or directed to an authorized repair center in the customer's area. In the latter case, the problem report is faxed to the repair center so that it is waiting when the customer arrives. MMM does not plan to change this procedure because it currently provides quick, excellent service to customers and alleviates the need for MMM to stock replacement parts. (Replacement parts are stocked by the authorized repair centers.)

Please register your Mighty-Mite Motors vehicle

By registering you receive the following benefits:

- Validation of the warranty on your vehicle, making it easier to obtain warranty service if ever necessary.
- Notification of product updates relating to your vehicle.
- Information mailings about enhancements to your vehicle and other products that may be of interest.

First name

Last name

Street

City   State   Zip

Phone #:

Model #   Serial #

Age of primary user of vehicle: _____

Gender: ☐ Male   ☐ Female

Fold Here. Tape closed; do not staple.

Date of purchase:

Place of purchase:

Where did you first learn about Mighty-Mite Motors?

☐ Advertisement in a magazine or newspaper
☐ Friend's recommendation
☐ In-store display
☐ Catalog
☐ Other

What features of the vehicle prompted your purchase?

☐ Size
☐ Color
☐ Speed
☐ Safety features
☐ Cost
☐ Other

What is the relationship of the purchaser to the primary user?

☐ Parent
☐ Grandparent
☐ Aunt/Uncle
☐ Friend
☐ Other

Figure 11-8:   Mighty-Mite Motors purchase registration form

Product test results are recorded on paper forms (Figure 11-10). After a testing period is completed, the forms are collated manually to produce a summary of how well a new product performed. MMM would like the test results stored within an information system so that the testing report can be produced automatically, saving time and effort. Such a report will be used to help decide which new models should be placed in production.

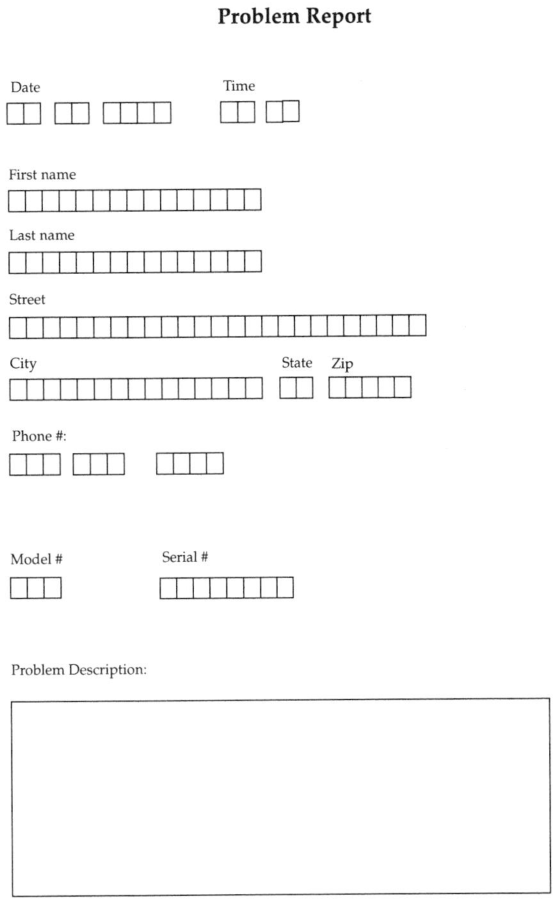

Problem Report

Date   Time
☐☐ ☐☐ ☐☐☐☐   ☐☐ ☐☐

First name
☐☐☐☐☐☐☐☐☐☐☐☐☐☐

Last name
☐☐☐☐☐☐☐☐☐☐☐☐☐

Street
☐☐☐☐☐☐☐☐☐☐☐☐☐☐☐☐☐☐☐☐☐☐

City   State   Zip
☐☐☐☐☐☐☐☐☐☐☐☐☐☐   ☐☐   ☐☐☐☐☐

Phone #:
☐☐☐ ☐☐☐   ☐☐☐☐

Model #   Serial #
☐☐☐   ☐☐☐☐☐☐☐

Problem Description:

Figure 11-9:   Mighty-Mite Motors problem report

Designing the Database

The most effective approach to the design of a database (or collection of databases) for an environment as diverse as that presented by Mighty-Mite Motors usually involves breaking the design into components indicated by the organization of the company. As the design evolves, the designer can examine the entities and their relationships to determine where parts of the organization will need to

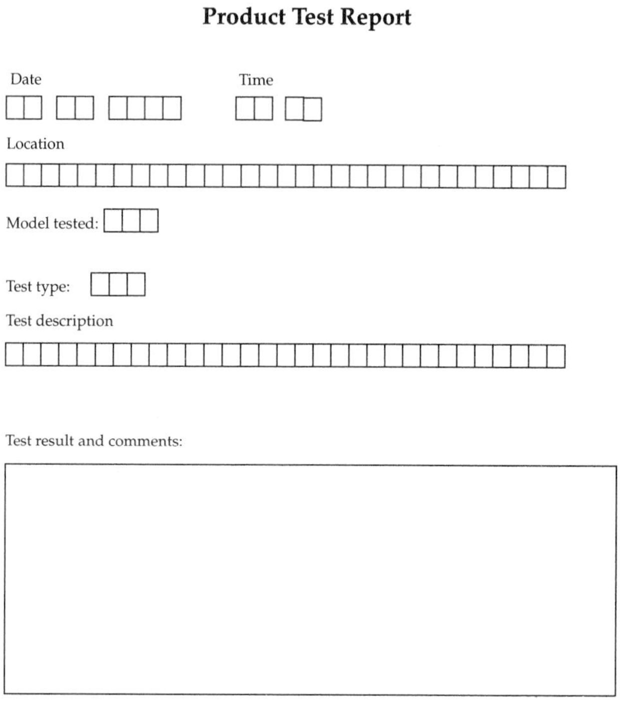

Product Test Report

Date   Time

Location

Model tested:

Test type:

Test description

Test result and comments:

Figure 11-10:   Mighty-Mite Motors product test report

share data. Working on one portion of the design at a time also simplifies dealing with what might at first seem to be an overwhelmingly large database environment.

The Mighty-Mite Motors database environment seems to fall naturally into the following areas:

- ◆ Manufacturing (including finished goods inventory and raw materials ordering)
- ◆ Sales to toy stores and shipping of products ordered
- ◆ Reported purchases
- ◆ Testing
- ◆ Problem handling

Examining the Data Flows

In this particular situation, a data flow diagram can be of enormous use in identifying where data are shared by various parts of an organization. The top-level DFD (the *context diagram*) in Figure 11-11 actually tells us very little. It indicates that three sources outside the company provide data: customers (the stores to which the company sells), purchasers (the individuals who purchase products from the stores), and raw materials suppliers. Somehow, all that data is used by a general process named "Manufacture & Sell Products" to keep the company in business.

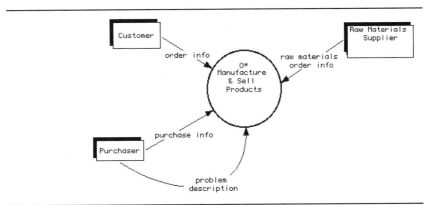

Figure 11-11:   Context DFD for Mighty-Mite Motors

However, the level 1 DFD (Figure 11-12) is much more telling. As the data handling processes are broken down, five data stores emerge:

- ◆ Raw materials: This data store holds both the raw materials inventory and the orders for raw materials.
- ◆ Product data: The product data store contains data about the products being manufactured and the finished goods inventory.
- ◆ Customer orders: This data store contains customer information as well as order data.

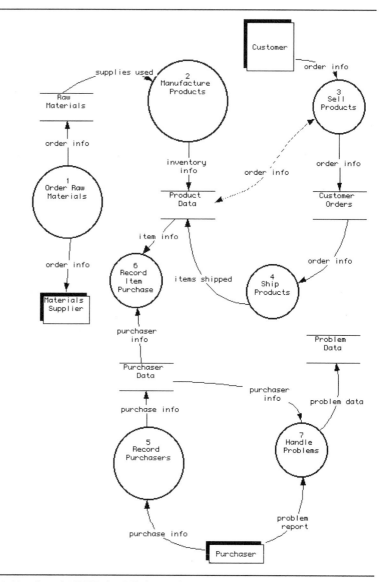

Figure 11-12:   Level 1 DFD for Mighty-Mite Motors

♦ Purchaser data: The purchaser data store contains information about the individuals who purchase products and the products they have purchased.

◆ Problem data: This final data store contains problem reports.

As you examine the processes that interact with these five data stores, you will find a number of processes that manipulate data in more than one data store as well as data stores that are used by more than one process:

◆ The raw materials data store is used by the raw materials ordering and the manufacturing processes.
◆ Product data are used by manufacturing, sales, shipping, and purchaser registration.
◆ Customer order data are used by sales and shipping.
◆ The purchaser data store is used by purchaser registration and problem handling.
◆ The problem data store, used only by problem handling, is the only data store not shared by multiple processes.

The raw materials ordering process is the only process that uses only a single data store. Nonetheless, the level 1 DFD makes it very clear that there is no instance in which a single process uses a single data store without interaction with other data stores and processes. Given that each process in the DFD probably represents all or part of an application program, this suggests that the database designer should probably consider a single database, rather than a set of databases.

The DFD makes it very clear that the need for the integration of the various data stores is very strong. In addition, Mighty-Mite Motors is a relatively small business and therefore a single database that manages all needed aspects of the company will not grow unreasonably large. Ultimately, the database designer may decide to distribute the database onto multiple servers, placing portions of it that are used most frequently in the divisions where that use occurs. The database design, however, will be the same regardless of whether the final implementation is centralized or distributed. The essential decision is to create a single database rather than several smaller, isolated databases that must somehow share data.

Creating the ER Diagram

The database designer working for Mighty-Mite Motors has two very good sources of information about exactly what needs to be stored in the database: the employees of the company and the paper documents the company has been using.

The designer needs to capture all the information on the paper documents. Some documents are used only for input (for example, the product registration form or the order form). Others represent outputs that an application program must be able to generate (for example, the line schedule report). Although the current documents do not necessarily represent all the outputs application programs running against the database will eventually prepare, they do provide a good starting place for the database design. Whenever the designer has questions, he or she can then turn to Mighty-Mite's employees for clarification.

Working from the documents, information gathered from employees, and the data flow diagram, the database developer puts together the ER diagram. Because there are so many entities, all of which interconnect, the diagram is very wide. It has therefore been split into three pieces so you can see it. As you look at each piece, keep in mind that entities that appear in more than one piece represent the connections between the three illustrations.

The first part (found in Figure 11-13) contains the entities for raw materials and manufacturing. This portion of the data model is dealing with three many-to-many relationships:

- ◆ material_order to raw_material (resolved by the composite entity material_order_line)
- ◆ raw_material to model (resolved by the composite entity material_needed)
- ◆ manufacturing_line to model (resolved by the composite entity line_schedule)

The second portion of the ERD (Figure 11-14) contains entities for product testing and sales. (Remember that in this instance, the cus-

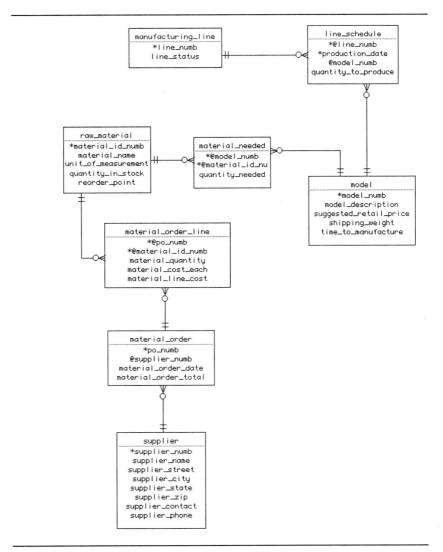

Figure 11-13:   Mighty-Mite Motors ERD (part I)

tomers are toy stores rather than individual purchasers.) There are two many-to-many relationships:

- ◆ test_type to model (resolved by the test entity)
- ◆ order to model (resolved by the order_line composite entity)

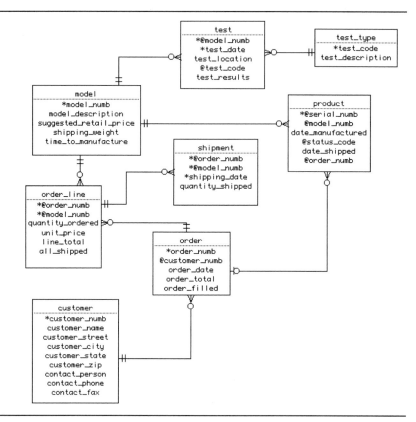

Figure 11-14:   Mighty-Mite Motors ERD (part II)

In this instance, the test entity is not a composite entity. It is an activity that someone performs and as such has an existence outside the database. It is not an entity created just to resolve a many-to-many relationship.

At this point the diagrams become a bit unusual, because of the need to keep track of individual products rather than simply groups of products of the same model. The model entity, which you first saw in Figure 11-13, represents a type of vehicle manufactured by Might-Mite Motors. However, the product entity, which first appears in Figure 11-14, represents a single vehicle that is uniquely identified by a serial number. This means that the relationships between an order, the line items on an order, and the models and products are more complex than for most other sales database designs.

The order and line_item entities are fairly typical. They indicate how many of a given model are required to fill a given order. The shipment entity then indicates how many of a specific model are shipped on a specific date. However, the database must also track the order in which individual products are shipped. As a result, there is a direct relationship between the product entity and the order entity, in addition to the relationships between order_line and model. In this way Mighty-Mite Motors will know exactly where each product has gone. At the same time, the company will be able to track the status of orders (in particular, how many units of each model have yet to ship).

The final portion of the ERD (Figure 11-15) deals with the purchasers and problem reports. There are two many-to-many relationships:

- ♦ problem_type to product (resolved with the entity problem_report)
- ♦ purchase to feature (resolved with the composite entity purchase_feature)

As with the test entity that you saw earlier, the problem_report entity acts like a composite entity to resolve a many-to-many relationship but is really a simple entity. It is an entity that has an existence outside the database and was not created simply to take care of the M:N relationship.

> *Note: Calling an entity "problem_report" can be a bit misleading. In this case, the word "report" does not refer to a piece of paper but to the action of reporting a problem. A "problem_report" is therefore an activity rather than a document. In fact, the printed documentation of a problem report will probably include data from several entities, including the product, problem_report, purchase, and owner entities.*

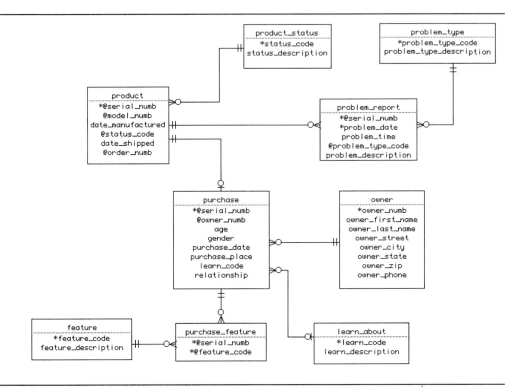

Figure 11-15:   Might-Mite Motors ERD (part III)

If you look closely at the diagram, you'll notice that there is a one-to-one relationship between the product and purchase entities. The handling of the data supplied by a purchaser on the product registration card presents an interesting dilemma for a database designer. Each product will be registered by only one purchaser. (Even if the product is later sold or given to someone else, the new owner will not have a registration card to send in.) There will be only one set of registration data for each product, at first thought suggesting that all the registration data should be part of the product entity.

However, there is a *lot* of registration data—including one repeating group (the features for which the purchaser chose the product, represented by the feature and purchase_feature entities)—and the product is involved in a number of relationships that have nothing to do with product registration. If the DBMS has to retrieve the registration data along with the rest of the product data, database performance will suffer. It therefore makes sense in this case to keep the purchase data separate and to retrieve it only when absolutely needed.

> *Note: One common mistake made by novice database designers is to create an entity called a "registration card." It is important to remember that the card itself is merely an input document. What is crucial is the data the card contains and the entity those data describe, rather than the medium on which the data are supplied.*

Creating the Tables

The tables for the Mighty-Mite Motors database can come directly from the ER diagram. They are as follows:

```
model (model_numb, model_description, suggested_retail_price,
    shipping_weight, time_to_manufacture)
test (model_numb, test_date, test_location, test_code, test_results)
test_types (test_code, test_description)
customers (customer_numb, customer_name, customer_street,
    customer_street, customer_city, customer_state, customer_zip,
    contact_person, contact_phone, contact_fax)
orders (order_numb, customer_numb, order_date, order_total,
    order_filled)
order_line (order_numb, model_numb, quantity_ordered, unit_price,
    line_total, all_shipped)
shipments (order_numb, model_numb, shipping_date, quantity_shipped)
product (serial_numb, model_numb, date_manufactured, status_code,
    order_numb, date_shipped)
product_status (status_code, status_description)
raw_material (material_id_numb, material_name, unit_of_measurement,
    quantity_in_stock, reorder_point)
supplier (supplier_numb, supplier_name, supplier_street,
    supplier_city, supplier_state, supplier_zip, supplier_contact,
    supplier_phone)
material_order (po_numb, supplier_numb, material_order_date,
    material_order_total)
material_order_line (po_numb, material_id_numb, material_quantity,
    material_cost_each, material_line_cost)
material_needed (model_numb, material_id_numb, quantity_needed)
manufacturing_line (line_numb, line_status)
line_schedule (line_numb, production_date, model_numb,
    quantity_to_produce)
```

```
owner (owner numb, owner_first_name, owner_last_name, owner_street,
    owner_city, owner_state, owner_zip, owner_phone)
purchase (serial numb, owner_numb, age, gender, purchase_date,
    purchase_place, learn_code, relationship)
purchase_feature (serial numb, feature code)
learn_about (learn code, learn_description)
feature (feature code, feature_description)
problem_report (serial numb, problem date, problem_time,
    problem_type_code, problem_description)
problem_type (problem type code, problem_type_description)
```

Generating the SQL

Assuming that the designers of the Mighty-Mite Motors database are working with a CASE tool, then generating SQL statements to create the database can be automated. For example, in Figure 11-16 you will find the SQL generated by Mac A&D from the ER diagram you saw earlier in this chapter.

```
CREATE TABLE model
(
    model_numb INTEGER,
    model_description CHAR (40),
    suggested_retail_price DECIMAL (6,2),
    shipping_weight DECIMAL (6,2),
    time_to_manufacture TIME,
    PRIMARY KEY (model_numb)
);

CREATE TABLE test_type
(
    test_code INTEGER,
    test_description CHAR (40),
    PRIMARY KEY (test_code)
);
```

Figure 11-16 :   SQL statements needed to create the Mighty-Mite Motors
database

```
CREATE TABLE test
(
    model_numb INTEGER,
    test_date DATE,
    test_location CHAR (40),
    test_code INTEGER,
    test_results CHAR (40),
    PRIMARY KEY (model_numb, test_date),
    FOREIGN KEY (model_numb) REFERENCES model,
    FOREIGN KEY (test_code) REFERENCES test_type
);

CREATE TABLE customer
(
    customer_numb INTEGER,
    customer_name CHAR (40),
    customer_street CHAR (40),
    customer_city CHAR (30),
    customer_state CHAR (2),
    customer_zip CHAR (5),
    contact_person CHAR (40)CHAR (30),
    contact_phone CHAR (12),
    contact_fax CHAR (12),
    PRIMARY KEY (customer_numb)
);

CREATE TABLE order
(
    order_numb INTEGER,
    customer_numb INTEGER,
    order_date DATE,
    order_total DECIMAL (8,2),
    order_filled CHAR (1),
    PRIMARY KEY (order_numb),
    FOREIGN KEY (customer_numb) REFERENCES customer
);
```

Figure 11-16 (Continued): **SQL statements needed to create the Mighty-Mite Motors database**

```
CREATE TABLE order_line
(
    order_numb INTEGER,
    model_numb INTEGER,
    quantity_ordered INTEGER,
    unit_price DECIMAL (6,2),
    line_total DECIMAL (8,2),
    all_shipped CHAR (1),
    PRIMARY KEY (order_numb, model_numb),
    FOREIGN KEY (order_numb) REFERENCES order,
    FOREIGN KEY (model_numb) REFERENCES model
);


CREATE TABLE shipment
(
    order_numb INTEGER,
    model_numb INTEGER,
    shipping_date DATE,
    quantity_shipped INTEGER,
    PRIMARY KEY (order_numb, model_numb, shipping_date),
    FOREIGN KEY (order_numb) REFERENCES order_line,
    FOREIGN KEY (model_numb) REFERENCES order_line
);

CREATE TABLE product
(
    serial_numb INTEGER,
    model_numb INTEGER,
    date_manufactured DATE,
    status_code INTEGER,
    date_shipped DATE,
    order_numb INTEGER,
    PRIMARY KEY (serial_numb),
    FOREIGN KEY (serial_numb) REFERENCES purchase,
    FOREIGN KEY (model_numb) REFERENCES model,
    FOREIGN KEY (status_code) REFERENCES product_status,
    FOREIGN KEY (order_numb) REFERENCES order
);

CREATE TABLE product_status
(
    status_code INTEGER,
    status_description CHAR (40),
    PRIMARY KEY (status_code)
);
```

Figure 11-16 (Continued):   SQL statements needed to create the Mighty-Mite Motors database

```
CREATE TABLE raw_material
(
    material_id_numb INTEGER,
    material_name CHAR (30),
    unit_of_measurement CHAR (12),
    quantity_in_stock INTEGER,
    reorder_point INTEGER,
    PRIMARY KEY (material_id_numb)
);

CREATE TABLE material_needed
(
    model_numb INTEGER,
    material_id_numb INTEGER,
    quantity_needed INTEGER,
    PRIMARY KEY (model_numb, material_id_numb),
    FOREIGN KEY (model_numb) REFERENCES model,
    FOREIGN KEY (material_id_numb) REFERENCES raw_material
);

CREATE TABLE supplier
(
    supplier_numb INTEGER,
    supplier_name CHAR (40),
    supplier_street CHAR (30),
    supplier_city CHAR (15),
    supplier_state CHAR (2),
    supplier_zip CHAR (5),
    supplier_contact CHAR (40),
    supplier_phone CHAR (12),
    PRIMARY KEY (supplier_numb)
);

CREATE TABLE material_order
(
    po_numb INTEGER,
    supplier_numb INTEGER,
    material_order_date DATE,
    material_order_total DECIMAL (6,2),
    PRIMARY KEY (po_numb),
    FOREIGN KEY (supplier_numb) REFERENCES supplier
);
```

Figure 11-16 (Continued):   SQL statements needed to create the Mighty-Mite Motors database

```
CREATE TABLE material_order_line
(
    po_numb INTEGER,
    material_id_numb INTEGER,
    material_quantity INTEGER,
    material_cost_each DECIMAL (6,2),
    material_line_cost DECIMAL (8,2),
    PRIMARY KEY (po_numb, material_id_numb),
    FOREIGN KEY (po_numb) REFERENCES material_order,
    FOREIGN KEY (material_id_numb) REFERENCES raw_material
);

CREATE TABLE manufacturing_line
(
    line_numb INTEGER,
    line_status CHAR (12),
    PRIMARY KEY (line_numb)
);

CREATE TABLE line_schedule
(
    line_numb INTEGER,
    production_date DECIMAL (6,2)DATE,
    model_numb INTEGER,
    quantity_to_produce INTEGER,
    PRIMARY KEY (line_numb, production_date),
    FOREIGN KEY (line_numb) REFERENCES manufacturing_line,
    FOREIGN KEY (model_numb) REFERENCES model
);

CREATE TABLE owner
(
    owner_numb INTEGER,
    owner_first_name CHAR (15),
    owner_last_name CHAR (15),
    owner_street CHAR (30),
    owner_city CHAR (15),
    owner_state CHAR (2),
    owner_zip CHAR (5),
    owner_phone CHAR (12),
    PRIMARY KEY (owner_numb)
);
```

Figure 11-16 (Continued):   SQL statements needed to create the Mighty-Mite Motors database

```
CREATE TABLE purchase
(
    serial_numb INTEGER,
    owner_numb INTEGER,
    age INTEGER,
    gender CHAR (1),
    purchase_date DATE,
    purchase_place CHAR (40),
    learn_code INTEGER,
    relationship CHAR (15),
    PRIMARY KEY (serial_numb),
    FOREIGN KEY (serial_numb) REFERENCES product,
    FOREIGN KEY (owner_numb) REFERENCES owner
);

CREATE TABLE feature
(
    feature_code INTEGER,
    feature_description CHAR (40),
    PRIMARY KEY (feature_code)
);

CREATE TABLE purchase_feature
(
    serial_numb INTEGER,
    feature_code INTEGER,
    PRIMARY KEY (serial_numb, feature_code),
    FOREIGN KEY (serial_numb) REFERENCES purchase,
    FOREIGN KEY (feature_code) REFERENCES feature
);

CREATE TABLE learn_about
(
    learn_code INTEGER,
    learn_description CHAR (40),
    serial_numb INTEGER,
    PRIMARY KEY (learn_code),
    FOREIGN KEY (serial_numb) REFERENCES purchase
);

CREATE TABLE problem_type
(
    problem_type_code INTEGER,
    problem_type_description CHAR (30),
    PRIMARY KEY (problem_type_code)
);
```

Figure 11-16 (Continued):   SQL statements needed to create the Mighty-Mite Motors database

```
CREATE TABLE problem_report
(
    serial_numb INTEGER,
    problem_date DATE,
    problem_time TIME,
    problem_type_code INTEGER,
    problem_description CHAR (40),
    PRIMARY KEY (serial_numb, problem_date),
    FOREIGN KEY (serial_numb) REFERENCES product,
    FOREIGN KEY (problem_type_code) REFERENCES problem_type
);
```

Figure 11-16 (Continued):   SQL statements needed to create the Mighty-Mite Motors database

The Object-Relational Design

One of the most challenging aspects of having object-oriented capabilities added to a relational DBMS is deciding whether a particular schema can benefit from a design that incorporates objects. Mighty-Mite Motors is one of those schemas that does not benefit greatly from a hybrid approach.

Why not? The major entities, such as products and models, participate in multiple relationships. Therefore, changing them into objects and then placing entire objects into related tables would result in unnecessary duplicated data and the introduction of significant data integrity problems.

The best use of the object technology in this particular database environment is to handle complex values, such as addresses and telephone numbers. Such objects can be reused throughout the database, simplifying the formatting, searching, and general handling of these elements.

> Note: The ER diagrams that you will see in the remainder of this chapter share the same data dictionary as the ERD for the pure relational design. Therefore, the names of some entities were changed slightly so that multiple entities with similar, but not identical, structure could exist in the data dictionary.

The first portion of the ER diagram for the hybrid MMM design can be found in Figure 11-17. There are three classes in this illustration: LineCost, Address, and Phone. The LineCost class contains the number of items of something that have been ordered and the cost of each item. One of the class's operations then computes and stores the line cost.

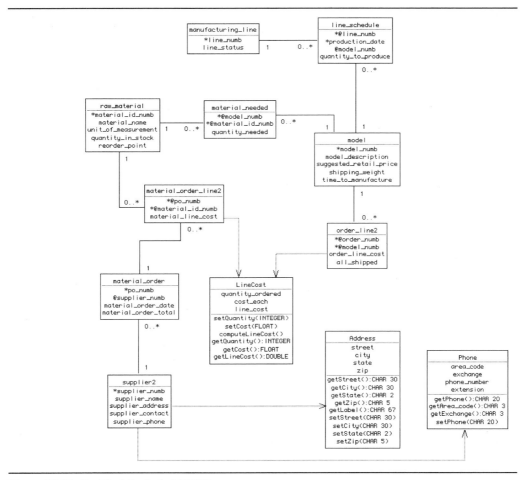

Figure 11-17: Part I of the hybrid ERD

The Address class takes a value that may consume multiple columns in a relation and collapses them down to a single column. The major value in doing this is conceptual clarity. You also gain simplicity in the relational design.

In a typical relational database, a telephone number is stored as a single text string. However, breaking it up into its constituent parts makes it possible to search the database by any of those parts and therefore enables access that was not previously available. (You could do so by searching in a text string, but such a search would be quite slow.) Marketing personnel, for example, could search for all customers within a specific exchange or map purchases by exchange to see purchasing patterns.

The second portion of the MMM hybrid ER diagram appears in Figure 11-18. Notice that the Customer2 entity has two lines going from the entity to the Phone class. This occurs because the customer_phone and customer_fax attributes have the same domain: the Phone class. The remainder of this portion of the design is exactly the same as the pure relational design.

Figure 11-19 contains the final portion of the ER diagram. The Owner2 relation is the most significantly changed relation when compared with the pure relational design. The owner's name is now an object of the Name class. The owner's address and telephone number are now objects of the Address and Phone classes, respectively.

The resulting relations are as follows:

```
model (model_numb, model_description, suggested_retail_price,
    shipping_weight, time_to_manufacture)
test (model_numb, test_date, test_location, test_code, test_results)
test_types (test_code, test_description)
customers (customer_numb, customer_name, customer_address,
    contact_person, contact_phone, contact_fax)
orders (order_numb, customer_numb, order_date, order_total,
    order_filled)
order_line (order_numb, model_numb, order_line_cost, all_shipped)
shipments (order_numb, model_numb, shipping_date, quantity_shipped)
product (serial_numb, model_numb, date_manufactured, status_code,
    order_numb, date_shipped)
product_status (status_code, status_description)
raw_material (material_id_numb, material_name, unit_of_measurement,
    quantity_in_stock, reorder_point)
```

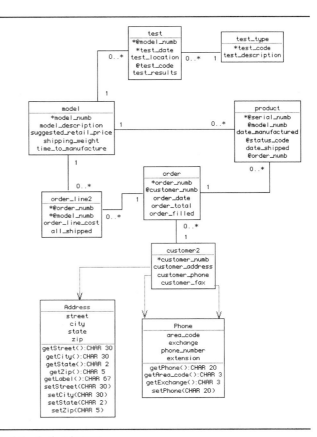

Figure 11-18: Part II of the hybrid ERD

```
supplier (supplier_numb, supplier_name, supplier_address,
     supplier_contact, supplier_phone)
material_order (po_numb, supplier_numb, material_order_date,
     material_order_total)
material_order_line (po_numb, material_id_numb, material_line_cost)
material_needed (model_numb, material_id_numb, quantity_needed)
manufacturing_line (line_numb, line_status)
line_schedule (line_numb, production_date, model_numb,
     quantity_to_produce)
owner (owner_numb, owner_name, owner_address, owner_phone)
purchase (serial_numb, owner_numb, age, gender, purchase_date,
     purchase_place, learn_code, relationship)
purchase_feature (serial_numb, feature_code)
learn_about (learn_code, learn_description)
feature (feature_code, feature_description)
problem_report (serial_numb, problem_date, problem_time,
     problem_type_code, problem_description)
```

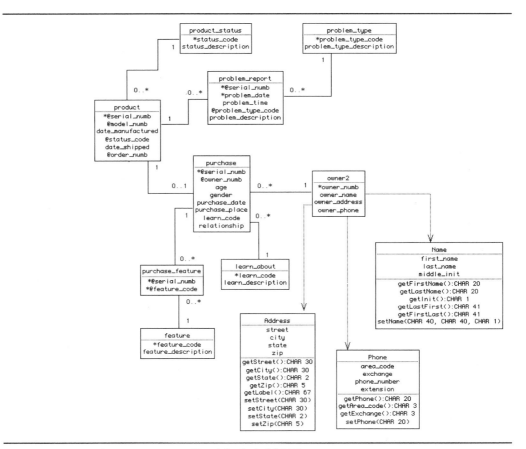

Figure 11-19: Part III of the hybrid ERD

```
problem_type (problem type code, problem_type_description)
```

When you compare the hybrid design with the traditional relational design, you will notice that the hybrid design is smaller. Because multiple values—such as the parts of an address—can now be stored in a single column, the design is somewhat simpler. In addition, because the classes are common enough to appear in several places in the design, code for commonly performed operations can be written once and reused as needed, saving application development time. Therefore, although the design does not take advantage of any of the more sophisticated characteristics of object-orientation, there is still some justification for using objects.

The major drawback to adding objects to this relational design is the need for programmers to complete the objects. You do not need to be a programmer to use SQL to create and manipulate a pure relational schema. However, to complete the hybrid schema and to make the data stored in objects available to users, a programmer must write the code for the LineCost, Name, Address, and Phone class operations.

Creating the Classes

You will find the Oracle SQL syntax for creating MMM's utility classes in Figure 11-20. The most important thing to notice is that these classes do not have the accessor and mutator methods that you might expect to see. This is because Oracle's SQL has been extended to include syntax for manipulating the objects, including inserting, modifying, deleting, and retrieving values. Therefore, other than the initialize method that sets attributes to NULL, you need to include only operations that manipulate the contents of the class in some other way.

```
CREATE TYPE Address AS OBJECT (
    street CHAR (25),
    city CHAR (20),
    state CHAR (2),
    zip CHAR (10),
    MEMBER PROCEDURE initialize );

CREATE TYPE BODY Address AS
    MEMBER PROCEDURE initialize IS
    BEGIN
        street := NULL;
        city := NULL;
        state := NULL;
        zip := NULL;
    END initialize;
END;
```

Figure 11-20 : Oracle syntax for creating utility classes

```
CREATE TYPE Phone AS OBJECT (
    area_code CHAR (6),
    exchange CHAR (6),
    phone_number CHAR (6),
    extension CHAR (5),
    MEMBER PROCEDURE initialize );

CREATE TYPE BODY Phone AS OBJECT
    MEMBER PROCEDURE initialize IS
    BEGIN
        area_code := NULL;
        exchange := NULL;
        phone_number := NULL;
        extension := NULL;
    END initialize;
END;

CREATE TYPE LineCost AS OBJECT (
    quantity_ordered INTEGER,
    cost_each REAL (5,2),
    line_cost REAL (8,2),
    MEMBER PROCEDURE initialize );

CREATE TYPE BODY LineCost AS
    MEMBER PROCEDURE initialize IS
    BEGIN
        quantity_ordered := NULL;
        cost_each := NULL;
        line_cost := NULL;
    END initialize;
END;

CREATE TYPE Name AS OBJECT (
    first_name CHAR (20),
    last_name CHAR (20),
    middle_init CHAR (1),
    MEMBER PROCEDURE initialize );

CREATE TYPE BODY Name AS
    MEMBER PROCEDURE initialize IS
    BEGIN
        first_name := NULL;
        last_name := NULL;
        middle_init = :NULL;
    END initialize;
END;
```

Figure 11-20 (Continued): Oracle syntax for creating utility classes

Using the Classes in the Schema

Once the classes have been declared and implemented, they can be used as data types in table declarations, using standard SQL syntax (see the CREATE TABLE statements in Figure 11-21). As you look through this schema, you will notice that it is only marginally different from a pure relational schema: Some of the user-defined data types may be classes, but they are used in the same way as any other user-defined data type (UDT).

```
CREATE TABLE model
(
    model_numb INTEGER,
    model_description CHAR (40),
    suggested_retail_price DECIMAL (6,2),
    shipping_weight DECIMAL (6,2),
    time_to_manufacture TIME,
    PRIMARY KEY (model_numb)
);

CREATE TABLE test_type
(
    test_code INTEGER,
    test_description CHAR (40),
    PRIMARY KEY (test_code)
);

CREATE TABLE test
(
    model_numb INTEGER,
    test_date DATE,
    test_location CHAR (40),
    test_code INTEGER,
    test_results CHAR (40),
    PRIMARY KEY (model_numb, test_date),
    FOREIGN KEY (model_numb) REFERENCES model,
    FOREIGN KEY (test_code) REFERENCES test_type
);
```

Figure 11-21 :   Oracle schema for the hybrid version of the MMM database

```
CREATE TABLE customer
(
    customer_numb INTEGER,
    customer_name CHAR (40),
    customer_address Address
    contact_person Name,
    contact_phone Phone,
    contact_fax Phone,
    PRIMARY KEY (customer_numb)
);

CREATE TABLE order
(
    order_numb INTEGER,
    customer_numb INTEGER,
    order_date DATE,
    order_total DECIMAL (8,2),
    order_filled CHAR (1),
    PRIMARY KEY (order_numb),
    FOREIGN KEY (customer_numb) REFERENCES customer
);

CREATE TABLE order_line
(
    order_numb INTEGER,
    model_numb INTEGER,
    order_line_cost LineCost,
    all_shipped CHAR (1),
    PRIMARY KEY (order_numb, model_numb),
    FOREIGN KEY (order_numb) REFERENCES order,
    FOREIGN KEY (model_numb) REFERENCES model
);


CREATE TABLE shipment
(
    order_numb INTEGER,
    model_numb INTEGER,
    shipping_date DATE,
    quantity_shipped INTEGER,
    PRIMARY KEY (order_numb, model_numb, shipping_date),
    FOREIGN KEY (order_numb) REFERENCES order_line,
    FOREIGN KEY (model_numb) REFERENCES order_line
);
```

Figure 11-21 (Continued):   Oracle schema for the hybrid version of the MMM

```
CREATE TABLE product
(
    serial_numb INTEGER,
    model_numb INTEGER,
    date_manufactured DATE,
    status_code INTEGER,
    date_shipped DATE,
    order_numb INTEGER,
    PRIMARY KEY (serial_numb),
    FOREIGN KEY (serial_numb) REFERENCES purchase,
    FOREIGN KEY (model_numb) REFERENCES model,
    FOREIGN KEY (status_code) REFERENCES product_status,
    FOREIGN KEY (order_numb) REFERENCES order
);

CREATE TABLE product_status
(
    status_code INTEGER,
    status_description CHAR (40),
    PRIMARY KEY (status_code)
);

CREATE TABLE raw_material
(
    material_id_numb INTEGER,
    material_name CHAR (30),
    unit_of_measurement CHAR (12),
    quantity_in_stock INTEGER,
    reorder_point INTEGER,
    PRIMARY KEY (material_id_numb)
);

CREATE TABLE material_needed
(
    model_numb INTEGER,
    material_id_numb INTEGER,
    quantity_needed INTEGER,
    PRIMARY KEY (model_numb, material_id_numb),
    FOREIGN KEY (model_numb) REFERENCES model,
    FOREIGN KEY (material_id_numb) REFERENCES raw_material
);
```

Figure 11-21 (Continued): Oracle schema for the hybrid version of the MMM

```
CREATE TABLE supplier
(
    supplier_numb INTEGER,
    supplier_name CHAR (40),
    supplier_address Address,
    supplier_contact Phone,
    supplier_phone Phone,
    PRIMARY KEY (supplier_numb)
);

CREATE TABLE material_order
(
    po_numb INTEGER,
    supplier_numb INTEGER,
    material_order_date DATE,
    material_order_total DECIMAL (6,2),
    PRIMARY KEY (po_numb),
    FOREIGN KEY (supplier_numb) REFERENCES supplier
);

CREATE TABLE material_order_line
(
    po_numb INTEGER,
    material_id_numb INTEGER,
    material_line_cost LineCost,
    PRIMARY KEY (po_numb, material_id_numb),
    FOREIGN KEY (po_numb) REFERENCES material_order,
    FOREIGN KEY (material_id_numb) REFERENCES raw_material
);

CREATE TABLE manufacturing_line
(
    line_numb INTEGER,
    line_status CHAR (12),
    PRIMARY KEY (line_numb)
);

CREATE TABLE line_schedule
(
    line_numb INTEGER,
    production_date DECIMAL (6,2)DATE,
    model_numb INTEGER,
    quantity_to_produce INTEGER,
    PRIMARY KEY (line_numb, production_date),
    FOREIGN KEY (line_numb) REFERENCES manufacturing_line,
    FOREIGN KEY (model_numb) REFERENCES model
);
```

Figure 11-21 (Continued):   Oracle schema for the hybrid version of the MMM

```
CREATE TABLE owner
(
    owner_numb INTEGER,
    owner_name Name,
    owner_addres Address,
    owner_phone Phone,
    PRIMARY KEY (owner_numb)
);

CREATE TABLE purchase
(
    serial_numb INTEGER,
    owner_numb INTEGER,
    age INTEGER,
    gender CHAR (1),
    purchase_date DATE,
    purchase_place CHAR (40),
    learn_code INTEGER,
    relationship CHAR (15),
    PRIMARY KEY (serial_numb),
    FOREIGN KEY (serial_numb) REFERENCES product,
    FOREIGN KEY (owner_numb) REFERENCES owner
);

CREATE TABLE feature
(
    feature_code INTEGER,
    feature_description CHAR (40),
    PRIMARY KEY (feature_code)
);

CREATE TABLE purchase_feature
(
    serial_numb INTEGER,
    feature_code INTEGER,
    PRIMARY KEY (serial_numb, feature_code),
    FOREIGN KEY (serial_numb) REFERENCES purchase,
    FOREIGN KEY (feature_code) REFERENCES feature
);

CREATE TABLE learn_about
(
    learn_code INTEGER,
    learn_description CHAR (40),
    serial_numb INTEGER,
    PRIMARY KEY (learn_code),
    FOREIGN KEY (serial_numb) REFERENCES purchase
);
```

Figure 11-21 (Continued): Oracle schema for the hybrid version of the MMM

```
CREATE TABLE problem_type
(
    problem_type_code INTEGER,
    problem_type_description CHAR (30),
    PRIMARY KEY (problem_type_code)
);

CREATE TABLE problem_report
(
    serial_numb INTEGER,
    problem_date DATE,
    problem_time TIME,
    problem_type_code INTEGER,
    problem_description CHAR (40),
    PRIMARY KEY (serial_numb, problem_date),
    FOREIGN KEY (serial_numb) REFERENCES product,
    FOREIGN KEY (problem_type_code) REFERENCES problem_type
);
```

Figure 11-21 (Continued):   **Oracle schema for the hybrid version of the MMM**

12

Database Design Case Study #2: East Coast Aquarium

Many-to-many relationships are often the bane of the relational database designer. Sometimes it is not completely clear that you are dealing with that type of relationship. However, failure to recognize the many-to-many can result in serious data integrity problems.

The organization described in this chapter actually needs two databases, the larger of which is replete with many-to-many relationships. In some cases it will be necessary to create additional entities for composite entities to reference merely to ensure data integrity.

Perhaps the biggest challenge facing a database designer working for East Coast Aquarium is the lack of complete specifications. As you will read, the people who will be using the application programs created to manipulate the aquarium's two new databases have only a general idea of what they need the programs to do. Unlike Mighty-Mite Motors, which had the luxury of working from a large collection of existing forms and documents, East Coast Aquarium has nothing of that sort.

The situation therefore lends itself to a technique known as *prototyping*, in which the designers prepare the user interface of an application program and let the end users evaluate it. Based on user feedback, the designers modify the prototype until the output design matches what the users want. This iterative process helps the end users focus their requirements. The designers also gather the necessary information to create a database design that can provide the outputs the users need. A CASE tool that can model screen forms will therefore be an invaluable tool in preparing the prototype.

Organizational Overview

The East Coast Aquarium is a nonprofit organization dedicated to the study and preservation of marine life. Located on the Atlantic coast in the heart of a major northeastern U.S. city, it provides a wide variety of educational services to the surrounding area. The aquarium is supported by donations, memberships, charges for private functions, gift shop revenues, class fees, and the small admission fees it charges to the public. To help keep costs down, many of the public service jobs (leading tours, staffing the admissions counter, running the gift shop) are handled by volunteers.

The aquarium grounds consist of three buildings: the main facility, a dolphin house, and a marina where the aquarium's research barge is docked.

The centerpiece of the main building is a three-story center tank that is surrounded by a spiral walkway. The sides of the tank are primarily glass, so that visitors can walk around the tank, observing the residents at various depths.

Note: If you happen to recognize the layout of this aquarium, please keep in mind that only the physical structure of the environment is modeled after something that really exists. The way in which the organization functions is purely a product of the author's imagination and no commentary, positive or negative, is intended with regard to the real-world aquarium.

The height of the tank makes it possible to simulate the way in which habitats change as the ocean depth changes. Species that dwell on the ocean floor, coral reef fish, and sand bar dwellers therefore are all housed in the same tank, interacting in much the same way as they would in the ocean.

The remaining space on the first floor of the main building (Figure 12-1) includes the gift shop and a quarantine area for newly arrived animals. The latter area is not accessible to visitors.

The second floor (Figure 12-2) contains a classroom and the volunteers office. Small tanks containing single-habitat exhibits are installed in the outside walls. These provide places to house species that have special habitat requirements or that don't coexist well with other species.

The third floor (Figure 12-3) provides wall space for additional small exhibits. It also houses the aquarium's administrative offices.

East Coast Aquarium has two very different areas in which it needs data management. The first is in the handling of its animals— where they are housed in the aquarium, where they came from, what they are to be fed, problems that occur in the tanks, and so on. The second area concerns the volunteers, including who they are, what they have been trained to do, and when they are scheduled to work. For this particular organization, the two data enviroments are completely separate; they share no data. A database designer who volunteers to work with the aquarium staff will therefore prepare two database designs, one to be used by the volunteer staff in the volunteers office and another to be used by the administrative and animal-care staff through the aquarium grounds.

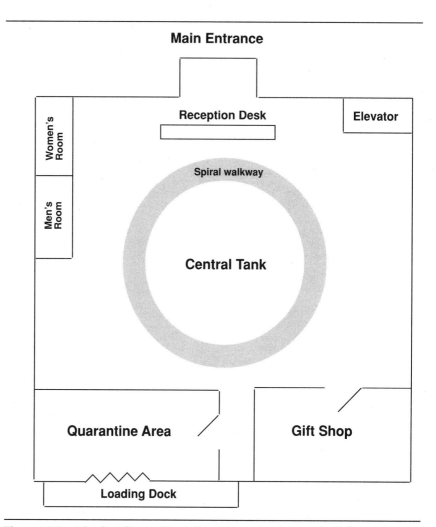

Figure 12-1:   The first floor of East Coast Aquarium's main building

Animal Tracking Needs

Currently, East Coast Aquarium uses a general-purpose PC accounting package to handle its data processing needs. The software takes care of payroll as well as purchasing and the accompanying accounts payable. Because the aquarium is a nonprofit organization, it does not have accounts receivables as does a for-profit business.

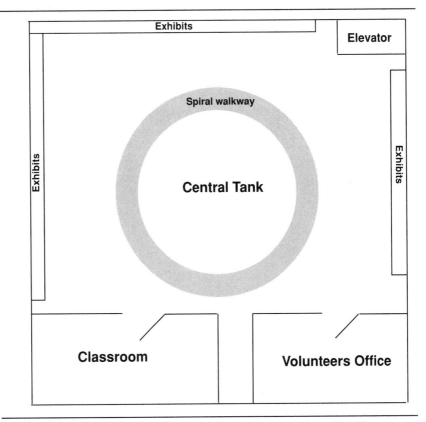

Figure 12-2: The second floor of East Coast Aquarium's main building

Instead, income from the gift shop, admissions, and donations is handled on a cash basis. Grant income is managed by special-purpose software designed to monitor grant awards and how they are spent.

Although the accounting and grant management packages adquately handle the aquarium's finances, there is no data processing that tracks the actual animals housed in the aquarium. The three people in charge of the animals have expressed a need for the following:

> ◆ An "inventory" of which species are living in which locations in the aquarium. Some species can be found in more

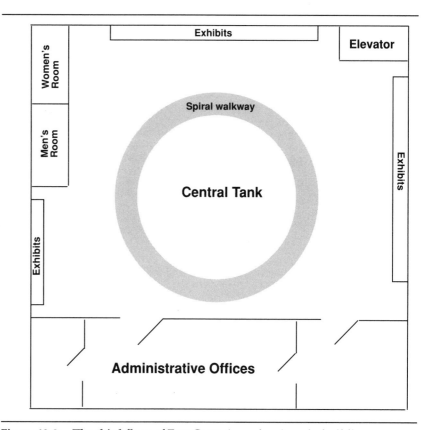

Figure 12-3:   The third floor of East Coast Aquarium's main building

than one tank, and several tanks in addition to the central tank contain more than one species. For larger animals, such as sharks and dolphins, the head animal keeper would like a precise count. However, for small fish that are often eaten by larger fish and that breed in large numbers, only an estimate is possible. The animal handling staff would like to be able to search for information about animals using either the animal's English name or its Latin name.

◆ Data about the foods each species eats, including how much should be fed at what interval. The head animal keeper would like to be able to print out a feeding instruction list every morning to give to staff. In addition, the animal-feeding staff would like to store information about their food inventory. Although the purchasing of food is handled by the administrative office, the head animal keeper would like an application program to decrement the food inventory automatically by the amount fed each day and to generate a tickle report whenever the stock level of a type of food drops below the reorder point. This will make it much easier to ensure that the aquarium does not run short of animal feed.

♦ Data about the sizes, locations, and habitats of the tanks on the aquarium grounds. Some tanks, such as the main tank, contain more than one habitat, and the same habitat can be found in more than one tank.

♦ Data about tank maintenance. Although the main tank is fed directly from the ocean, the smaller tanks around the walls of the main building are closed environments, much like a saltwater aquarium someone might have at home. This means that the pH and salinity of the tanks must be monitored closely. The head animal keeper therefore would like to print out a maintenance schedule each day as well as be able to keep track of what maintenance is actually performed.

♦ Data about the habitats in which a given species can live. When a new species arrives at the aquarium, the staff can use this information to determine which locations could possibly house that species.

♦ Data about where species can be obtained. If the aquarium wants to increase the population of a particular species and the increase cannot be generated through in-house breeding, then the staff would like to know which external supplier can be contacted. Some of the suppliers sell animals; others, such as zoos or other aquariums, will trade or donate animals.

♦ Problems that arise in the tanks. When animals become ill, the veterinarian wants to be able to view a history of both the animal and the tank in which it is currently living.

♦ Data about orders placed for animals and, in particular, the shipments in which animals arrive. Since any financial arrangements involved in securing animals are handled by the administrative office, these data indicate only how many individuals of each species are included on a given order or shipment.

The shipment and problem data are particularly important to the aquarium. When animals first arrive, they are not placed immediately into the general population. Instead, they are held in special tanks in the quarantine area at the rear of the aquarium's first floor. The length of the quarantine is determined by the species.

After the quarantine period has passed and the animals are declared disease free, they can be placed on exhibit in the main portion of the aquarium. Nonetheless, animals do become ill after they have been released from quarantine. It is therefore essential that records are kept of the sources of animals so that patterns of illness can be tracked back to specific suppliers, if such patterns appear. By the same token, patterns of illnesses in various species housed in the same tank can be an indication of serious problems with the environment in the tank.

The Volunteer Organization

The volunteer organization (the Friends of the Aquarium) is totally separate from the financial and animal-handling areas of the aquarium. Volunteers perform tasks that do not involve direct contact with animals, such as leading tours, manning the admissions desk, and running the gift shop. The aquarium has provided office space and a telephone line for the volunteer coordinator and her staff. Beyond that, the Friends of the Aquarium organization has been on its own to secure office furniture and equipment.

The recent donation of a PC now makes it possible for the volunteers to automate some of their scheduling. Currently, the scheduling processing works in the following way:

> ♦ The person on duty in the volunteers office receives requests for volunteer services from the aquarium's administrative office. Some of the jobs are regularly scheduled

(for example, staffing the gift shop and the admissions desk). Others are ad hoc, such as the request by a school-teacher to bring a class of children for a tour.

♦ The volunteer doing the scheduling checks the list of volunteers to see who is trained to do the job requested. Each volunteer's information is recorded on an index card, along with the volunteer's skills. A skill is a general expression of something the volunteer knows how to do, such as lead a tour for elementary school children. The volunteer's information also includes an indication of when that person is available to work.

♦ The volunteer doing the scheduling separates the cards for those people who have the required skill and have indicated that they are available at the required time. Most volunteers work on a regularly scheduled basis either at the admissions desk or in the gift shop. However, for ad hoc jobs, the person doing the scheduling must start making telephone calls until someone who is willing and able to do the job is found.

♦ The volunteer is scheduled for the job by writing in the master schedule notebook. As far as the volunteer coordinator is concerned, a job is an application of a skill. Therefore, a skill is knowing how to lead a tour for elementary school students, while a job that applies that skill is leading a tour of Mrs. Brown's third graders at 10 AM on Thursday.

One of the things that is very difficult to do with the current scheduling process is to keep track of the work record of each individual volunteer. The aquarium holds a volunteer recognition luncheon once a year, and the volunteer organization would like to find an easy way to identify volunteers who have put in an extra effort so that they can be recognized at that event. In contrast, the volunteer organization would also like to be able to identify volunteers who rarely participate —the people who stay on the volunteer rolls only to get free admission to the aquarium—as well as people who make commitments to work but do not show up. (The latter are actually far more of a problem than the former.)

The Volunteers Database

In terms of scope, the volunteers database is considerably smaller than the animal tracking database. It therefore makes sense to tackle the smaller project first. The database designers will create the application prototype and review it with the users. When the users are satisfied and the designers feel they have enough detailed information to actually design a database, they will move on to the more traditional steps of creating an ER diagram, tables, and SQL statements.

> Note: As you will see, there is a lot involved in creating a prototype. It requires very detailed intensive work and produces a significant number of diagrams. We will therefore look at the volunteers prototype in full, but in the interest of length we will look at only selected aspects of the animal tracking prototype.

Creating the Application Prototype

Given that the specifications of the database are rather general, the first step is to create a prototype of an application program interface. It begins with the opening screen and its main menu bar (Figure 12-4). As you can see, when in browse mode, the CASE tool allows users and designers to pull down the menus in the menu bar.

The complete menu tree (with the exception of the Help menu, whose contents are determined by the user interface guidelines of the operating system on which the application is running) can be found in Figure 12-5. Looking at the menu options, users can see that their basic requirements have been fulfilled. The details, however, must be specified by providing users with specific output designs.

Each menu option in the prototype's main menu has therefore been linked to a screen form. For example, to modify or delete a volunteer, a user must first *find* the volunteer's data. Therefore the Modify or Delete a Volunteer menu option leads to a dialog box that allows

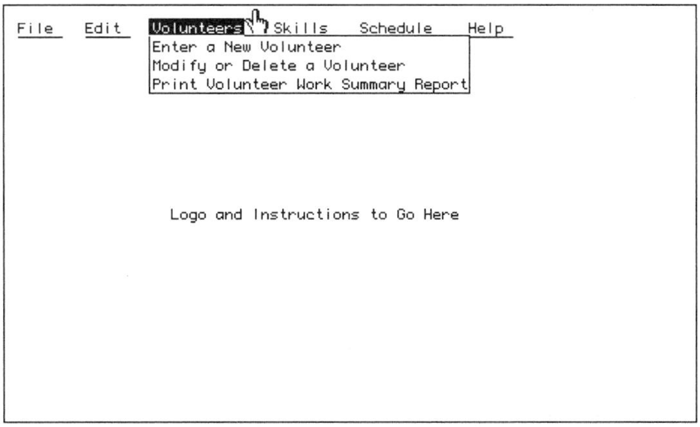

```
        File    Edit    Volunteers    Skills    Schedule    Help
                        Enter a New Volunteer
                        Modify or Delete a Volunteer
                        Print Volunteer Work Summary Report




                         Logo and Instructions to Go Here
```

Figure 12-4:   Main menu prototype for the volunteers application

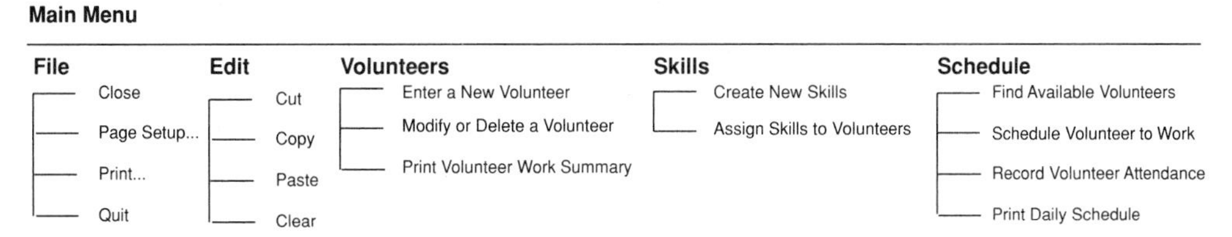

Main Menu

File	**Edit**	**Volunteers**	**Skills**	**Schedule**
Close	Cut	Enter a New Volunteer	Create New Skills	Find Available Volunteers
Page Setup...	Copy	Modify or Delete a Volunteer	Assign Skills to Volunteers	Schedule Volunteer to Work
Print...	Paste	Print Volunteer Work Summary		Record Volunteer Attendance
Quit	Clear			Print Daily Schedule

Figure 12-5:   Menu tree of the volunteers database prototype application

the user either to enter a volunteer number or to select a volunteer by name and phone number from a list (Figure 12-6). With the prototype, clicking the Find button opens the modify–delete form (Figure 12-7). Users can click in the data entry fields and tab between them, but the buttons at the right of the window are not functional.

While in browse mode, the CASE tool presents a form as it would appear to the user. However, in design mode, a database designer can see the names of the fields on the form (for example, Figure 12-8). These field names will ultimately guide the design of the database.

In the case of the volunteer data, it is apparent to the designers that there are at least two entities (and perhaps three) involved with the data that describe a volunteer. The first entity is represented by the

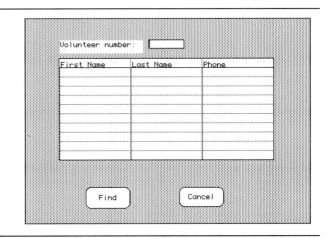

Figure 12-6:   Prototype of a dialog box for finding a volunteer for modification

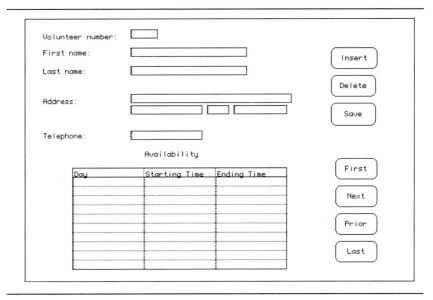

Figure 12-7:   Prototype of a form for modifying and deleting a volunteer

single-valued fields occupying the top half of the form (volunteer number, first name, last name, street, city, state, zip, and phone). However, the availability data—day of the week, starting time, and ending time—are multivalued and therefore must be given an entity of their own. This also implies that there will be a one-to-many

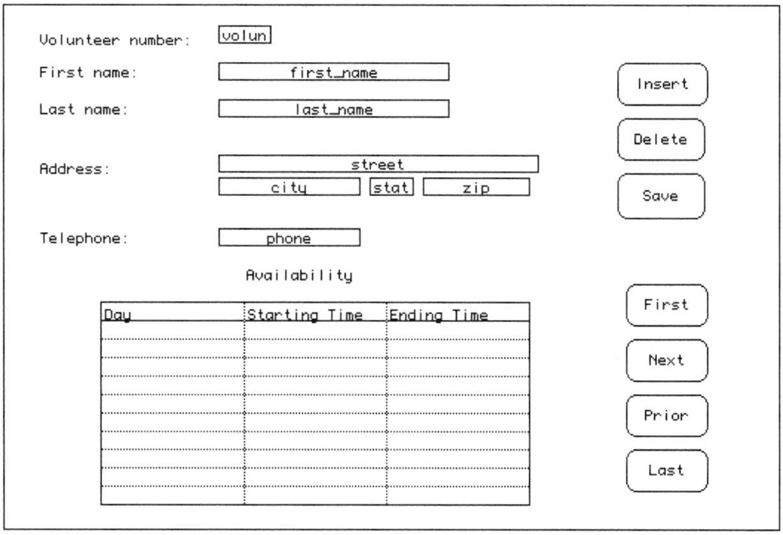

Figure 12-8: **Prototype data modification form showing field names**

relationship between a volunteer and a period of time during which he or she is available.

> *Note: Should you choose, the field names on a screen prototype can become part of the data dictionary. However, if the field names do not ultimately correspond to column names, their inclusion may add unnecessary complexity to the data dictionary.*

The remainder of the prototype application and its forms are designed and analyzed in a similar way:

♦ The volunteer work summary report has been designed to let the user enter a range of dates that the report will cover (see Figure 12-9). The report itself (Figure 12-10) is a control-break report that displays the work performed by each volunteer along with the total hours worked and the number of times the volunteer was a "no show." The latter number was included because the volunteer coordinator had indicated that it was extremely important to know which volunteers consistently signed up to work and then didn't report when scheduled.

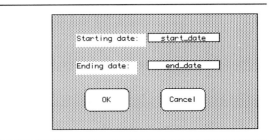

Figure 12-9:   A dialog box layout for entering dates for the work summary report

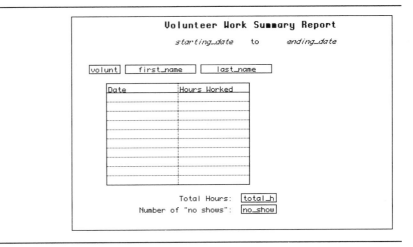

Figure 12-10:   Prototype layout for the work summary report

The need to report the "no shows" tells the designers that the schedule table needs to include a boolean column that indicates whether a person showed up for a scheduled shift. The report layout also includes some computed fields (total hours worked and number of no shows) that contain data that do not need to be stored but can be generated when the report is displayed.

♦ Entering a new skill into the master list of skills requires only a simple form (Figure 12-11). The end user sees only the description of a skill. However, the database designers know that the best way to handle unstructured blocks of text is to assign each description a skill number, which can then be used as a foreign key throughout the database. Users, however, do not necessarily need to know that a skill number is being used; they will always see just the text descriptions.

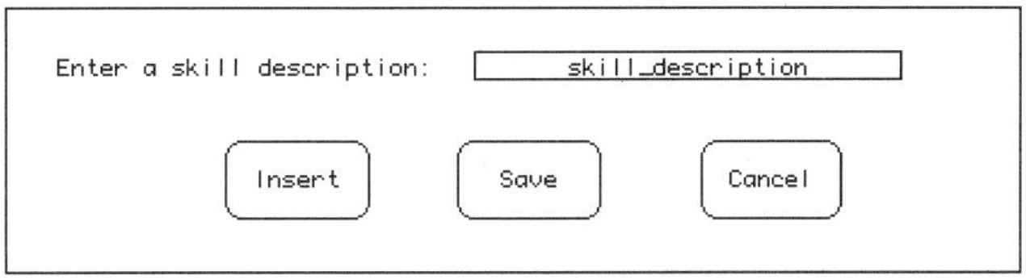

Figure 12-11:   Entering a new skill

♦ To assign skills to a volunteer, the end user must first find the volunteer. The application can therefore use a copy of the dialog box in Figure 12-6. In this case, however, the Find button leads to the form in Figure 12-12.

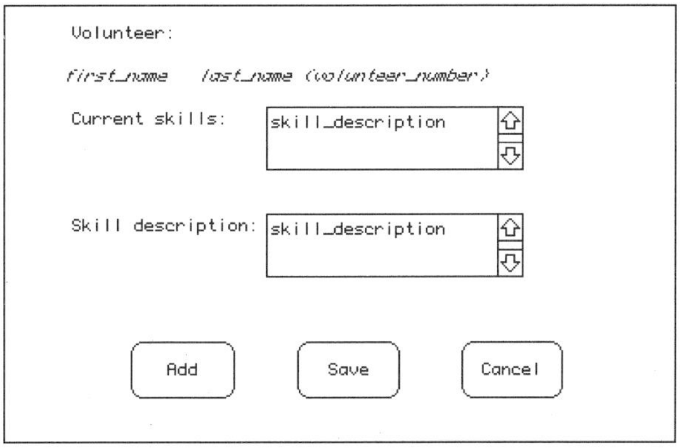

Figure 12-12:   Assigning skills to a volunteer

A database designer will quickly recognize that there is a many-to-many relationship between a skill and a volunteer. There are actually three entities behind Figure 12-12: the skill, the volunteer, and the composite entity that represents the relationship between the two. The skill entry form displays data from the volunteer entity at the top, data from the composite entity in the current skills list, and all skills not assigned from the skills table in the skill description list. Of course, the actual foreign key used in the composite entity is a skill number, but the user sees only the result of a join back to the skills table that retrieves the skill description.

> *Note: Database integrity constraints will certainly prevent anyone from assigning the same skill twice to the same volunteer. However, it is easier if the user can see currently assigned skills. Then, the application can restrict what appears in the skill description list to all skills not assigned to that volunteer. In this case, it is a matter of user interface design rather than database design.*

♦ To find the volunteers available to perform a specific job, the volunteers application needs a form something like Figure 12-13. The end user enters the date and time of the job and chooses the skill required by the job. Clicking the Search button fills in the table at the bottom of the form with the names and phone numbers of volunteers who are theoretically available.

Of all the outputs produced by this application, finding available volunteers is probably the most difficult to implement. The application program must not only work with overlapping intervals of time but also consider both when a volunteer indicates he or she will be available and when a volunteer is already scheduled to work. In most cases, however, a database designer does not have to write the application program code. The designer needs only to ensure that the data necessary to produce the output are present in the database.

> *Note: A smart database designer, however, would discuss any output that involves evaluating overlapping time intervals with application programmers to ensure that the output is feasible. There is no point in specifying infeasible output.*

♦ Once the person doing the volunteer scheduling has located a volunteer to fill a specific job, then the volunteer's

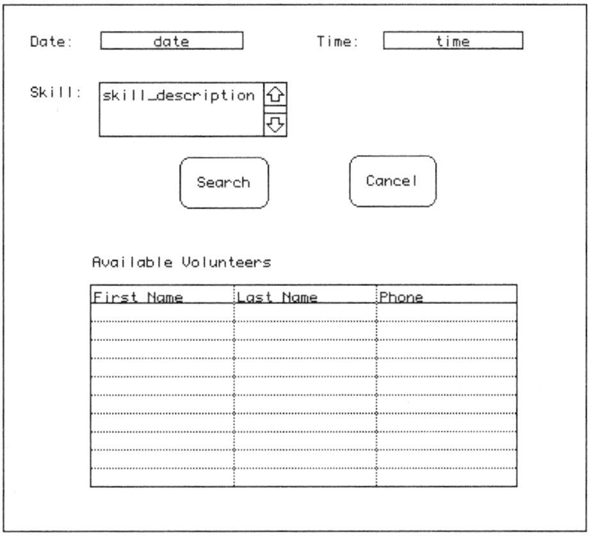

Figure 12-13: **Finding available volunteers**

commitment to work needs to become a part of the database. The process begins by presenting the user with a Find Volunteer dialog box like that in Figure 12-6. In this case, the Find button is linked to the Schedule Volunteer window (Figure 12-14). A database designer will recognize that this is not all the data that needs to be stored about a job, however. In particular, someone will need to record whether the volunteer actually appeared to do the scheduled job on the day of the job; this cannot be done when the job is scheduled initially.

♦ To record attendance, an end user first locates the volunteer using a Find Volunteer dialog box (Figure 12-6), which then leads to a display of the jobs the volunteer has been scheduled to work in reverse chronological order (see Figure 12-15). For those jobs that have not been worked, the End Time and Worked? columns will be empty. The user can then scroll the list to find the job to be modified and enter values for the two empty columns. The fields on this form, plus those on the job scheduling

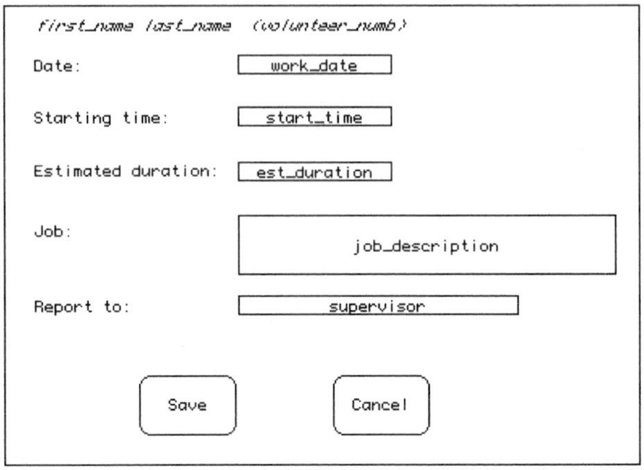

Figure 12-14:   Scheduling a volunteer to perform a job

form, represent the attributes that will describe the job entity.

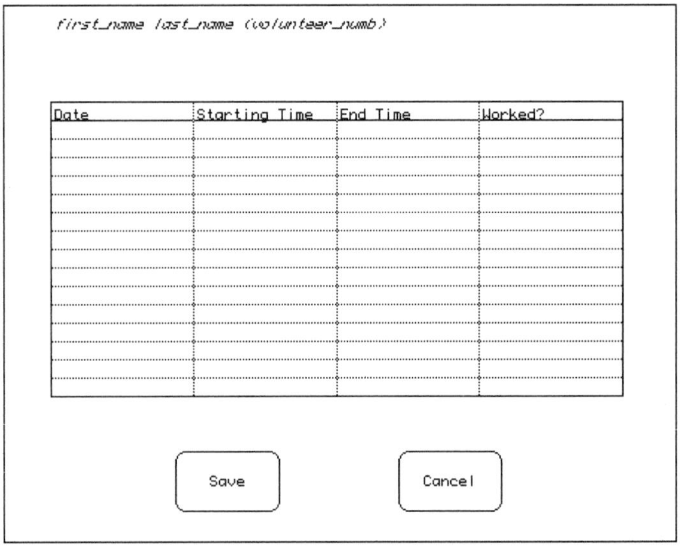

Figure 12-15:   Recording jobs worked

♦ To print a daily schedule, an end user first uses a dialog box to indicate the date for which a schedule should be displayed (Figure 12-16). The application program then assembles the report (Figure 12-17). To simplify working with the program, the application developers should probably allow users to double-click on any line in the listing to open the form in Figure 12-15 for the scheduled volunteer. However, this capability has no impact on the database design.

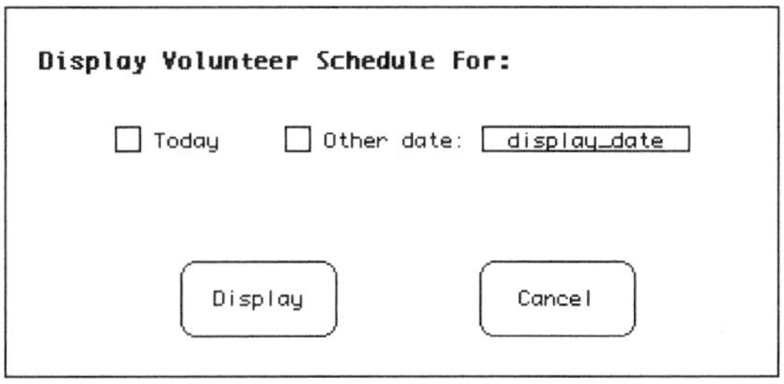

Figure 12-16:   Choosing a date for schedule display

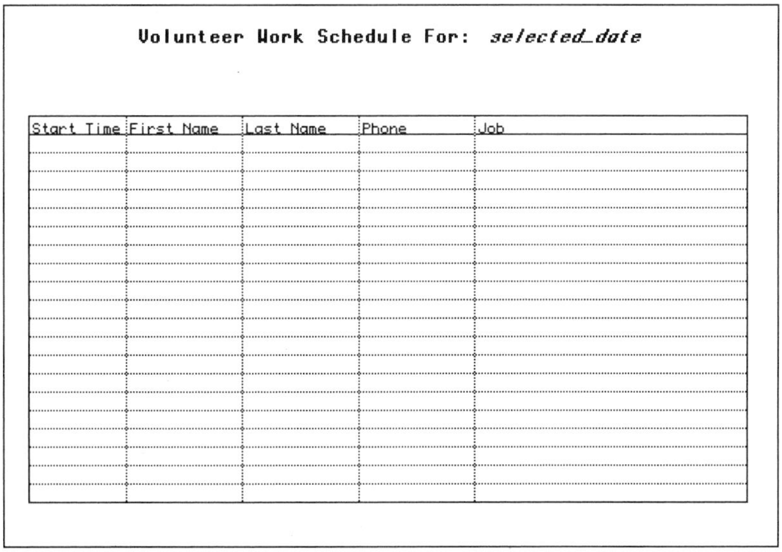

Figure 12-17:   Volunteer work schedule

Creating the ER Diagram

From the approved prototype of the application design, the database designers can gather enough information to create a basic ER diagram for the volunteers organization. The designers examine each screen form carefully to ensure that the database design provides the attributes and relationships necessary to generate the output.

Although the application prototype consumes many screen forms, the underlying database design is surprisingly simple. The complete ER diagram can be found in Figure 12-18. The Skills Known entity serves as a composite entity between Volunteer and Skill. Given that there is no direct relationship between a skill and a job, then scheduling data (the Job entity) is related to the volunteer entity in a simple one-to-many relationship. The same is true of the availability data.

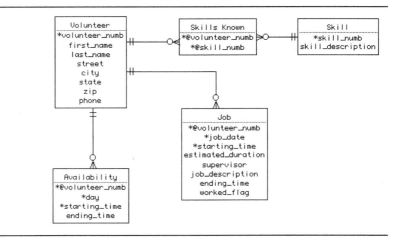

Figure 12-18:   ER diagram for the volunteers database

Designing the Tables

The ER diagram in Figure 12-18 produces the following tables:

```
Volunteer (volunteer numb, first_name, last_name, street, city,
     state, zip, phone)
Availability (volunteer_numb, day, starting_time, ending_time)
```

```
Job (volunteer_numb, job_date, starting_time, estimated_duration,
     supervisor, job_description, ending_time, worked_flag)
Skill (skill_numb, skill_description)
Skills_known (volunteer_numb, skill_numb)
```

The Job table presents a question that must be answered before a correct primary key can be chosen. In particular, can a volunteer perform more than one job on a single day? If so, then the starting time must be concatenated with the volunteer number and the job date to form a unique primary key. However, if volunteers are limited to only one job in a given day, then the starting time does not need to be part of the key.

Generating the SQL

The five tables that make up the volunteers database can be created with the SQL in Figure 12-19. Notice that some of the attributes in the Volunteer table have been specified as NOT NULL. This constraint ensures that at least a name and phone number are available for each volunteer.

> Note: The domain of INTERVAL was introduced with the SQL-92 standard and may not be available with all of today's DBMSs. When INTERVALS are not available, you can store the duration of an event as an integer (number of minutes) that can later be added to a starting time.

The Animal Tracking Database

The animal tracking database is considerably larger than the volunteers database. The application that will manipulate that database therefore is concomitantly larger, as demonstrated by the menu tree in Figure 12-20. (The File and Edit menus have been left off so that the diagram will fit across the width of the page. However, they are intended to be the first and second menus from the left, respectively. A Help menu can also be added along the right edge.)

```
CREATE TABLE volunteer
(
    volunteer_numb INT,
    first_name CHAR (15) NOT NULL,
    last_name CHAR (15) NOT NULL,
    street CHAR (30),
    city CHAR (15),
    state CHAR (2),
    zip CHAR (5),
    phone CHAR (12) NOT NULL,
    PRIMARY KEY (volunteer_numb) );

CREATE TABLE availability
(
    volunteer_numb INT,
    day CHAR (10),
    starting_time TIME,
    ending_time TIME,
    PRIMARY KEY (volunteer_numb, day, starting_time),
    FOREIGN KEY (volunteer_numb) REFERENCES volunteer );

CREATE TABLE skill
(
    skill_numb INT,
    skill_description CHAR (30),
    PRIMARY KEY (skill_numb) );

CREATE TABLE skills_known
(
    volunteer_numb INT,
    skill_numb INT,
    PRIMARY KEY (volunteer_numb, skill_numb),
    FOREIGN KEY (volunteer_numb) REFERENCES volunteer,
    FOREIGN KEY (skill_numb) REFERENCES skill );

CREATE TABLE Job
(
    volunteer_numb INT,
    job_date DATE,
    starting_time TIME,
    estimated_duration INTERVAL,
    supervisor CHAR (30),
    job_description CHAR (255),
    ending_time TIME,
    worked_flag CHAR (1),
    PRIMARY KEY (volunteer_numb, job_date, starting_time),
    FOREIGN KEY (volunteer_numb) REFERENCES volunteer );
```

Figure 12-19:   SQL statements needed to create the tables for the volunteers database

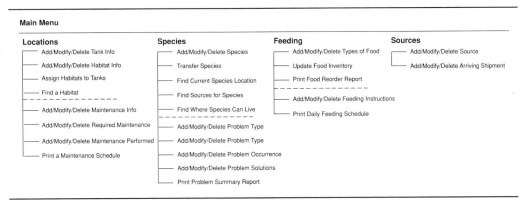

Figure 12-20: Menu tree for the animal tracking database

The functionality requested by the animal handlers falls generally into four categories: the locations (the tanks) and their habitats, the species, the food, and the sources for animals. The organization of the application interface was therefore guided by those groupings.

Highlights of the Application Prototype

The screen and report layouts designed for the animal tracking application provide a good starting place for the database designers to identify the entities and attributes needed in the database. As with the volunteers application, there is not necessarily a one-to-one correspondence between an entity and an output.

> *Note: One of the common mistakes novices make when designing the interfaces of database application programs is to use one data entry form per table. Users do not look at their environment in the same way as a database designer, however, and often the organization imposed by tables does not make sense to the users. Another benefit of prototype is therefore that it forces database and application designers to adapt to what the users really need, rather than the other way around.*

Food Management

One of the important functions mentioned by the aquarium's animal handlers was management of the animal feeding schedule and the food inventory. First, they wanted a daily feeding schedule, such as that in Figure 12-21. Knowing that each species can eat many types of food and that a type of food can be eaten by many species, a database designer realizes that there are at least four entities behind the sample output:

- ◆ An entity that indicates which species lives in which tank (a composite entity between the tank and species entities)
- ◆ An entity describing a type of food
- ◆ An entity describing a species
- ◆ An entity that indicates which species eats which food and how often that food should be fed (a composite entity between the food and species entities)

Food inventory management—although it sounds like a separate function to the animal handlers—actually requires nothing more than the food entity. The food entity needs to store data about how

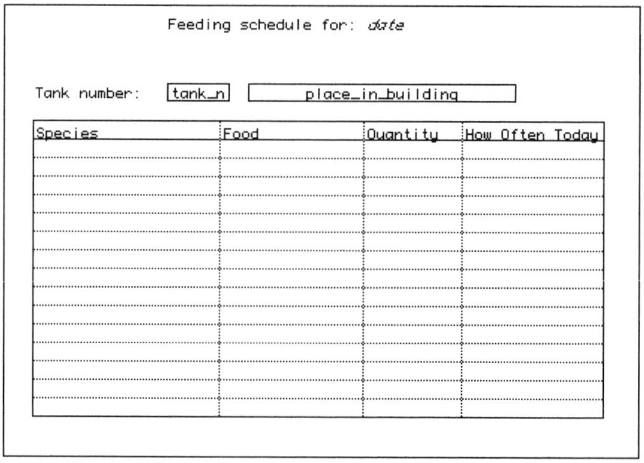

Figure 12-21:   Daily feeding schedule

much food is currently in stock and a reorder point. The application program can take care of decrementing how much has been fed when the animal handlers run the Update Food Inventory function.

Handling Arriving Animals

When a shipment arrives at the aquarium, animal handlers first check the contents of the shipment against the shipment's paperwork. They then take the animals and place them in the aquarium's quarantine area. The data entry form that the animal handlers will use to store data about arrivals therefore includes a place for entering an identifier for the tank in which the new animals have been placed (Figure 12-22). Given that the aquarium staff needs to be able to locate animals at any time, this suggests that the quarantine tanks should be handled no differently from the exhibit tanks and that there is only one entity for a tank.

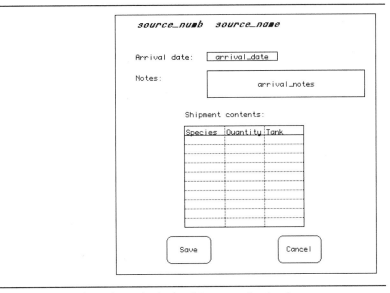

Figure 12-22:   Recording the arrival of a shipment of animals

After the quarantine period has expired and the animals are certified as healthy, they can be transferred to another location in the building. This means an application program must delete the species from their current tank (regardless of whether it is a quarantine tank or an exhibit tank) and insert data for the new tank. The screen form (Figure 12-23) therefore lets the user identify the species and its current location using popup menus. The user also uses a popup menu to indicate the new location. To a database designer, this translates into the deletion of one row from a table—a table representing a composite entity between tank and species entities—and an insertion of a new row. All the database design needs to do, however, is provide the table; the application program will take care of managing the data modification.

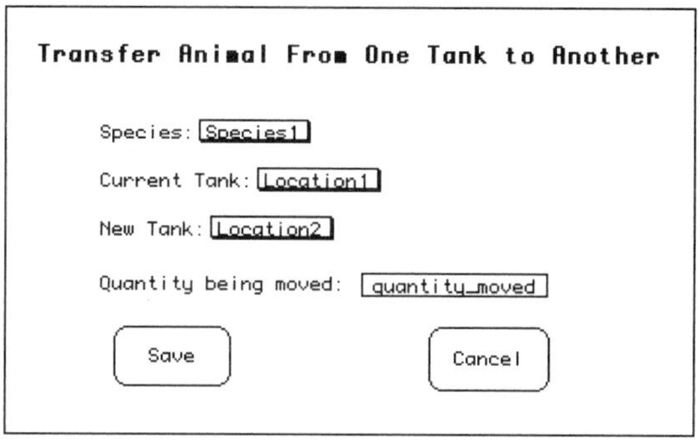

Figure 12-23:   Moving a species between tanks

Problem Analysis

The health of the animals in the aquarium is a primary concern of the animal handlers. They are therefore anxious to be able to analyze the problems that occur in the tanks for patterns. Perhaps a single species is experiencing more problems than any other; perhaps an animal handler is not paying as much attention to the condition of the tanks for which he or she is responsible.

The animal handlers want the information in Figure 12-24 included in the problem summary report. What cannot be seen from the sample screen created by the CASE tool is that the data will appear in a control-break layout. For example, each tank number will appear only once; each species will appear once for each tank in which it was the victim of a problem. By the same token, each type of problem will appear once for each tank and species it affected. Only the problem solutions will contain data for every row in the sample output table.

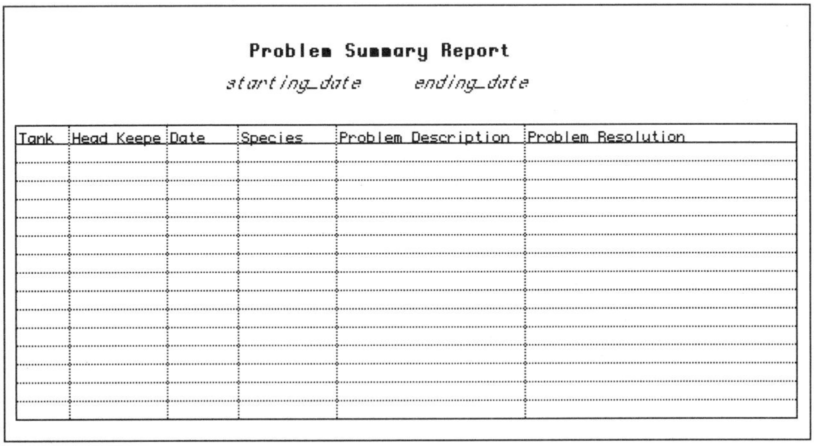
Problem Summary Report

starting_date *ending_date*

Tank	Head Keepe	Date	Species	Problem Description	Problem Resolution

Figure 12-24: Problem summary report

To a database designer, the form in Figure 12-24 suggests the need for five entities:

- The species
- The tank
- The type of problem
- A problem occurrence (a type of problem occurring in one tank and involving one species)
- A problem solution (a solution that has been tried for one problem occurrence). There may be many solutions to a single problem occurrence.

One of the best ways to handle problems is to avoid them. For this reason, the animal handlers also want to include maintenance data in their database. To make data entry simpler for the end users, the form for entering required maintenance (Figure 12-25) allows a user to select a tank and then enter as many maintenance activities as needed.

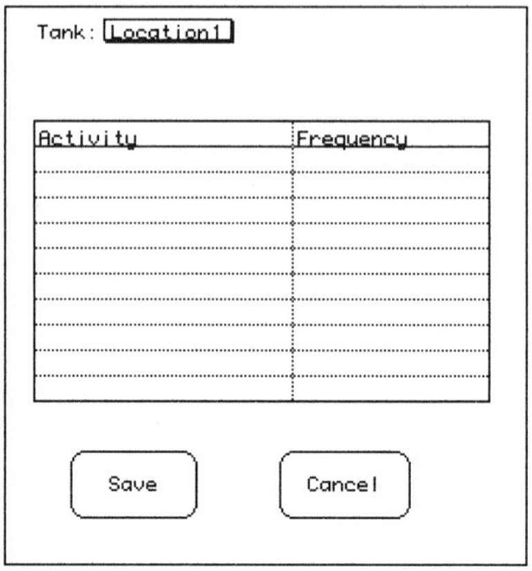

Figure 12-25:   Entering required maintenance

A database designer views such a form as requiring three entities: the tank, the maintenance activity, and the maintenance required for the tank (a composite entity between the tank and maintenance activity entities).

Creating the ER Diagram

After refining the entire application prototype, the database designers for the East Coast Aquarium generate a large interconnected ER diagram. (Part I can be found in Figure 12-26; part II appears in Figure 12-27.) As you can see when examining both diagrams, the centerpiece is the Species entity, which participates in six different relationships.

There are at least 10 many-to-many relationships represented by this design:

- ◆ Species to Location
- ◆ Location to Habitat
- ◆ Species to Habitat
- ◆ Location to Maintenance Activity for required maintenance
- ◆ Location to Maintenance Activity for maintenance performed

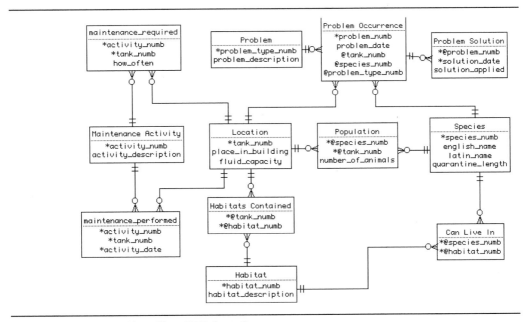

Figure 12-26: **Animal handling ERD (part I)**

♦ Location to Problem
♦ Species to Problem
♦ Species to Food
♦ Species to Source for ability of source to supply the species
♦ Shipment to Species

The relationships involving Location, Problem, and Species are particularly interesting. On the surface, there appears to be a many-to-many relationship between a tank and a type of problem. By the same token, there appears to be another many-to-many relationship between a species and a type of problem. The problem is that if the database maintains the two separate relationships, each with its own individual composite entity, then it will be impossible to determine which species was affected by which problem in which tank. To resolve the issue, the design uses a three-way composite entity—Problem Occurrence—that relates three parent entities (Location, Problem, and Species) rather than just the traditional two. Semantically, a problem occurrence is one type of problem affecting one

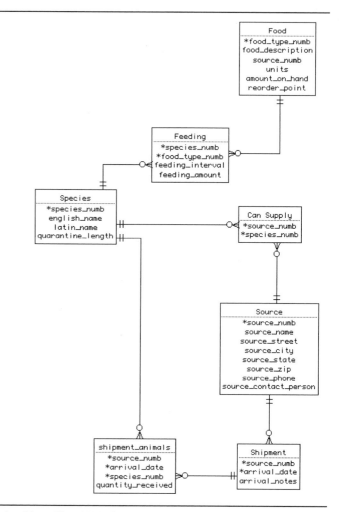

Figure 12-27:   Animal handling ERD (part II)

species in one location and therefore identifying it in the database requires all three parent entities.

In contrast, why is there no three-way composite entity between Species, Location, and Habitat? As with the preceding example, there is a many-to-many relationship between Species and Location and a many-to-many relationship between Habitat and Location. The answer once again lies in the meaning of the relationships.

Were we to create a single composite entity relating all three entities, we would be asserting that a given species lives in a given habitat in a given location. However, the animal handlers at the aquarium know that this type of data is not valid, particularly because if an animal lives in a tank with many habitats, the animal may move between multiple habitats. Instead, the relationship between Species and Habitat indicates all habitats in which a species can live successfully; the relationship between Location and Habitat indicates the habitats provided by a tank.

The remainder of the many-to-many relationships are the typical two-parent relationships that you have been seeing throughout this book. The only aspect of these relationships that is the least bit unusual is the two relationships between Maintenance Activity and Location. Each relationship has a different meaning (scheduled maintenance versus maintenance actually performed). Therefore, the design must include two composite entities, one to represent the meaning of each individual relationship.

> Note: There is no theoretical restriction to the number of relationships that can exist between the same parent entities. As long as each relationship has a different meaning, then there is usually justification for including all of them in a database design.

Creating the Tables

The ER diagrams translate to the following tables:

```
species (species_numb, english_name, latin_name, quarantine_length)
location (tank_numb, place_in_building, fluid_capacity)
population (species_numb, tank_numb, number_of_animals)
habitat (habitat_numb, habitat_description)
can_live_in (species_numb, habitat_numb)
habitats_contained (tank_numb, habitat_numb)
problem (problem_type_numb, problem_description)
problem_occurrence (problem_numb, problem_date, tank_numb,
    species_numb, problem_type_numb)
problem_solution (problem_numb, solution_date, solution_applied)
source (source_numb, source_name, source_street, source_city,
    source_state, source_zip, source_phone, source_contact_person)
can_supply (source_numb, species_numb)
shipment (source_numb, shipment_date, arrival_notes)
```

```
shipment_animals (source numb, arrival date, species numb,
    quantity_received)
food (food type numb, food_description, source_numb, units,
    amount_on_hand, reorder_point)
feeding (species numb, food type numb, feeding_interval,
    feeding_amount)
maintenance_activity (activity numb, activity_description)
maintenance_required (activity numb, tank numb, how_often)
maintenance_performed (activity numb, tank numb, activity_date)
```

Choosing a primary key for the problem occurrence table presents a bit of a dilemma. Given that a problem occurrence represents a relationship between a problem type, tank, and species, the theoretically appropriate primary key is a concatenation of the problem type number, tank number, species number, and the date of the problem. However, this is an extremely awkward primary key to use as a foreign key in the Problem Solution table. Although it is unusual to give composite entities arbitrary unique identifiers, in this case it makes good practical sense.

There are several tables in this design that are "all key" (made up of nothing but the primary key). According to the CASE tool used to draw the ER diagram, this represents an error in the design. However, there is nothing in relational database theory that states that all-key relations are not allowed. In fact, they are rather common when they are needed to represent a many-to-many relationship that has no accompanying relationship data.

Generating the SQL

The SQL CREATE statements that generate the animal tracking database for East Coast Aquarium can be found in Figure 12-28. Because of the large number of composite entities, there are also a large number of foreign keys. Other than that, the SQL presents no unusual features.

```
CREATE TABLE species
(
    species_numb INT,
    english_name CHAR (100),
    latin_name CHAR (100),
    quarantine_length INT,
    PRIMARY KEY (species_numb) );

CREATE TABLE location
(
    tank_numb INT,
    place_in_building CHAR (30),
    fluid_capacity DECIMAL (9,2),
    PRIMARY KEY (tank_numb) );

CREATE TABLE can_live_in
(
    species_numb INT,
    habitat_numb INT,
    PRIMARY KEY (species_numb, habitat_numb),
    FOREIGN KEY (species_numb) REFERENCES species,
    FOREIGN KEY (habitat_numb) REFERENCES habitat );

CREATE TABLE population
(
    species_numb INT,
    tank_numb INT,
    number_of_animals INT,
    PRIMARY KEY (species_numb, tank_numb),
    FOREIGN KEY (species_numb) REFERENCES species,
    FOREIGN KEY (tank_numb) REFERENCES location );

CREATE TABLE habitat
(
    habitat_numb INT,
    habitat_description CHAR (100),
    PRIMARY KEY (habitat_numb) );

CREATE TABLE problem
(
    problem_type_numb INT,
    problem_description CHAR (100),
    PRIMARY KEY (problem_type_numb) );
```

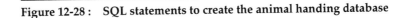

Figure 12-28 : SQL statements to create the animal handing database

```
CREATE TABLE problem_occurrence
(
    problem_numb INT,
    problem_date DATE,
    tank_numb INT,
    species_numb INT,
    problem_type_numb INT,
    PRIMARY KEY (problem_numb),
    FOREIGN KEY (tank_numb) REFERENCES location,
    FOREIGN KEY (species_numb) REFERENCES species,
    FOREIGN KEY (problem_type_numb) REFERENCES problem );

CREATE TABLE problem_solution
(
    problem_numb INT,
    solution_date DATE,
    solution_applied CHAR (100),
    PRIMARY KEY (problem_numb, solution_date),
    FOREIGN KEY (problem_numb) REFERENCES problem_occurrence );

CREATE TABLE source
(
    source_numb INT,
    source_name CHAR (30),
    source_street CHAR (30),
    source_city CHAR (30),
    source_state CHAR (2),
    source_zip CHAR (5),
    source_phone CHAR (12),
    source_contact_person CHAR (30),
    PRIMARY KEY (source_numb) );

CREATE TABLE shipment
(
    source_numb INT,
    arrival_date DATE,
    arrival_notes CHAR (255),
    PRIMARY KEY (source_numb, arrival_date),
    FOREIGN KEY (source_numb) REFERENCES source );

CREATE TABLE can_supply
(
    source_numb INT,
    species_numb INT,
    PRIMARY KEY (source_numb, species_numb),
    FOREIGN KEY (source_numb) REFERENCES source,
    FOREIGN KEY (species_numb) REFERENCES species );
```

Figure 12-28 (Continued):   **SQL statements to create the animal handing database**

```
CREATE TABLE shipment_animals
(
    source_numb INT,
    arrival_date DATE,
    species_numb INT,
    quantity_received INT,
    PRIMARY KEY (source_numb, arrival_date, species_numb),
    FOREIGN KEY (source_numb) REFERENCES shipment,
    FOREIGN KEY (arrival_date) REFERENCES shipment,
    FOREIGN KEY (species_numb) REFERENCES species );

CREATE TABLE food
(
    food_type_numb INT,
    food_description CHAR (30),
    source_numb INT,
    units CHAR (15),
    amount_on_hand INT,
    reorder_point INT,
    PRIMARY KEY (food_type_numb) );

CREATE TABLE feeding
(
    species_numb INT,
    food_type_numb INT,
    feeding_interval CHAR (15),
    feeding_amount CHAR (15),
    PRIMARY KEY (species_numb, food_type_numb),
    FOREIGN KEY (species_numb) REFERENCES species,
    FOREIGN KEY (food_type_numb) REFERENCES food );

CREATE TABLE habitats_contained
(
    tank_numb INT,
    habitat_numb INT,
    PRIMARY KEY (tank_numb, habitat_numb),
    FOREIGN KEY (tank_numb) REFERENCES location,
    FOREIGN KEY (habitat_numb) REFERENCES habitat );

CREATE TABLE maintenance_activity
(
    activity_numb INT,
    activity_description CHAR (30),
    PRIMARY KEY (activity_numb) );
```

Figure 12-28 (Continued): SQL statements to create the animal handing database

```
CREATE TABLE maintenance_required
(
    activity_numb INT,
    tank_numb INT,
    how_often INTERVAL,
    PRIMARY KEY (activity_numb, tank_numb),
    FOREIGN KEY (activity_numb) REFERENCES maintenance_activity,
    FOREIGN KEY (tank_numb) REFERENCES location
);

CREATE TABLE maintenance_performed
(
    activity_numb INT,
    tank_numb INT,
    activity_date DATE,
    PRIMARY KEY (activity_numb, tank_numb, activity_date),
    FOREIGN KEY (activity_numb) REFERENCES maintenance_activity,
    FOREIGN KEY (tank_numb) REFERENCES location
);
```

Figure 12-28 (Continued):   SQL statements to create the animal handing database

The Object-Relational Design

As with the relational databases, the object-relational designs for the East Coast Aquarium consist of two separate databases, one for the volunteers and the other for the animals.

The Volunteers Database

Like the database for the Mighty-Mite Motors company, the design for the volunteers database presents only a few simple opportunities to take advantage of the integration of objects into a relational design. The ER diagram in Figure 12-29 contains objects for a name, address, and phone number. When you consider the entities closely, there are no other attributes that it makes sense to group together into objects.

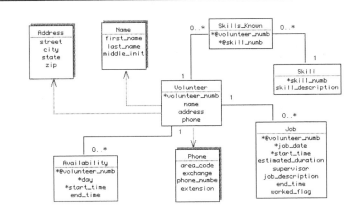

Figure 12-29:   The hybrid design for the volunteers database

The resulting tables are as follows:

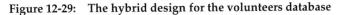

```
Volunteer (volunteer numb, name, address, phone)
Availability (volunteer numb, day, starting time, ending_time)
Job (volunteer numb, job date, starting time, estimated_duration,
     supervisor, job_description, ending_time, worked_flag)
Skill (skill numb, skill_description)
Skills_known (volunteer numb, skill numb)
```

The only benefit of moving to an object–relational model for this small database is the ability to reuse the Name, Address, and Phone classes, assuming that they have been declared for use elsewhere.

> *Note: For delcarations and implementations of the Name, Address, and Phone classes, see the discussion beginning on page 273 in Chapter 11.*

The Animal Tracking Database

Of all of the sample databases you have seen so far, the animals portion of the East Coast Aquarium database environment benefits the least from a hybrid design. The first portion of the ER diagram (Figure 12-30) is identical to the relational design. It does gain some clarity in the move from the Information Engineering model to UML in

that it can use the n-ary association symbol to show the three-way relationship between location, species, and problem. This technique
makes it very clear that the problem report is related to all three parent entities.

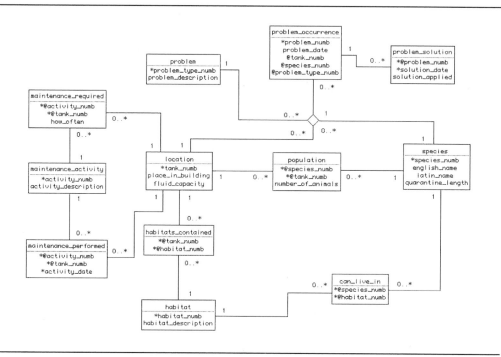

Figure 12-30:   A hybrid design for the animals database (part I)

The second portion of the ER diagram (Figure 12-31) incorporates
the utility classes that you have seen already. Beyond those three
classes, there is nothing that lends itself to grouping into a class
rather than using individual columns.

The hybrid schema therefore differs from the relational schema in
only one relation:

```
source (source_numb, source_name, source_address, source_phone,
    source_contact_person)
```

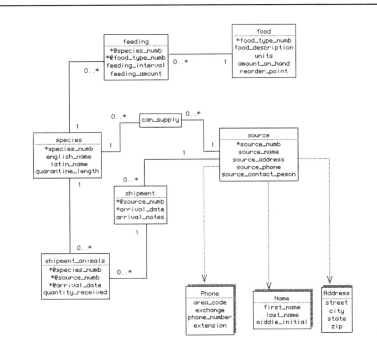

Figure 12-31:   A hybrid design for the animals database (part II)

The domain for the source_address attribute is the Address class, for the source_phone attribute the Phone class, and for the source_contact_person attribute the Name class.

13

Database Design Case Study #3: Independent Intelligence Agency

In the preceding two case studies, we have encountered several database design challenges, including the need to determine whether one or more databases are required, incomplete specifications, and a large number of many-to-many relationships. The final case study we are going to consider presents two different challenges: First, the specifications have been written by people who are more concerned with security than they are with helping database designers; second, the environment contains an enormous number of repeating groups. In addition, this is the largest database you have seen so far. Although at the outset it may appear that there are two or three separate databases, the parts of the database share just enough data that the only way to meet all the organization's requirements is to maintain a single schema.

Note: The cases in the two preceding chapters to some extent have been based on real organizations. However, this case is a pure flight of fancy. (The author had been watching too many spy movies when she wrote it!)

Organizational Overview

A group of database designers have been hired to provide updated information systems for the Independent Intelligence Agency (IIA). Given the nature of the agency's work, the designers realize that they will, in some cases, be working with limited information about the way in which the organization functions. In particular, the design team must accept specifications in whatever format they are provided; team members are not permitted to identify or question agency personnel other than the Vice President for Information Services, who has been their sole contact with the organization. In addition, they will be given few details about the application programs that will be interacting with the database they design.

The Independent Intelligence Agency, headquartered in Geneva, is a nonaligned, worldwide organization that specializes in the gathering and dissemination of covert intelligence. Established during the aftermath of World War II (1947), the IIA is quick to emphasize that while it employs undercover field agents and uses other methods common to intelligence agencies, it has not, is not, and will not be involved in manipulating or in any way influencing the affairs of any country; its sole purpose is to gather information and to sell it to whoever is willing to pay. The IIA will accept commissions to gather specific intelligence as long as doing so does not violate the restriction on becoming active in the affairs of governments. All of IIA's financial resources come from fees paid by clients for information and from investments made with those fees. All transactions are strictly confidential; unauthorized disclosure of information by any employee is cause for immediate dismissal.

The IIA's headquarters building in Geneva contains offices for the Executive Director, Internal Affairs (responsible for monitoring the conduct of field agents, readers, and administrative personnel), Human Resources, and Finance. Because space in the headquarters building is limited, Information Systems has been moved to a renovated warehouse behind the headquarters.

IIA's organization divides the planet into six bureaus, one for each continent except Antarctica. (Any intelligence that comes out of the research stations in Antarctica is handled through an Australian station.) Within the bureaus there are separate *stations* that conduct field operations. Each bureau has a Director, and each station has a Chief who reports to his or her bureau Director. (Note that the central offices for the European Bureau and the Geneva station are on the other side of the city. This arrangement was created to give the Director of the European Bureau and the Chief of the Geneva station the freedom to operate without the constant surveillance of top-level management.)

Stations have three types of people with whom they interact:

- ◆ *Field agents* are actively involved in the collection of intelligence. They are typically full-time employees of the IIA.
- ◆ *Readers* work inside station buildings reviewing print, audio, video, and electronic materials. Much of a reader's work involves intercepting and decoding international cable and satellite transmissions. Readers are typically full-time employees of the IIA.
- ◆ *Informants* are people who are contacted by field agents for information. Informants are usually paid based on the perceived value of the information they provide. They are not IIA employees. Some informants have become so valuable to the IIA, however, that they have been hired as field agents.

Occasionally field agents and readers will exchange roles. For example, a field agent who has spent too long in the field may become a reader and work at that job until retirement. By the same token, a promising reader may undergo field agent training and move into that role.

Stations also have administrative personnel. Although many administrative personnel have little contact with intelligence data or client lists, the security requirements for those employees are as rigorous as for field agents and readers.

Each station has its own budget and manages its own accounting. The Finance Department works at the top organizational level to determine the budget, but once funds are allocated, each station handles the ordering of its own supplies, pays its own expenses (including payments to informants), and cuts its own paychecks. Sales of information may be handled by any level in the organizational hierarchy. Payment is received by the agency making the sale, but all funds are deposited in a single, centralized account in Geneva. The Finance Department's auditors and Internal Affairs staff keep close watch to ensure that all funds collected end up in the bank.

Current Information Systems

IIA maintains a distributed file processing system using ISAM file organization that has been in place since 1974. Each station has its own minicomputer or server that is used to handle the station's accounting functions. These data are available to the Finance Department at the Geneva headquarters building, the station's bureau, and the station's area. Personnel files are kept on the Geneva headquarters' mainframe. The data are available to all stations.

The personnel files, however, contain data about IIA employees only. Each field agent keeps his or her own list of informants. In some cases, those lists have been placed on station computers, but the use is not consistent and in many cases, agents have been reluctant to share their sources.

Data gathered by field agents are stored in the file processing system. The files containing these raw facts are then indexed to allow retrieval by major topics—countries, individuals, and events. An online query language is available, but attempts to retrieve by a characteristic on which there is no index are unacceptably slow.

The IIA does not sell raw facts, but instead sells verified pieces of intelligence. To obtain a saleable piece of intelligence, the IIA must receive confirmation of the same raw fact from several sources. When a field agent or reader reports raw data, he or she also reports a confidence level (from 0 to 100) in the accuracy of that data. Printouts of sorted raw data along with their confidence levels are then examined by readers to find data that support each other with increasing confidence levels. When the confidence levels reach a specific point—IIA will not reveal exactly what that level is—a saleable piece of intelligence is entered into the data file containing saleable merchandise. The reader certifying the piece of intelligence affixes an approximate price, but the exact selling price will be negotiated when the intelligence is actually sold. Of all the tasks that the IIA undertakes, this is the most labor-intensive and delays in certifying saleable intelligence can cost the IIA a significant amount in sales.

The IIA has informed the database designers working on a new information system that application programmers will be preparing an expert system to automate the verification of raw data into saleable pieces of intelligence. Although the database designers will not be given any details on how the expert system will work, they will be told exactly what data the expert system will need to function.

The file processing system has become difficult to maintain. The volume of data added to the files is so high that the station IS staff must reblock the files as often as once every two weeks. The reblocking is time consuming and results in unacceptable downtime during working hours.

Security Concerns

Many of IIA's clients are extremely sensitive to the exclusiveness of the data they are buying: They wish to be the *only* purchasers. Exclusive sales command much higher fees than those for pieces of intelligence that can be sold to more than one buyer.

Some data are also extremely sensitive. The IIA believes that the release of those data to the public would violate the IIA's policy against manipulating or influencing existing governments. Therefore, the security of the intelligence data is of primary concern to the IIA.

The ISAM file system they are currently using has no built-in security. Instead, each record of data added to the files contains a field with a security classification. Each user name that the computer recognizes has a security classification as well. Access to data is granted if the user has a classification equal to or above the classification of the data. The classification scheme is an all-or-nothing affair. Anyone who can supply a user name and password that the computer will recognize receives the classification level of the user name and can read all data at that level or below and can modify all data at that classification level. Since users can modify only data at their classification level, highly privileged users who need to modify data at lower classification levels will have more than one account on the system, once for each classification level below them.

The need for a single user to maintain more than one account has led to numerous security breaches. Users who could not remember all of the user names, passwords, and their associated classification levels have written the information down and either taped it to their monitors in full view of an entire office or placed it in the top center drawer of a desk that is never locked. IIA would therefore like a security system where access can be more tightly tailored to an individual's needs so that only a single account is needed for each user.

The IIA's VP for Information Services has told the design team that the IIA is willing to install retina scanners for user identification in all locations. Portable scanners are also available to be issued with laptop computers.

Equipment Development

To augment its intelligence collection activities, the IIA develops and manufactures about half of its own intelligence gathering equipment. Some of this equipment is then sold to intelligence agencies around the world. In keeping with its position of strict neutrality, the IIA sells equipment to any government that has the money to purchase it.

Currently, control over equipment inventory, usage, testing, and sales is very lax. The VP for Information Services, however, has informed the database design team that a new system must include equipment tracking. Although the equipment development is managed separately from the intelligence gathering, most field equipment tests are performed by field agents and most equipment sales are to clients who also purchase intelligence.

Subject Classifications

The current indexing of the existing data files by commonly used keywords has given the IIA's IS staff an idea that could potentially increase sales of pieces of intelligence. The staff would like to assign subject classifications to verified saleable merchandise, much in the same way a library assigns subject headings to books.

Classifications would then be matched with customers in three ways:

- Subject areas about which a customer wants to be notified whenever something is available
- Subject areas from which the customer has previously made a purchase
- Subject areas about which a customer has made a request but then subsequently declined to purchase

Searches on these matchings of customers and subject classifications could potentially tailor sales calls to client purchasing habits, providing a better use of administrative personnel time.

Summary of IS Needs

The IIA is therefore faced with four major IS problems:

- The file processing system is slow and hard to maintain.
- The file processing system does not provide enough flexibility for current application program technologies. In

particular, it cannot support the expert system that will be created to verify saleable pieces of intelligence.
- ◆ The system is far less secure than IIA requires.
- ◆ The distributed file system has led to inconsistencies in the types of data that are stored on the organization's various computers.

To remedy these problems, the IIA has hired a number of IS teams that will be working independently on various parts of the organization's new system. (The isolation of the teams is for security purposes.) The database will still be distributed, but because it will be a true database rather than a file processing system, it will be possible to use a common schema throughout the entire organization.

Accounting functions, which are of interest only to each local station and its supervising bureau, will continue to use the file processing system, at least temporarily. Any upgrades to that system will take place as a separate project.

System Specifications

Prior to hiring the database design team, the bureau directors, continent directors, and local station chiefs came together to prepare a document that described the data they needed in a database. Input for the meeting came from discussions at the stations with field agents, readers, and administrative personnel.

The following outline of data dealing with intelligence gathering and sales that should be stored in the IIA's database was presented to the database design team:

- ◆ Personnel
  - Classification (field agent, reader, or administrative)
  - Real name
  - Birthdate
  - Local country identification number (for example, U.S. social security number)

- Driver's license country (and state, if applicable) and number
- Photo
- Fingerprints
- Retina print
- Height in centimeters
- Weight in kilograms
- Eye color
- Vision
- Current address and phone number
- Aliases (all aliases used, currently or in the past)
  § Name
  § Photo
  § Birthdate
  § Local country identification number (for example, U.S. social security number)
  § Driver's license country (and state, if applicable) and number
  § Height
  § Weight
  § Eye color
  § Address and phone number (if any)
  § Date last used
- All previous addresses including dates of residence
- Family members (parents; all spouses; biological, adopted, step, and foster children; biological, adopted, step, and foster siblings)
  § Real name
  § Birthdate
  § Current address and phone number
  § Highest level of education
  § Current job
  § Photo
- Education (all schools attended and degrees earned)
- Work history
- Criminal record
- Religion
- Organizations other than IIA to which person belongs

- ◆ Informants
  - Real name
  - Birthdate
  - Local country identification number (for example, U.S. social security number)
  - Driver's license country (and state, if applicable) and number
  - Photo
  - Fingerprints
  - Height
  - Weight
  - Eye Color
  - Vision
  - Current address and phone number
  - Aliases (all aliases used, currently or in the past)
    - § Name
    - § Photo
    - § Birthdate
    - § Local country identification number (for example, U.S. social security number)
    - § Driver's license country (and state, if applicable) and number
    - § Height
    - § Weight
    - § Eye color
    - § Address and phone number (if any)
    - § Date last used
  - All previous addresses including dates of residence
  - Family members (parents; all spouses; biological, adopted, step, and foster children; biological, adopted, step, and foster siblings)
    - § Real name
    - § Birthdate
    - § Current address and phone number
    - § Highest level of education
    - § Current job
    - § Photo
  - Education (all schools attended and degrees earned)
  - Work history

- Criminal record
- Religion
- Organizations to which person belongs
- Field agent who recruited the informant
- Contacts made with agents
  § Date of contact
  § Outcome of contact
  § Payment received at contact
  § Data presented at contact
  § Agent making the contact

◆ Intelligence data (raw facts)
  - Date collected
  - Source (for example, informant, printed document, agent observation)
  - Location collected (country, city or town)
  - How gathered
  - The data itself
  - Confidence level
  - Cost of the data

◆ Verified piece of intelligence
  - The piece of intelligence itself
  - Subject classifications
  - Customers who purchased the piece of intelligence
  - Price paid by each customer
  - Date each purchase was made
  - Whether sold exclusively

◆ Customers
  - Name
  - Contact person
  - Address
  - Phone number
  - Fax number
  - Subject classifications of previous purchases
  - Subject classification of previous inquiries that did not lead to purchases

- Subject classifications for which the customer has requested notification
- Purchases made
- Whether customer requires exclusive sales

Internal Affairs, the department responsible, among other things, for monitoring security, wants additional data kept about access to the database:

- ◆ System logon data (kept about each attempt to log on to the system)
    - User ID
    - Date
    - Time on
    - Workstation ID (if access was not from an IIA workstation, but over a phone line, then the phone number from which the call was placed)
    - Time off (will be null if logon attempt is unsuccessful)

- ◆ Information request data
    - User ID
    - Date
    - Time
    - Workstation ID or phone number of remote call
    - Data item requested
        § Table name
        § Row identifier(s)
    - Result (access granted or denied)
    - Action performed (retrieve, insert, modify, delete)

The final portion of the database will handle the equipment inventory, testing, use, and sales:

- ◆ Current equipment inventory
    - Classification (for example, tape recorder, microphone, camera)
    - Description
    - Location (station at which equipment is stored when not in use)

- Current condition
- Restrictions on use

♦ Equipment use records
  - Classification
  - Date used
  - Agent using equipment
  - Where used
  - How used
  - Result of use

♦ Equipment sales
  - Customer
  - Date of purchase
  - Items purchased
  - Amount paid for each item
  - Total amount of purchase

♦ Equipment under development
  - Classification
  - Description
  - Intended use
  - Station where development is taking place
  - Employees involved in development
  - Estimated date of completion
  - Testing data
    § Date of test
    § Type of test
    § Test results
    § Location of test
    § Agent performing test

Designing the Database

One of the drawbacks to the way in which the specifications for the IIA's database have been presented is that they initially appear to be quite well prepared. Each top-level heading seems to correspond to an entity. However, a closer examination of the specifications indicates that each grouping of required data includes multiple entities and often a number of repeating groups.

Probably the easiest way to approach a database design where the specifications are presented in this way is to begin to create an ER diagram. When the database is as large as this one appears to be, it is also easier to break the design into several components (people, intelligence gathering and sales, system security, and equipment tracking).

ER Diagram for People

When looking at the data that are to be stored about people, a database designer is immediately faced with a major decision before drawing a single entity: Should there be separate entities for IIA employees and informants, or should they be a single entity?

When faced with a choice of this type, you need to look carefully at the data that describe the entities. Will the database store the same data about employees as it will about informants? If so, then you are probably dealing with a single entity.

> Note: An exception to the rule of "same attributes, same entity" occurs when the two entities have different meanings. For example, in an accounting database you may have line item entities for purchase orders that you place to your suppliers and orders that your customers place with you. Although the two entities have exactly the same attributes, their meaning and use are very different and they should be kept as separate entities.

With the exception of the agent that recruited an informant, the data describing employees and informants is identical. Add to this the fact that informants sometimes become agents and it becomes clear that it makes sense to represent all people as a single entity.

What about that extra attribute that belongs to the informants (the agent that recruited the informant)? There are two ways to handle it. One is to include it as an attribute of the single person entity. Its value will simply be null for employees. The cost of this solution is the disk space wasted by the large number of nulls. The alternative is to create a separate entity that has a one-to-one relationship with the person entity and contains the person identifier and the agent recruiting the informant. Obtaining the recruiting agent would then require a join between the person entity and the entity holding the extra data. Given that disk space is relatively inexpensive and processor time is very dear, the better choice is to add the attribute to the person entity and allow it to be null where necessary.

Assuming that the design uses one entity for people (named "person"), the portion of the ER diagram that contains data describing people can be found in Figure 13-1. There are eight entities that represent repeating groups of data:

♦ Fingerprint: Each instance of the Fingerprint entity represents one finger on one hand. Of all the repeating groups, fingerprints are the only ones for which we can make a reasonable estimate of how many there will be. An alternative to including this entity therefore is to use 10 attributes in the Person entity (one for each finger). However, there is no way to guarantee that the IIA has exactly 10 prints for each person. There may be fewer … or there may be more! (Some people are born with six fingers.) In addition, searching fingerprints would be very clumsy if there were separate attributes for each finger because an application program would need to contain logic to search each individual attribute. However, the current design, which places the repeating group in its own entity, has all fingers in a single attribute. The database stores one instance for each print, regardless of how many there are, and a search routine needs to worry about only one attribute.

♦ Former Address: Each instance of the Former Address entity represents one place a person has lived. Under the assumption that a person has only one primary residence at any given time, the addresses are distinguished by the date the person moved into the location.

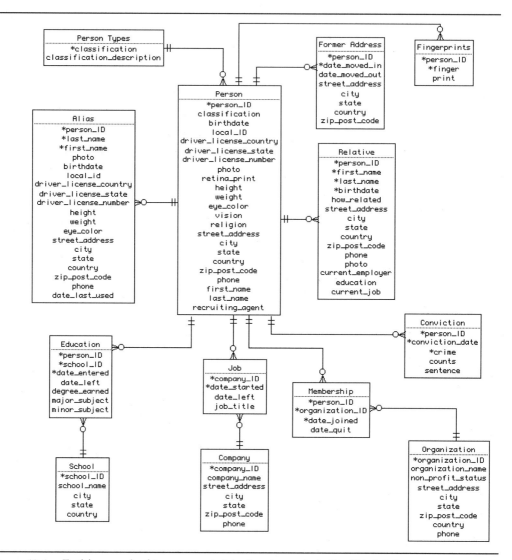

Figure 13-1: Entities required to represent data about people in the IIA database

♦ Relative: There is one instance of the Relative entity for each person that is related to an IIA employee. Choosing a unique identifier for this entity can be a bit tricky. However, it seems reasonable to assume that no one has two relatives with exactly the same name born on the same day.

- ◆ Conviction: Each instance of the Conviction entity represents a conviction for a specific crime on a specific date.
- ◆ Membership: Each instance of the Membership entity represents joining a given organization on a given date. By distinguishing memberships by date, the database can track multiple members in the same organization over time.
- ◆ Job: Each instance of the Job entity represents one job the person has held. The entity identifier is based on the assumption that a person starts only one job with a given company on one day. This entity takes care of a person's job history both at the IIA and prior to joining the IIA. A person's current job will have a date_left value of null.
- ◆ Education: There is one instance of the Education entity for each time a person enrolls in a school. By including the date entered in the entity identifier, the entity can track people who attend a school, take a break, and then return to same school.
- ◆ Alias: Each instance of the alias entity represents one entity used by a person. The entity identifier is based on the assumption that no person has more than one alias with the same name.

ER Diagram for Intelligence Gathering and Sales

The ER diagram that supports intelligence gathering and sales can be found in Figure 13-2. There are three aspects of this diagram that are of particular interest.

First, consider what appear to be the two identical relationships between the Person and Contact entities. If we were to label those relationships, one would represent the agent involved in a contact; the other would represent the informant. As you can see in the Contact entity, there are actually two foreign keys—informant_ID and agent_ID—both of which reference the person_ID in the Person entity. However, the integrity constraint for the foreign key checking is a bit more complicated than simply verifying that a person_ID exists in the Person entity.

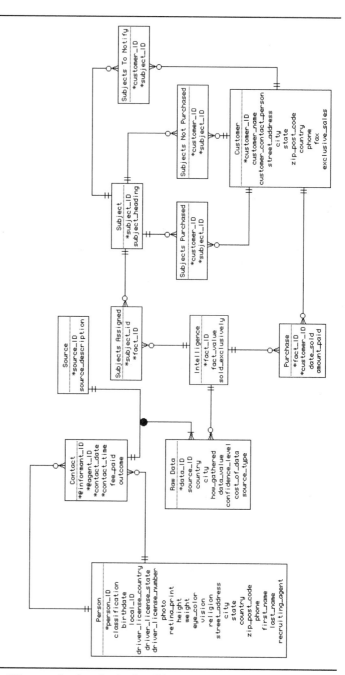

Figure 13-2:   Entities required to depict intelligence gathering and sales

An informant_ID must not only match a person_ID, but the classification of that person must be "informant." By the same token, an agent_ID must have a classification of "agent" as well as matching a person_ID. This is the only way to represent a relationship between two entities of the same type in a relational database. Although other data models may allow circular relationships such as that in Figure 13-3, the relational data model cannot support it because it is a many-to-many relationship. The Contact entity therefore is a composite entity that resolves the relationship between multiple person entities.

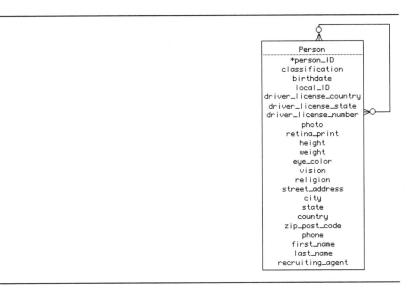

Figure 13-3:   A circular relationship

The drawback to this approach is a practical one: Most CASE tools are not capable of recognizing primary key–foreign key relationships when the attributes involved do not have the same name. Nor can it automatically recognize the need to verify the classification of a person along with the person's ID. A database designer will therefore need to add a CHECK clause for each column that performs this unusual referential integrity verification.

The second unusual facet of this ER diagram is a type of relationship that you have not seen before: a *mutually exclusive relationship*.

A piece of raw data can come from an informant (the result of a contact) or it can come from another type of source (print, video, electronic, and so on), but it cannot come from both. Therefore, if an instance of the Raw Data entity is related to an instance of the Source entity, it cannot be related to an instance of the Contact entity, and vice versa. We represent this in an ER diagram with a solid black circle between the entities that mutually exclude one another. In this particular case, the relationship can be read: "A piece of raw data comes from one and only one contact or a piece of raw data comes from one and only one source, but not both."

To handle the constraint on the source_ID entity, a database designer must place a CHECK constraint on the entire table created from the entity. (You will see this and other CHECK constraints in the last section of this chapter as part of the discussion of the SQL needed to create this database.) Although source_ID appears to a CASE tool as a foreign key referencing the entity identifier of the Source table, a normal foreign key constraint will not include the possibility that the value is an information ID rather than a source ID.

The third interesting aspect of this ERD is the three relationships between the Subject entity and the Customer entity. As discussed earlier, each of these many-to-many relationships has a different meaning, so although the attributes belonging to each of the three composite entities are identical, they represent completely different things. This is another example of an exception to the rule that if two entities have the same attributes, they are probably the same entity.

ER Diagram for System Security

The ER diagram for the portion of the database that handles system security can be found in Figure 13-4. This diagram contains one mutually exclusive relationship: the relationship between a data access and raw data or intelligence. A person can access either a piece of raw data or a piece of verified intelligence, but not both in the same access. The remaining relationships between entities are all simple one-to-many relationships.

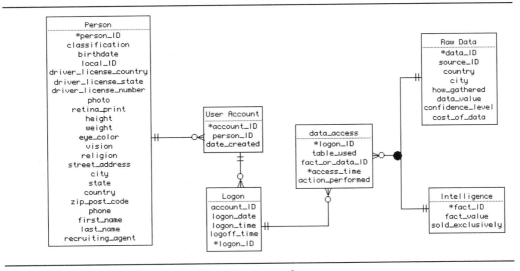

Figure 13-4:   Entities needed to depict system access data

ER Diagram for Equipment Tracking

Equipment tracking (use, development, and sales) requires a fairly straightforward group of entities and relationships (see Figure 13-5). Notice that each piece of equipment is first classified by general type (for example, tape recorder or microphone). It is then given a unique ID so its use can be tracked.

Sale data do not require the individual identifiers of items being sold but only how many of each given type were included. It is therefore up to an application program to delete items sold from inventory. This means that each time an item is sold, an instance of the Equipment Item entity must be deleted. It will therefore be up to the individual who is preparing a shipment of items sold to enter the item identifiers of those items.

The Equipment Item and Under Development Item entities have the same primary key. Should they be combined into one entity? In this case, probably not. Notice that other than the primary key, the entities have no attributes in common. This alone suggests that we are dealing with two different entities. Adding to that the fact that

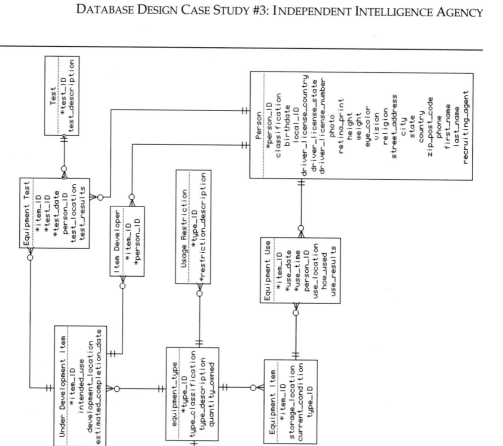

Figure 13-5:   Entities for tracking equipment development, use, and sales

the IIA does not want to retain testing data once a piece of equipment has been certified as ready for everyday use, it is clear that the two entities are indeed distinct.

Designing the Tables

The ER diagrams you have seen translate into the following 37 tables:

```
person (person ID, classification, first_name, last_name, birthdate,
    local_ID, driver_license_country, driver_license_state,
    driver_license_number, photo, retina_print, height, weight,
    eye_color, vision, religion, street_address, city, state,
    country, zip_post_code, phone, recruiting_agent)
person_types (classification, classification_description)
alias (person ID, last name, first name, photo, birthdate, local_ID,
    driver_license_country, driver_license_state,
    driver_license_number, height, weight, eye_color,
    streeet_address, city, state, country, zip_post_code, phone,
    date_last_used)
former_address (person ID, date moved in, date_moved_out,
    street_address, city, state, country, zip_post_code)
education (person ID, school ID, date entered, date_left,
    degree_earned, major_subject, minor_subject)
relative (person ID, first name, last name, birthdate, how_related,
    street_address, city, state, country, zip_post_code, phone,
    photo, current_employer, education, current_job)
school (school ID, school_name, city, state, country)
job (person ID, company ID, date started, date_left, job_title)
company (company ID, company_name, street_address, city, state,
    zip_post_code, phone)
conviction (person ID, conviction date, crime, counts, sentence)
organization (organization ID, organization_name,
    non_profit_status, street_address, city, state, zip_post_code,
    country, phone)
membership (person ID, organization ID, date joined, date_quit)
fingerprints (person ID, finger, print)
contact (informant ID, agent ID, contact date, contact time,
    fee_paid, outcome)
raw_data (data ID, source_ID, source_type, country, city,
    how_gathered, data_value, confidence_level, fact_ID)
source (source ID, source_description)
intelligence (fact ID, fact_value, sold_exclusively)
subject (subject ID, subject_heading)
subjects_assigned (subjectID, fact ID)
customer (customer ID, customer_name, customer_contact_person,
    street_address, city, state, zip_post_code, country, phone, fax,
    exclusive_sales)
```

```
purchase (fact_ID, customer_ID, date_sold, amount_paid)
subjects_purchased (customer_ID, subject_ID)
subjects_not_purchased (customer_ID, subject_ID)
subjects_to_notify (customer_ID, subject_ID)
user_account (account_ID, person_ID, date_created)
logon (logon_ID, account_ID, logon_date, logon_time, logoff_time)
data_access (logon_ID, access_time, table_used, fact_or_data_ID,
    action_performed)
equipment_item (item_ID, storage_location, current_condition,
    type_ID)
usage_restriction (type_ID, restriction_description)
equipment_use (item_ID, use_date, use_time, person_ID, use_location,
    how_used, use_results)
equipment_type (type_ID, type_classification, type_description,
    quantity_owned)
equipment_sale (customer_ID, sale_date, sale_total)
sale_item (customer_ID, sale_date, type_ID, quantity_purchased,
    price_each, line_cost)
under_development_item (item_ID, intended_use,
    development_location, estimated_completion_date, type_ID)
item_developer (item_ID, person_ID)
equipment_test (item_ID, test_ID, test_date, person_ID,
    test_location, test_results)
test (test_ID, test_description)
```

Because of the circular and mutually exclusive relationships, this set of tables does not document itself as well as other designs, even with its meaningful column and table names. To be understandable, this design definitely needs to be accompanied by a data dictionary that contains explanations for the unusual relationships.

Generating the SQL

The SQL CREATE statements used to install the IIA database appear in Figure 13-6. They contain two elements with which you may not be familiar: BLOBs and CHECK constraints.

BLOBs

Unlike the databases discussed previously in this book, the IIA database contains images. DBMSs use two general strategies for storing images. The first is to link image files to the database by storing a path name to a separate image file. The second is to actually store

```
CREATE TABLE person
(
    person_ID INT,
    classification INT,
    birthdate DATE,
    local_ID CHAR (15),
    driver_license_country CHAR (15),
    driver_license_state CHAR (15),
    driver_license_number CHAR (15),
    photo BLOB,
    retina_print BLOB,
    height DECIMAL (5,1),
    weight DECIMAL (5,1),
    eye_color CHAR (10),
    vision CHAR (10),
    religion CHAR (15),
    street_address CHAR (30),
    city CHAR (30),
    state CHAR (30),
    country CHAR (30),
    zip_post_code CHAR (10),
    phone CHAR (15),
    first_name CHAR (15),
    last_name CHAR (15),
    recruiting_agent INT,
    PRIMARY KEY (person_ID),
    FOREIGN KEY (classification) REFERENCES person_types
);

CREATE TABLE person_types
(
    classification INT,
    classification_description CHAR (15),
    PRIMARY KEY (classification)
);

CREATE TABLE former_address
(
    person_ID INT,
    date_moved_in DATE,
    date_moved_out DATE,
    street_address CHAR (30),
    city CHAR (30),
    state CHAR (30),
    country CHAR (30),
    zip_post_code CHAR (10),
    PRIMARY KEY (person_ID, date_moved_in),
    FOREIGN KEY (person_ID) REFERENCES person
);
```

Figure 13-6 :   SQL statements to create the IIA database

```
CREATE TABLE alias
(
    person_ID INT,
    last_name CHAR (15),
    first_name CHAR (15),
    photo BLOB,
    birthdate DATE,
    local_id CHAR (15),
    driver_license_country CHAR (15),
    driver_license_state CHAR (15),
    driver_license_number CHAR (15),
    height DECIMAL (5,1),
    weight DECIMAL (5,1),
    eye_color CHAR (10),
    street_address CHAR (30),
    city CHAR (30),
    state CHAR (30),
    country CHAR (30),
    zip_post_code CHAR (10),
    phone CHAR (15),
    date_last_used DATE,
    PRIMARY KEY (person_ID, last_name, first_name),
    FOREIGN KEY (person_ID) REFERENCES person
);

CREATE TABLE relative
(
    person_ID INT,
    first_name CHAR (15),
    last_name CHAR (15),
    birthdate DATE,
    how_related CHAR (30),
    street_address CHAR (30),
    city CHAR (30),
    state CHAR (30),
    country CHAR (30),
    zip_post_code CHAR (10),
    phone CHAR (15),
    photo BLOB,
    current_employer CHAR (30),
    education CHAR (30),
    current_job CHAR (30),
    PRIMARY KEY (person_ID, first_name, last_name, birthdate),
    FOREIGN KEY (person_ID) REFERENCES person
);
```

Figure 13-6 (Continued): SQL statements to create the IIA database

```
CREATE TABLE education
(
    person_ID INT,
    school_ID INT,
    date_entered DATE,
    date_left DATE,
    degree_earned CHAR (10),
    major_subject CHAR (15),
    minor_subject CHAR (15),
    PRIMARY KEY (person_ID, school_ID, date_entered) );

CREATE TABLE school
(
    school_ID INT,
    school_name CHAR (50),
    city CHAR (30),
    state CHAR (30),
    country CHAR (30),
    PRIMARY KEY (school_ID) );

CREATE TABLE job
(
    company_ID INT,
    date_started DATE,
    date_left DATE,
    job_title CHAR (50),
    person_ID INT,
    PRIMARY KEY (company_ID, date_started),
    FOREIGN KEY (company_ID) REFERENCES company,
    FOREIGN KEY (person_ID) REFERENCES person );

CREATE TABLE company
(
    company_ID INT,
    company_name CHAR (50),
    street_address CHAR (30),
    city CHAR (30),
    state CHAR (30),
    zip_post_code CHAR (10),
    phone CHAR (15),
    PRIMARY KEY (company_ID) );

CREATE TABLE fingerprints
(
    person_ID INT,
    finger CHAR (15),
    print BLOB,
    PRIMARY KEY (person_ID, finger),
    FOREIGN KEY (person_ID) REFERENCES person );
```

Figure 13-6 (Continued):   SQL statements to create the IIA database

```
CREATE TABLE conviction
(
    person_ID INT,
    conviction_date DATE,
    crime CHAR (50),
    counts INT,
    sentence CHAR (50),
    PRIMARY KEY (person_ID, conviction_date, crime) );

CREATE TABLE organization
(
    organization_ID INT,
    organization_name CHAR (50),
    non_profit_status CHAR (1),
    street_address CHAR (30),
    city CHAR (30),
    state CHAR (30),
    zip_post_code CHAR (10),
    country CHAR (30),
    phone CHAR (15),
    PRIMARY KEY (organization_ID) );

CREATE TABLE membership
(
    person_ID INT,
    organization_ID INT,
    date_joined DATE,
    date_quit DATE,
    PRIMARY KEY (person_ID, organization_ID, date_joined),
    FOREIGN KEY (person_ID) REFERENCES person,
    FOREIGN KEY (organization_ID) REFERENCES organization );

CREATE TABLE contact
(
    informant_ID INT
        CHECK (EXISTS (SELECT * FROM person
            WHERE VALUE = person_ID and classification = 4)),
    agent_ID INT
        CHECK (EXISTS (SELECT * FROM person
            WHERE VALUE = person_ID and classification = 1)),
    contact_date DATE,
    contact_time TIME,
    fee_paid DECIMAL (8,2),
    outcome CHAR (50),
    PRIMARY KEY (informant_ID, agent_ID, contact_date,
        contact_time));
```

Figure 13-6 (Continued): SQL statements to create the IIA database

```
CREATE TABLE raw_data
(
    data_ID INT,
    source_ID INT,
    source_type CHAR (!5),
    country CHAR (30),
    city CHAR (30),
    how_gathered CHAR (50),
    data_value CHAR (255),
    confidence_level INT,
    cost_of_data DECIMAL (8,2),
    fact_ID INT,
    PRIMARY KEY (data_ID),
    FOREIGN KEY (fact_ID) REFERENCES intelligence
    CHECK (source_type = 'informant' AND
        EXISTS (SELECT * FROM person
        WHERE source_ID = person_ID AND classification = 4)
        OR
        source_type = 'document' AND
        EXISTS (SELECT * FROM source
        WHERE source_ID = source.source_ID)));

CREATE TABLE source
(
    source_ID INT,
    source_description CHAR (255),
    PRIMARY KEY (source_ID) );

CREATE TABLE intelligence
(
    fact_ID INT,
    fact_value CHAR (255),
    sold_exclusively CHAR (1),
    PRIMARY KEY (fact_ID) );

CREATE TABLE subject
(
    subject_ID INT,
    subject_heading CHAR (50),
    PRIMARY KEY (subject_ID) );

CREATE TABLE subjects_assigned
(
    subject_ID INT,
    fact_ID INT,
    PRIMARY KEY (subject_ID, fact_ID),
    FOREIGN KEY (subject_ID) REFERENCES subject,
    FOREIGN KEY (fact_ID) REFERENCES intelligence );
```

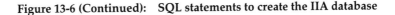

Figure 13-6 (Continued):   SQL statements to create the IIA database

```
CREATE TABLE customer
(
    customer_ID INT,
    customer_name CHAR (50),
    customer_contact_person CHAR (50),
    street_address CHAR (30),
    city CHAR (30),
    state CHAR (30),
    zip_post_code CHAR (10),
    country CHAR (30),
    phone CHAR (15),
    fax CHAR (15),
    exclusive_sales CHAR (1),
    PRIMARY KEY (customer_ID) );

CREATE TABLE purchase
(
    fact_ID INT,
    customer_ID INT,
    date_sold DATE,
    amount_paid DECIMAL (8,2),
    PRIMARY KEY (fact_ID, customer_ID),
    FOREIGN KEY (fact_ID) REFERENCES intelligence,
    FOREIGN KEY (customer_ID) REFERENCES customer );

CREATE TABLE subjects_purchased
(
    customer_ID INT,
    subject_ID INT,
    PRIMARY KEY (customer_ID, subject_ID),
    FOREIGN KEY (customer_ID) REFERENCES customer,
    FOREIGN KEY (subject_ID) REFERENCES subject );

CREATE TABLE subjects_not_purchased
(
    customer_ID INT,
    subject_ID INT,
    PRIMARY KEY (customer_ID, subject_ID),
    FOREIGN KEY (customer_ID) REFERENCES customer,
    FOREIGN KEY (subject_ID) REFERENCES subject );

CREATE TABLE subjects_to_notify
(
    customer_ID INT,
    subject_ID INT,
    PRIMARY KEY (customer_ID, subject_ID),
    FOREIGN KEY (customer_ID) REFERENCES customer,
    FOREIGN KEY (subject_ID) REFERENCES subject );
```

Figure 13-6 (Continued):   SQL statements to create the IIA database

```
CREATE TABLE user_account
(
    account_ID INTCHAR (10),
    person_ID INT,
    date_created DATE,
    PRIMARY KEY (account_ID),
    FOREIGN KEY (person_ID) REFERENCES person
);

CREATE TABLE logon
(
    account_ID INTCHAR (10),
    logon_date DATE,
    logon_time TIME,
    logoff_time TIME,
    logon_ID INT,
    PRIMARY KEY (logon_ID),
    FOREIGN KEY (account_ID) REFERENCES user_account
);

CREATE TABLE data_access
(
    logon_ID INT,
    table_used CHAR (30),
    fact_or_data_ID INT,
    access_time TIME,
    action_performed CHAR (30),
    PRIMARY KEY (logon_ID, access_time),
    FOREIGN KEY (logon_ID) REFERENCES logon
    CHECK (table_used = 'raw_data' AND
        EXISTS (SELECT * FROM raw_date
        WHERE fact_or_data_ID = data_ID)
        OR
        (table_used = 'intelligence' AND
        EXISTS (SELECT * FROM intelligence
        WHERE fact_or_data_ID = fact_ID))
);

CREATE TABLE equipment_item
(
    item_ID INT,
    storage_location CHAR (30),
    current_condition CHAR (10),
    type_ID INT,
    PRIMARY KEY (item_ID),
    FOREIGN KEY (type_ID) REFERENCES equipment_type
);
```

Figure 13-6 (Continued):   SQL statements to create the IIA database

```
CREATE TABLE usage_restriction
(
    type_ID INT,
    restriction_description CHAR (50),
    PRIMARY KEY (type_ID, restriction_description),
    FOREIGN KEY (type_ID) REFERENCES equipment_type );

CREATE TABLE equipment_use
(
    item_ID INT,
    use_date DATE,
    use_time TIME,
    person_ID INT,
    use_location CHAR (50),
    how_used CHAR (255),
    use_results CHAR (255),
    PRIMARY KEY (item_ID, use_date, use_time),
    FOREIGN KEY (item_ID) REFERENCES equipment_item,
    FOREIGN KEY (person_ID) REFERENCES person );

CREATE TABLE equipment_type
(
    type_ID INT,
    type_classification CHAR (15),
    type_description CHAR (50),
    quantity_owned INT,
    PRIMARY KEY (type_ID) );

CREATE TABLE equipment_sale
(
    customer_ID INT,
    sale_date DATE,
    sale_total DECIMAL (8,2),
    PRIMARY KEY (customer_ID, sale_date),
    FOREIGN KEY (customer_ID) REFERENCES customer );

CREATE TABLE sale_item
(
    customer_ID INT,
    sale_date DATE,
    type_ID INT,
    quantity_purchased INT,
    price_each DECIMAL (8,2),
    line_cost DECIMAL (8,2),
    PRIMARY KEY (customer_ID, sale_date, type_ID),
    FOREIGN KEY (customer_ID) REFERENCES equipment_sale,
    FOREIGN KEY (sale_date) REFERENCES equipment_sale,
    FOREIGN KEY (type_ID) REFERENCES equipment_type );
```

Figure 13-6 (Continued): SQL statements to create the IIA database

```
CREATE TABLE under_development_item
(
    item_ID INT,
    intended_use CHAR (50),
    development_location CHAR (50),
    estimated_completion_date DATE,
    type_ID INT,
    PRIMARY KEY (item_ID),
    FOREIGN KEY (type_ID) REFERENCES equipment_type
);

CREATE TABLE item_developer
(
    item_ID INT,
    person_ID INT,
    PRIMARY KEY (item_ID, person_ID),
    FOREIGN KEY (person_ID) REFERENCES person
);

CREATE TABLE equipment_test
(
    item_ID INT,
    test_ID INT,
    test_date DATE,
    person_ID INT,
    test_location CHAR (50),
    test_results CHAR (255),
    PRIMARY KEY (item_ID, test_ID, test_date),
    FOREIGN KEY (item_ID) REFERENCES under_development_item,
    FOREIGN KEY (test_ID) REFERENCES test,
    FOREIGN KEY (person_ID) REFERENCES person
);

CREATE TABLE test
(
    test_ID INT,
    test_description CHAR (255),
    PRIMARY KEY (test_ID)
);
```

Figure 13-6 (Continued):   SQL statements to create the IIA database

the images as part of the database itself, usually in a column with a data type of BLOB (binary large object).

The first strategy keeps the database smaller, but you run the risk of not being able to access an image if the image file is moved or deleted. By keeping the image within the database, you can be assured that the image is always available. That is why the columns in the IIA database that will hold images have a data type of BLOB.

> *Note: You may not have a choice in the way in which you store images in a database because often a DBMS will not support both image storage strategies.*

CHECK Constraints

The IIA database has three instances of unusual relationships: one circular relationship and two mutually exclusive relationships. To enforce the integrity of those relationships, a database designer must add CHECK constraints to the SQL CREATE statements; standard foreign key constraints will not suffice.

To handle the circular relationship, a database designer adds the CHECK constraints to the columns:

```
informant_ID INT
    CHECK (EXISTS (SELECT * FROM person
        WHERE VALUE = person_ID and classification = 4)),
agent_ID INT
    CHECK (EXISTS (SELECT * FROM person
        WHERE VALUE = person_ID and classification = 1)),
```

The constraint is met if the expression within parentheses is true. Therefore, if some row exists in the Person table that has a value matching the informant_ID and a classification of informant (the code value 4), then the constraint is met. By the same token, if a row exists in the Person table that has a value matching the agent_ID and a classification of agent (the code value 1), then the constraint is met.

To handle the mutually exclusive relationships, each CHECK constraint contains two retrievals linked by an OR. Because the constraints require values from two columns in each table, the constraints are most easily implemented as table constraints:

```
CHECK (source_type = 'informant' AND
    EXISTS (SELECT * FROM person
    WHERE source_ID = person_ID AND classification = 4)
    OR
    source_type = 'document' AND
    EXISTS (SELECT * FROM source
    WHERE source_ID = source.source_ID))
```

```
CHECK (table_used = 'raw_data' AND
    EXISTS (SELECT * FROM raw_date
    WHERE fact_or_data_ID = data_ID)
    OR
    (table_used = 'intelligence' AND
    EXISTS (SELECT * FROM intelligence
    WHERE fact_or_data_ID = fact_ID)
```

In both cases, the constraint first determines which type of source or table has been used. It then verifies that a matching row exists in the correct table.

In most cases, it is impossible to enforce mutually exclusive relationships and verify their integrity without including a column in the table that indicates which of the mutually exclusive options has been chosen. This happens because the numeric identifiers assigned to entities are independent and meaningless and do not necessarily represent unique sets of values. Assume, for example, that a row is entered into the Data Access table with a fact_or_data_ID of 1019. As it so happens, this is a piece of raw data. However, there is a fact_ID of 1019 but no data_ID with that value. If the CHECK constraint were written

```
CHECK (EXISTS (SELECT * FROM raw_date
    WHERE fact_or_data_ID = data_ID)
    OR
    EXISTS (SELECT * FROM intelligence
    WHERE fact_or_data_ID = fact_ID)
```

then the constraint would be valid, even though there was no matching raw data ID.

The Object-Relational Design

The complexity of the IIA database allows it to take better advantage of classes as domains than the databases you have seen in the preceding two chapters. In Figure 13-7, the first of four parts, you will find the Person entity and the entities that are necessary to handle the many repeating groups in this database environment.

Figure 13-7 also contains the utility classes that are used as domains throughout the database.

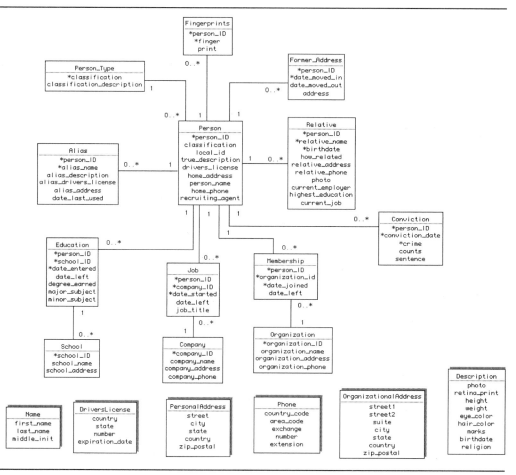

Figure 13-7:   The object–relational design (part I)

The utility classes, especially the Description class, significantly simplify the data that describe agents, informants, and their aliases. In addition, the Description class encapsulates a great deal of related data so that it can be handled as a whole. An application programmer or user working with SQL can therefore retrieve an entire description with a single attribute name, rather than needing to retrieve the individual pieces of the description.

The Description class exemplifies the two major benefits of adding objects as domains to a relational schema: You simplify the overall logical design of the database and you simplify the task of retrieving logically grouped attributes that will always be accessed together. On the other hand, there would appear to be no drawbacks to adding the objects.

The second portion of the ER diagram appears in Figure 13-8. Notice that the Contact entity is actually a composite entity that handles the many-to-many relationship between two Person entities, one of which is an agent and one of which is an informant. The two relationships between Contact and Person have therefore been labeled to clarify the meaning of each relationship.

As mentioned earlier in this chapter, the Raw_Data entity participates in a mutually exclusive relationship with either a Contact or a Source. In other words, a piece of raw data can come from a contact with an informant or another source (for example, print or video material) but not both. UML represents such a relationship by connecting the two relationships with a dashed line that is labeled with the word OR.

The third portion of the design (Figure 13-9) deals with online access to data by IIA employees. A person can access either raw data or a verified piece of intelligence but only one item at a time. Therefore, this second mutually exclusive relationship is represented between the Data_Access entity and either the Raw_Data or Intelligence entity. The remainder of the diagram is a standard relational design.

The final portion of the ER diagram (Figure 13-10) concerns the development and use of IIA's equipment. Because the attributes needed to describe equipment in use and equipment under development are so very different, it isn't practical to handle them in a single relation. Unlike the situation with people, where the informants have just one extra attribute, the two categories of equipment have only one attribute in common: the equipment ID. In a practical sense, this is rather awkward. When a piece of equipment is certified ready for use, a row must be removed from the Under_Development_Item

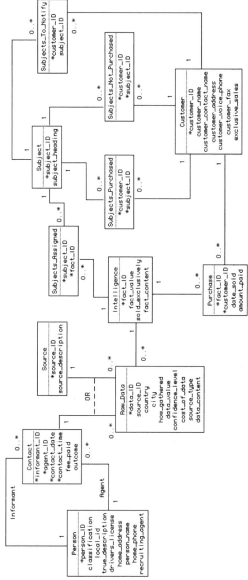

Figure 13-8: The object–relational design (part II)

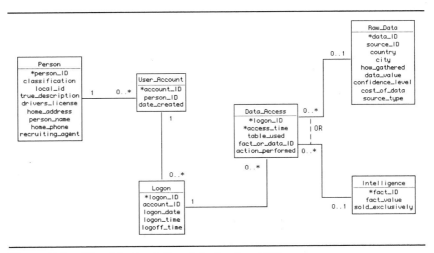

Figure 13-9: The object–relational design (part III)

table and a new row created for the Equipment_Item table. In addition, the integrity constraint that verifies the uniqueness of the item_ID attribute must apply to both tables rather than to each table individually. However, without the benefit of inheritance, it is impossible to generalize the two types of equipment into a single entity.

Given the issues that have just been discussed and the ER diagrams you have seen, an object–relational design for the IIA database could be written as follows:

```
person (person_ID, classification, local_ID, true_description,
    driver_license, home_address, person_name, home_phone,
    recruiting_agent)
person_type (classification, classification_description)
alias (person_ID, alias_name, alias_description,
    alias_drivers_license, alias_address, date_last_used)
former_address (person_ID, date_moved_in, date_moved_out, address)
education (person_ID, school_ID, date_entered, date_left,
    degree_earned, major_subject, minor_subject)
relative (person_ID, relative_name, birthdate, how_related,
    relative_address, relative_phone, photo, current_employer,
    education, current_job)
school (school_ID, school_name, school_address)
job (person_ID, company_ID, date_started, date_left, job_title)
company (company_ID, company_name, coompany_address, company_phone)
conviction (person_ID, conviction_date, crime, counts, sentence)
```

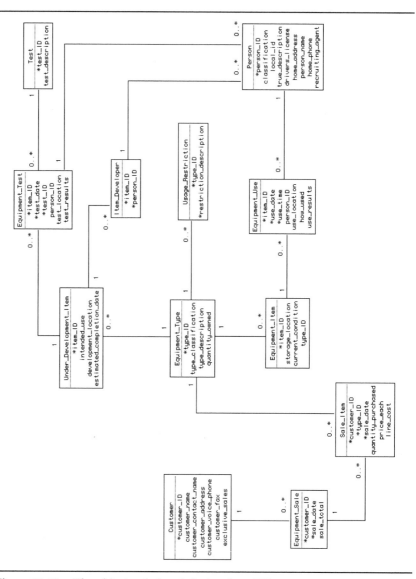

Figure 13-10: The object–relational design (part IV)

organization (<u>organization_ID</u>, organization_name,
    organization_address, organization_phone)
membership (<u>person_ID</u>, <u>organization_ID</u>, <u>date_joined</u>, date_quit)
fingerprints (<u>person_ID</u>, <u>finger</u>, print)
contact (<u>informant_ID</u>, <u>agent_ID</u>, <u>contact_date</u>, <u>contact_time</u>,
    fee_paid, outcome)

```
raw_data (data_ID, source_ID, source_type, country, city,
    how_gathered, data_value, confidence_level, data_content,
    fact_ID)
source (source_ID, source_description)
intelligence (fact_ID, fact_value, sold_exclusively, fact_content)
subject (subject_ID, subject_heading)
subjects_assigned (subjectID, fact_ID)
customer (customer_ID, customer_name, customer_contact_person,
    customer_address, customer_phone, customer_fax, exclusive_sales)
purchase (fact_ID, customer_ID, date_sold, amount_paid)
subjects_purchased (customer_ID, subject_ID)
subjects_not_purchased (customer_ID, subject_ID)
subjects_to_notify (customer_ID, subject_ID)
user_account (account_ID, person_ID, date_created)
logon (logon_ID, account_ID, logon_date, logon_time, logoff_time)
data_access (logon_ID, access_time, table_used, fact_or_data_ID,
    action_performed)
equipment_item (item_ID, storage_location, current_condition,
    type_ID)
usage_restriction (type_ID, restriction_description)
equipment_use (item_ID, use_date, use_time, person_ID, use_location,
    how_used, use_results)
equipment_type (type_ID, type_classification, type_description,
    quantity_owned)
equipment_sale (customer_ID, sale_date, sale_total)
sale_item (customer_ID, sale_date, type_ID, quantity_purchased,
    price_each, line_cost)
under_development_item (item_ID, intended_use,
    development_location, estimated_completion_date, type_ID)
item_developer (item_ID, person_ID)
equipment_test (item_ID, test_ID, test_date, person_ID,
    test_location, test_results)
test (test_ID, test_description)
```

Utility classes:

```
Name (first_name, last_name, middle_init)
Description (photo, retina_print, height, weight, eye_color,
    hair_color, marks, birthdate, religion)
DriversLicense (country, state, number, expiration_date)
PersonalAddress (street, city, state, country, zip_postal)
Phone (country_code, area_code, exchange, number, extension)
OrganizationalAddress (street1, street2, suite, city, state,
    country, zip_postal)
```

Like any relational schema, the object-relational schema for the IIA has difficulty representing a relationship between two entities whose primary keys are defined over the same domain. In particular, representing a contact—where two occurrences of the Person entity are related to one another—requires a concatenated key of which two parts are the person_ID attribute. The problem, of course, is that no two attributes in the same relation can have the same name. They must therefore be renamed, as they are in the Contact relation. Nonetheless, both agent_ID and informant_ID are defined over the person_ID domain.

The primary key constraint involving these two attributes is more complex than a standard primary key constraint. For example, the constraint for agent_ID is

```
agent_ID exists in Person and classification = "agent"
```

SQL does not allow expressions of this type as primary key constraints. Therefore, should the IIA choose to use an object-relational approach, it needs to look for a DBMS that not only supports the hybrid model, but also supports the SQL-92 CONSTRAINT syntax so that the additional primary key condition can be stored in the data dictionary.

The utility classes included in this design are classes, not relations. Although the preceding may seem like an obvious statement, its implications are significant. First, the classes may appear on paper here just like relations, but no attributes have been underlined to indicate primary keys: They do not require primary keys. In fact, keys are optional for classes. Second, the classes appear unconnected to any of the relations in the database. This is because they are really definitions of domains rather than entities. They are indeed unrelated to anything else in the database.

Creating the Classes

You will find the declarations and implementation of the utility classes for the IIA database in Figure 13-11. Like those for the object-relational databases in Chapters 11 and 12, the only procedure necessary for each class is initialize.

```
CREATE TYPE Name AS OBJECT (
    first_name CHAR (15),
    last_name CHAR (15),
    middle_init CHAR (1);
    MEMBER PROCEDURE initialize);

CREATE TYPE BODY Name AS
    MEMBER PROCEDURE initialize IS
    BEGIN
        first_name := NULL;
        last_name := NULL;
        middle_init := NULL;
    END initialize;
END;

CREATE TYPE DriversLicense AS OBJECT (
    country CHAR (20),
    state CHAR (2),
    number CHAR (20),
    expiration_date DATE,
    MEMBER PROCEDURE initialize );

CREATE TYPE BODY DriversLicense AS
    MEMBER PROCEDURE initialize IS
    BEGIN
        country := NULL;
        state := NULL;
        number := NULL;
        expiration_date := '1/1/1000'
    END initialize;
END;

CREATE TYPE PersonalAddress AS OBJECT (
    street CHAR (25),
    city CHAR (20),
    state CHAR (2),
    country CHAR (15),
    zip_postal CHAR (10),
    MEMBER PROCEDURE initialize );
```

Figure 13-11 : Oracle declarations and implementations for the IIA utility classes

```
REATE TYPE BODY PersonalAddress AS
    MEMBER PROCEDURE initialize IS
    BEGIN
        street := NULL;
        city := NULL;
        state := NULL;
        country := NULL;
        zip_postal := NULL;
    END initialize;
END;

CREATE TYPE OrganizationalAddress AS OBJECT
    street1 CHAR (25),
    street2 CHAR (25),
    suite CHAR (10),
    city CHAR (20),
    state CHAR (2),
    country CHAR (15),
    zip_postal CHAR (10),
    MEMBER PROCEDURE initialize );

CREATE TYPE BODY PersonalAddress AS
    MEMBER PROCEDURE initialize IS
    BEGIN
        street1 := NULL;
        street2 := NULL;
        suite := NULL:
        city := NULL;
        state := NULL;
        country := NULL;
        zip_postal := NULL;
    END initialize;
END;

CREATE TYPE Phone AS OBJECT (
    country_code CHAR (6),
    area_code CHAR (6),
    exchange CHAR (6),
    number CHAR (6),
    extension CHAR (5),
    MEMBER PROCEDURE initialize );
```

Figure 13-11 (Continued): Oracle declarations and implementations for the IIA utility classes

```
CREATE TYPE BODY Phone AS
    MEMBER PROCEDURE initialize IS
    BEGIN
        country_code := NULL;
        area_code := NULL;
        exchange := NULL;
        number := NULL;
        extension := NULL;
    END initialize;
END;

CREATE TYPE Description AS OBJECT (
    photo BLOB,
    retina_print BLOB,
    height REAL (5,2),
    weight INTEGER,
    eye_color CHAR (10),
    hair_color CHAR (10),
    marks VARCHAR (100),
    birthdate DATE,
    religion CHAR (15),
    MEMBER PROCEDURE initialize );

CREATE TYPE BODY Description AS
    MEMBER PROCEDURE initialize IS
    BEGIN
        photo = NULL;
        retina_print = NULL;
        height := 0.0;
        weight := 0;
        eye_color := NULL;
        hair_color := NULL;
        marks := NULL;
        birthdate := '1/1/1000';
        religion := NULL;
    END initialize;
END;
```

Figure 13-11 (Continued): Oracle declarations and implementations for the IIA utility classes

Writing the Schema

Once the classes have been declared and implemented, they can be used as data types in table declarations, using standard SQL syntax (see the CREATE TABLE statements in Figure 13-12). Notice how much the use of the classes simplifies the declaration of the tables.

```
CREATE TABLE person
(
    person_ID INT,
    classification INT,
    birthdate DATE,
    local_ID CHAR (15),
    driver_license DriversLicense,
    true_description Description,
    home_address PersonalAddress,
    phone Phone,
    person_name Name,
    recruiting_agent INT,
    PRIMARY KEY (person_ID),
    FOREIGN KEY (classification) REFERENCES person_types
);

CREATE TABLE person_types
(
    classification INT,
    classification_description CHAR (15),
    PRIMARY KEY (classification)
);

CREATE TABLE former_address
(
    person_ID INT,
    date_moved_in DATE,
    date_moved_out DATE,
    previous_address PersonalAddress,
    PRIMARY KEY (person_ID, date_moved_in),
    FOREIGN KEY (person_ID) REFERENCES person
);

CREATE TABLE alias
(
    person_ID INT,
    alias_name Name,
    alias_description Description
    local_id CHAR (15),
    alias_drivers_license DriversLicense,
    alias_address PersonalAddress,
    alias_phone Phone,
    date_last_used DATE,
    PRIMARY KEY (person_ID, last_name, first_name),
    FOREIGN KEY (person_ID) REFERENCES person
);
```

Figure 13-12 :   Oracle schema for the object-relational version of the IIA database

```
CREATE TABLE relative
(
    person_ID INT,
    relative_name Name,
    birthdate DATE,
    how_related CHAR (30),
    relative_address PersonalAddress,
    relative_phone Phone,
    photo BLOB,
    current_employer CHAR (30),
    education CHAR (30),
    current_job CHAR (30),
    PRIMARY KEY (person_ID, first_name, last_name, birthdate),
    FOREIGN KEY (person_ID) REFERENCES person
);

CREATE TABLE education
(
    person_ID INT,
    school_ID INT,
    date_entered DATE,
    date_left DATE,
    degree_earned CHAR (10),
    major_subject CHAR (15),
    minor_subject CHAR (15),
    PRIMARY KEY (person_ID, school_ID, date_entered) );

CREATE TABLE school
(
    school_ID INT,
    school_name CHAR (50),
    school_address OrganizationAddress,
    PRIMARY KEY (school_ID) );

CREATE TABLE job
(
    company_ID INT,
    date_started DATE,
    date_left DATE,
    job_title CHAR (50),
    person_ID INT,
    PRIMARY KEY (company_ID, date_started),
    FOREIGN KEY (company_ID) REFERENCES company,
    FOREIGN KEY (person_ID) REFERENCES person );
```

Figure 13-12 (Continued): Oracle schema for the object-relational version of the IIA database

```
CREATE TABLE company
(
    company_ID INT,
    company_name CHAR (50),
    company_address OrganizationalAddress,
    company_phone Phone,
    PRIMARY KEY (company_ID) );

CREATE TABLE fingerprints
(
    person_ID INT,
    finger CHAR (15),
    print BLOB,
    PRIMARY KEY (person_ID, finger),
    FOREIGN KEY (person_ID) REFERENCES person );

CREATE TABLE conviction
(
    person_ID INT,
    conviction_date DATE,
    crime CHAR (50),
    counts INT,
    sentence CHAR (50),
    PRIMARY KEY (person_ID, conviction_date, crime) );

CREATE TABLE organization
(
    organization_ID INT,
    organization_name CHAR (50),
    non_profit_status CHAR (1),
    organization_address OrganizationalAddress,
    organization_phone Phone,
    PRIMARY KEY (organization_ID) );

CREATE TABLE membership
(
    person_ID INT,
    organization_ID INT,
    date_joined DATE,
    date_quit DATE,
    PRIMARY KEY (person_ID, organization_ID, date_joined),
    FOREIGN KEY (person_ID) REFERENCES person,
    FOREIGN KEY (organization_ID) REFERENCES organization );
```

Figure 13-12 (Continued):   Oracle schema for the object-relational version of the IIA database

```
CREATE TABLE contact
(
    informant_ID INT
        CHECK (EXISTS (SELECT * FROM person
            WHERE VALUE = person_ID and classification = 4)),
    agent_ID INT
        CHECK (EXISTS (SELECT * FROM person
            WHERE VALUE = person_ID and classification = 1)),
    contact_date DATE,
    contact_time TIME,
    fee_paid DECIMAL (8,2),
    outcome CHAR (50),
    PRIMARY KEY (informant_ID, agent_ID, contact_date,
        contact_time));

CREATE TABLE raw_data
(
    data_ID INT,
    source_ID INT,
    source_type CHAR (!5),
    country CHAR (30),
    city CHAR (30),
    how_gathered CHAR (50),
    data_value CHAR (255),
    confidence_level INT,
    cost_of_data DECIMAL (8,2),
    fact_ID INT,
    PRIMARY KEY (data_ID),
    FOREIGN KEY (fact_ID) REFERENCES intelligence
    CHECK (source_type = 'informant' AND
        EXISTS (SELECT * FROM person
        WHERE source_ID = person_ID AND classification = 4)
        OR
        source_type = 'document' AND
        EXISTS (SELECT * FROM source
        WHERE source_ID = source.source_ID)));

CREATE TABLE source
(
    source_ID INT,
    source_description CHAR (255),
    PRIMARY KEY (source_ID) );
```

Figure 13-12 (Continued): Oracle schema for the object-relational version of the IIA database

```
CREATE TABLE intelligence
(
    fact_ID INT,
    fact_value CHAR (255),
    sold_exclusively CHAR (1),
    PRIMARY KEY (fact_ID) );

CREATE TABLE subject
(
    subject_ID INT,
    subject_heading CHAR (50),
    PRIMARY KEY (subject_ID) );

CREATE TABLE subjects_assigned
(
    subject_ID INT,
    fact_ID INT,
    PRIMARY KEY (subject_ID, fact_ID),
    FOREIGN KEY (subject_ID) REFERENCES subject,
    FOREIGN KEY (fact_ID) REFERENCES intelligence );

CREATE TABLE customer
(
    customer_ID INT,
    customer_name CHAR (50),
    customer_contact_person Name,
    customer_address OrganizationalAddress,
    phone Phone,
    fax Phone,
    exclusive_sales CHAR (1),
    PRIMARY KEY (customer_ID) );

CREATE TABLE purchase
(
    fact_ID INT,
    customer_ID INT,
    date_sold DATE,
    amount_paid DECIMAL (8,2),
    PRIMARY KEY (fact_ID, customer_ID),
    FOREIGN KEY (fact_ID) REFERENCES intelligence,
    FOREIGN KEY (customer_ID) REFERENCES customer );
```

Figure 13-12 (Continued): Oracle schema for the object-relational version of the IIA database

```
CREATE TABLE subjects_purchased
(
    customer_ID INT,
    subject_ID INT,
    PRIMARY KEY (customer_ID, subject_ID),
    FOREIGN KEY (customer_ID) REFERENCES customer,
    FOREIGN KEY (subject_ID) REFERENCES subject );

CREATE TABLE subjects_not_purchased
(
    customer_ID INT,
    subject_ID INT,
    PRIMARY KEY (customer_ID, subject_ID),
    FOREIGN KEY (customer_ID) REFERENCES customer,
    FOREIGN KEY (subject_ID) REFERENCES subject );

CREATE TABLE subjects_to_notify
(
    customer_ID INT,
    subject_ID INT,
    PRIMARY KEY (customer_ID, subject_ID),
    FOREIGN KEY (customer_ID) REFERENCES customer,
    FOREIGN KEY (subject_ID) REFERENCES subject );

CREATE TABLE user_account
(
    account_ID INTCHAR (10),
    person_ID INT,
    date_created DATE,
    PRIMARY KEY (account_ID),
    FOREIGN KEY (person_ID) REFERENCES person);

CREATE TABLE logon
(
    account_ID INTCHAR (10),
    logon_date DATE,
    logon_time TIME,
    logoff_time TIME,
    logon_ID INT,
    PRIMARY KEY (logon_ID),
    FOREIGN KEY (account_ID) REFERENCES user_account
);
```

Figure 13-12 (Continued): Oracle schema for the object-relational version of the IIA database

```
CREATE TABLE data_access
(
    logon_ID INT,
    table_used CHAR (30),
    fact_or_data_ID INT,
    access_time TIME,
    action_performed CHAR (30),
    PRIMARY KEY (logon_ID, access_time),
    FOREIGN KEY (logon_ID) REFERENCES logon
    CHECK (table_used = 'raw_data' AND
        EXISTS (SELECT * FROM raw_date
        WHERE fact_or_data_ID = data_ID)
        OR
        (table_used = 'intelligence' AND
        EXISTS (SELECT * FROM intelligence
        WHERE fact_or_data_ID = fact_ID)));

CREATE TABLE equipment_item
(
    item_ID INT,
    storage_location CHAR (30),
    current_condition CHAR (10),
    type_ID INT,
    PRIMARY KEY (item_ID),
    FOREIGN KEY (type_ID) REFERENCES equipment_type);

CREATE TABLE usage_restriction
(
    type_ID INT,
    restriction_description CHAR (50),
    PRIMARY KEY (type_ID, restriction_description),
    FOREIGN KEY (type_ID) REFERENCES equipment_type );

CREATE TABLE equipment_use
(
    item_ID INT,
    use_date DATE,
    use_time TIME,
    person_ID INT,
    use_location CHAR (50),
    how_used CHAR (255),
    use_results CHAR (255),
    PRIMARY KEY (item_ID, use_date, use_time),
    FOREIGN KEY (item_ID) REFERENCES equipment_item,
    FOREIGN KEY (person_ID) REFERENCES person );
```

Figure 13-12 (Continued): Oracle schema for the object-relational version of the IIA database

```
CREATE TABLE equipment_type
(
    type_ID INT,
    type_classification CHAR (15),
    type_description CHAR (50),
    quantity_owned INT,
    PRIMARY KEY (type_ID) );

CREATE TABLE equipment_sale
(
    customer_ID INT,
    sale_date DATE,
    sale_total DECIMAL (8,2),
    PRIMARY KEY (customer_ID, sale_date),
    FOREIGN KEY (customer_ID) REFERENCES customer );

CREATE TABLE sale_item
(
    customer_ID INT,
    sale_date DATE,
    type_ID INT,
    quantity_purchased INT,
    price_each DECIMAL (8,2),
    line_cost DECIMAL (8,2),
    PRIMARY KEY (customer_ID, sale_date, type_ID),
    FOREIGN KEY (customer_ID) REFERENCES equipment_sale,
    FOREIGN KEY (sale_date) REFERENCES equipment_sale,
    FOREIGN KEY (type_ID) REFERENCES equipment_type );

CREATE TABLE under_development_item
(
    item_ID INT,
    intended_use CHAR (50),
    development_location CHAR (50),
    estimated_completion_date DATE,
    type_ID INT,
    PRIMARY KEY (item_ID),
    FOREIGN KEY (type_ID) REFERENCES equipment_type );

CREATE TABLE item_developer
(
    item_ID INT,
    person_ID INT,
    PRIMARY KEY (item_ID, person_ID),
    FOREIGN KEY (person_ID) REFERENCES person );
```

Figure 13-12 (Continued):   Oracle schema for the object-relational version of the IIA database

```
CREATE TABLE equipment_test
(
    item_ID INT,
    test_ID INT,
    test_date DATE,
    person_ID INT,
    test_location CHAR (50),
    test_results CHAR (255),
    PRIMARY KEY (item_ID, test_ID, test_date),
    FOREIGN KEY (item_ID) REFERENCES under_development_item,
    FOREIGN KEY (test_ID) REFERENCES test,
    FOREIGN KEY (person_ID) REFERENCES person );

CREATE TABLE test
(
    test_ID INT,
    test_description CHAR (255),
    PRIMARY KEY (test_ID)
);
```

Figure 13-12 (Continued): Oracle schema for the object-relational version of the IIA database

Glossary

Abstract data type: An object-oriented term for a user-defined data type, usually a class.

Accessor: In an object-oriented environment, a procedure that returns the value of a private variable.

Aggregation: A container class.

Application class: A class representing an application program.

Attribute: A property of an entity; data that describe an entity; a column in a relation.

Base table: A table whose data are physically stored in a database.

BLOB (binary large object): A column data type specifying that the column will store the contents of a file (text and/or graphics) in its binary representation, without being searchable or readable in any way by the DBMS.

Cardinality (of a relationship): The type of relationship (one-to-one, one-to-many, or many-to-many).

Case sensitive: Distinguishing between upper- and lowercase letters.

CASE (computer-aided software engineering) tool: A piece of software used to support the design and development of information systems and application software.

Catalog: Another term for a data dictionary.

Class: A definition of an entity, including the data that describe an occurrence of the entity and procedures that operate on entity data.

Clustering: Grouping data together on the same disk page to improve retrieval performance.

CODASYL: See **Committee on Data Systems Languages**.

CODASYL database: A database that adheres to the CODASYL database standard.

Column homogeneous: A property of a relation stating that all the values in a given column are taken from the same domain.

Commit: End a transaction by making its changes permanent.

Committee on Data Systems Languages (CODASYL): A committee of government and industry technologists that developed the COBOL programming language and a standard for a simple network database.

Complex network data model: A navigational data model that supports direct many-to-many relationships.

Composite entity: An entity that represents the relationship between two other entities.

Concatenated identifier: An entity identifier made up of the values of more than one attribute.

Constraint: A rule to which some element in a database must adhere.

Constructor: In an object-oriented environment, a procedure that is run automatically whenever an object is created from a class.

Container class: A class that contains and manages multiple objects of another class.

Context diagram: The top-level diagram in a data flow diagram that shows the environmental context in which the information system exists.

Control class: A class that controls the operational flow of a program.

Copy constructor: In an object-oriented environment, a constructor that initializes an object with data values copied from another object of the same class.

Currency indicator: In a CODASYL database, a set of internal pointers maintained for each application running at any given time indicating the position of the application in the simple network.

Cylinder: The same track on all surfaces in a stack of platters in a hard disk.

Data dictionary: A repository for data describing the structural elements of a database.

Data dictionary driven: A property of relational databases in which all access to stored data is preceded by access to the data dictionary to determine if the requested data elements exist and if the user has the access rights to perform the requested action.

Data encapsulation: An object-oriented concept in which the details of how an object performs an action is hidden from objects or programs that invoke that action.

Data flow: The path taken by data as they are processed throughout an organization.

Data flow diagram: A diagram that shows the data flows in an organization, including sources of data, where data are stored, and processes that transform data.

Data model: A formal way of describing the relationship between entities in a database to a database management system.

Data store: In a data flow diagram, a place where data are stored.

Database: A place where data are stored along with definitions of the relationships between those data.

Database definition language: A special-purpose computer language used to define the logical structure of a database (in particular, those based on the hierarchical, simple network, and complex network data models).

Database key: In a CODASYL database, an internal pointer to the physical storage location of a record occurrence in a file.

Database management system: Software that provides access to the data in a database; translates a user's requests for data that are framed in terms of logical relationships into physical storage access commands.

Deletion anomaly: A problem that occurs in poorly designed relations such that a user accidentally loses data that should be kept when deleting part of a primary key forces removal of an entire row from a relation.

Destructor: In an object-oriented environment, a procedure that is executed automatically whenever an object is destroyed.

Determinant: An attribute upon which another attribute is functionally dependent.

Domain: An expression of the permissible values for an attribute.

Domain constraint: A rule that requires that all values of an attribute come from a specified domain.

Embedded SQL: SQL statements coded as part of a program written in a high-level language such as C++ or Java.

Entity: Anything about which data are stored in a database.

Entity class: A class that represents an entity.

Entity identifier: An attribute or combination of attributes whose values will uniquely identify every instance of an entity.

Entity integrity: A constraint on a relation that states that no part of a primary key may be null.

Entity-relationship diagram: A diagram that shows the relationships between entities in a database environment.

Equi-join: A join based on matching identical values.

Extent: A data structure used by an object-oriented database to contain all objects created from a single class.

Field: In a file processing system, the smallest unit of meaningful data, such as a first name or street address.

Foreign key: A column or combination of columns that is the same as the primary key of a table in the same database.

Functional dependency: A relationship between two attributes such that at any given time, for each unique value of attribute A in the database, there is only one value of attribute B.

Hashing: A technique for providing fast access to data based on a key value by determining the physical storage location of that data.

Hierarchical data model: A navigational data model that supports only one-to-many relationships and includes the restriction that no entity can have more than one parent entity.

Horizontal partitioning: Splitting the rows of a table into multiple tables to improve retrieval performance.

Hybrid database: An object-relational database.

Index: An ordered list of key values that provides a fast access path to the data in a relation.

Indexed Sequential Access Method (ISAM): An IBM file structure that provided both sequential file access and fast access paths (via indexes) to data.

Information hiding: An object-oriented concept in which the details of how an object performs an action is hidden from objects or programs that invoke that action.

Inheritance: In an object-oriented environment, a general-specific ("is a") relationship between two classes.

Inner join: An equi-join.

Insertion anomaly: A problem that occurs in poorly designed relations such that a user is prevented from entering data because values for all the columns of a primary key are not available.

Instance (of a relation): A relation that contains rows of data values.

Instance (of an entity): A real-world occurrence of an entity represented by values for the entity's attributes.

Interface class: A class that represents something in a program's user interface, such as a window or menu.

ISAM: See **Indexed Sequential Access Method.**

Join: An operation from the relational algebra that combines two relations by matching rows based on values in columns in the two tables. The matching relationship is usually primary key to foreign key.

Many-to-many relationship: A relationship between two entities in which an instance of entity A can be related to zero, one, or more instances of entity B and an instance of entity B can be related to zero, one, or more instances of entity A.

Message: In an object-oriented environment, the way in which objects communicate with each other.

Metadata: Data about data; the data stored in a data dictionary.

Modification anomaly: A problem with a poorly designed relation that occurs when unnecessary duplicated data are not updated consistently and data that should have identical values do not.

Multivalued: Having the potential to contain more than one value at any given time.

Multivalued dependency: A dependency between three attributes in which attribute A determines a small but finite set of values for attribute B and attribute A also determines a small but finite set of values for attribute C, but attributes B and C are independent.

Mutator: In an object-oriented environment, a procedure that modifies the value of a private variable.

Mutually exclusive relationship: A relationship in which an instance of entity A can be related to either an instance of entity B or an instance of entity C, but not both.

Natural equi-join: An equi-join.

Navigational: A property of a data model such that the access paths to data are predefined and represented by pointers within the data space.

Normal form: Design criteria that a relation must meet.

Normalization: The process of placing attributes into tables that avoid the problems associated with poor database design.

Null: A special value meaning "unknown."

Object: An instance of a class.

Object-Relational database: A database that supports classes as column data types.

One-to-many relationship: A relationship between two entities in which an instance of entity A can be related to zero, one, or more instances of entity B and entity B can be related to at most one instance of entity A.

One-to-one relationship: A relationship between two entities in which an instance of entity A can be related to at most one instance of entity B and entity B can be related to at most one instance of entity A.

Overloading: In an object-oriented environment, providing multiple implementations of the same procedure, each with the same name but different input parameters.

Page: The size of the block of data that a computer (and therefore a database) transfers between disk and main memory at one time.

Partitioning: Breaking relations into parts to improve retrieval performance.

Physical schema: The physical storage structures used to store the data in a database.

Polymorphism: In an object-oriented inheritance hierarchy, giving the same function in related classes different implementations.

Post-relational database: An object-relational database.

Precision: The number of digits to the right of the decimal point in a number.

Predicate: A logical expression against which data are evaluated.

Primary key: One or more columns whose values uniquely identify every row in a relation.

Process: In a data flow diagram, something that is done to or with data.

Prototyping: A process for system and database design in which users respond to increasingly specific designs of the interface of an application program; useful in cases where system specifications are not thoroughly known in advance.

Query optimizer: That portion of a database management system that selects the most efficient strategy for processing a query.

Reblocking: For an ISAM file, rewriting the file to leave physical space on each track occupied by the file to allow the additional of records in key sequence order.

Record: In a file processing system, a collection of fields describing a single entity.

Referential integrity: A constraint on a relation that states that every nonnull foreign key value must reference an existing primary key value.

Relation: The definition of the structure of a two-dimensional table made up of columns and rows.

Relational database: A database in which the only data structures are relations.

Relationship data: Data that describe the relationship between two entities rather than each of the individual entities.

Repeating group: An attribute that has more than one value in each row of a relation.

Roll back: End a transaction by undoing all its actions so the database is restored to the state it was in when the transaction began.

Schema: The overall logical plan of a database.

Set: In a CODASYL database, a two-level hierarchy representing one or more one-to-many relationships.

Simple network data model: A navigational data model that supports only one-to-many relationships but allows an entity to have an unlimited number of parent entities.

Signature: In programming languages such C, C++, and Java as well as object-oriented DBMSs, the name and parameter list of a procedure/function.

Single-valued: Having only a single value at any given time.

System set: In a CODASYL database, a special set with only one owner occurrence that is used to collect all occurrences of a single entity.

Table: A relation in a relational database.

Temporary table: A base table that exists only in main memory and for the length of a given database session.

Three-schema architecture: Three ways of looking at a database through the physical schema, the logical schema, and user views of data.

Three-valued logic: A set of logical truth tables that include the values true, false, and unknown.

Transaction: A unit of work submitted to a database.

Transitive dependency: A group of functional dependencies such that attribute A determines attribute B, which in turn determines attribute C. Therefore, it is also true that attribute A determines attribute C.

Tuple: A row in a relation.

Unified modeling language (UML): A style of ER diagramming that includes support for objects and therefore can be used to model object-relational database designs.

Update anomaly: Another term for a modification anomaly.

Vertical partitioning: Splitting the columns of a table into multiple tables to improve retrieval performance.

View: A named query store in a data dictionary that is used to create a virtual table whenever a user includes the name of the view in a data access request.

Virtual table: A table in a relational database that exists only in main memory.

Weak entity: An entity that cannot exist in a database unless an instance of another entity is present and related to it.

Index